Telling the Santa Clara Story

Sesquicentennial Voices

Telling the
Santa Clara Story

Sesquicentennial Voices

Edited by
RUSSELL K. SKOWRONEK

Santa Clara University
Santa Clara, California

City of Santa Clara

Front cover photos (from the bottom up):
- Reconstructed Ohlone tule reed house, located in the de Saisset Museum, Santa Clara University. Skowronek Collection.
- Facial reconstruction of a 16-18 year old female who was buried on the Santa Clara University campus some 1300 years ago. Courtesy Kevin Richlin, Investigator for the Santa Clara County District Attorney's Office.
- Berryessa Adobe, constructed in the 1840s and currently a historic site in the City of Santa Clara. Skowronek Collection.
- Fr. Jerome Ricard in the 1920s. McKay Collection.
- Santa Clara Convention Center, constructed in 1986 in the City of Santa Clara. Skowronek Collection.

Back cover photos (from the bottom up):
- Santa Clara train depot, constructed in 1863 and still in use. Skowronek Collection
- One of Santa Clara's surviving Victorian houses constructed circa 1895 and located at 1116 Washington St. Skowronek Collection.
- One of the "Fighting 40" Lt. Leonard McKay, 1944. McKay Collection.
- Santa Clara Civic Center, constructed 1963. Skowronek Collection.

Cover design and interior typsetting in Goudy Old Style by Kenneth Guentert of Schueller House, Santa Clara, California.

Printed on acid-free paper by McNaughton and Gunn, Saline, Michigan

ISBN: 0-9720765-0-6.

Printed in the United States of America

5 4 3 2 1

To the People of Santa Clara
Past, Present, and Future

Table of Contents

.

Preface

Anniversaries are bittersweet occasions for reflection about past tragedies and triumphs, losses and gains. They are also times to look to the future and to build upon the foundations of the past. These truisms are applicable across the spectrum from weddings to the millennial jubilee of Christianity. Many will remember the acrimony that accompanied the Columbian Quincentennial observations of 1992 and might juxtapose those with the pride associated with the 1976 celebration of the American Revolution. The years 2000, 2001, and 2002, respectively, mark the sesquicentennials of California Statehood, the establishment of Santa Clara University, and the incorporation of the City of Santa Clara. These anniversaries provide us with an occasion to reflect on the good, the bad, and the ugly of our past, to re-evaluate history and, thus, discover its unrecognized potential. Most of all, what we learn from the past can help us chart the pathway to the future.

This book contains "stories" about yesterday, today, and tomorrow. They are stories told by "eyewitnesses" or constructed through a combination of archaeology, documentary, and oral history research. Many of the authors have deep roots in the valley. Some can trace their roots to the first inhabitants of the valley, the Ohlone, others to the Anza expedition of 1776, or to Irish-Anglo migrants of the 1840s, or to Italian immigrants of the late-nineteenth century. Generations of these families have seen the valley change. Their oral traditions enliven their accounts. Others, though more recent migrants to the "Golden State," have used their skills as investigators to describe changes in the cultural and natural environment and so reveal how the "*llano de los robles*" or "Plains of the Oaks" came to be transformed into the Valley of Heart's Delight, and today's Silicon Valley. And, the central focus for these changes was Santa Clara.

The seeds for this book were sown in the closing years of the last millennium. Santa Clara University planned to celebrate the sesquicentennial of its 1851 founding during the 2000-2001 and Fall 2001 academic years. In 1999 it solicited its faculty and staff for ideas on how to mark this anniversary. The result was funding for a series of symposia and lectures, the publication of a major illustrated history of the university[1] and other minor research publications,[2] interpretive historical wayside exhibits and tour guides,[3] exhibits at the de Saisset Museum on Fr. Bernard Hubbard and on Mission Santa Clara de Asís, and two classes. These courses, developed by Ms. JoAnne Northrup, Curator for the de Saisset Museum, and Dr. Russell Skowronek, Associate Professor of Anthropology, in the Department of Anthropology and Sociology were titled, *Telling the Santa Clara Story*, and *Re-Telling the Santa Clara Story*, and were taught as Anthropology 193, Museum Anthropology. Enrolled students included Kevin Bender, Brendan Devine, Michael Frank, Michael Gonzales, Steven McEvoy, Sarah Naumes, Katrina Osland, Linh Pham, Vanessa Rodriguez, Sarah Skinner, Eileen Vollert, Melissa Walker, Dorothy Wall, and Tani Yuen. Docent participants from the de Saisset Museum included Lisa Santana-Bakewell, Marion Bratton, Laura Brickman, Carmen Burke, Diane Clark, Margaret Demorest, Patricia Enfantino, Carole Guentert, John Ross Jackson, Connie Jennings, Berta Landwehr, Simone Morrow, Joyce Osborn, Esther Elizabeth "Liz" Pike, Ursula Ramos, Joseph "Spike" Standifer, Sharon Stewart, Julie Tomlin, Ida Tonnelli, Betty Torres, and Marge Verga.

The class was seen as a way to not only educate students and museum docents about Santa Clara's history, but to give voice to the diverse peoples whose legacy is part of today's Santa Clara. Furthermore, it was envisioned as a catalyst for compiling information toward the refurbishment of the interpretive exhibits on California history at the de Saisset Museum. During the Fall quarter of 2000, 26 lectures were delivered by the following individuals: Linda Yamane; Andrew Galvan; Ann-Marie Sayers; Russell Skowronek; Randall Milliken; Lorie Garcia; Constance Cortez; Elise Schlick; Robert Senkewicz; Wells Twombly; Leon Pappanastos; Gerald McKevitt, S.J.; George F. Giacomini Jr.; Paul Fitzgerald, S.J.; Nancy Unger; Carl Hayn, S.J.; Robert Parden; Phil Kesten; Robert H. Jackson; Leonard

McKay; Ramon Chacon; Barbara Molony; Patricia Mahan; Michael Malone; and Paul Locatelli, S.J. These individuals represented the Native American community, local historians, local scholars, visiting scholars, alumni, members of the Santa Clara City Council, and Santa Clara University faculty. Lectures were grouped into four topics:

The First Santa Clarans
Mission Santa Clara
Nineteenth Century Santa Clara
Santa Clara in the Twentieth Century and Beyond

All of the public lectures were video taped by Harvey D. "Doug" Gross with the aid of Lorie Garcia, both with the City of Santa Clara. These were shown on the City of Santa Clara's public access channel during their sesquicentennial in 2002. Copies of the tapes were deposited at the Santa Clara University Archives, along with a complete set of the notes from the class. Perhaps they will be of interest during the university's bicentennial observations in 2051.

The Spring 2001 course, *Re-Telling the Santa Clara Story,* challenged students to tell, using the venue of a museum, part of **The Santa Clara Story.** This meant planning an entire exhibition (dealing with student life) and doing a mock-up of one exhibit.

Students enjoyed field trips to History San Jose (Kelley Park), and the Oakland Historical Museum, as well as presentations by Beth Redmond-Jones (an independent museum exhibition developer); Edward Von der Porten (past Director of the Treasure Island Museum); Alida Bray (Curator, History San Jose); Steve Gelber (Santa Clara University Department of History); Rebecca Schapp (Director, de Saisset Museum); JoAnne Northrup (Curator, de Saisset Museum); and Russell Skowronek (Santa Clara University Department of Anthropology and Sociology).

It is unlikely that the "exhibitions" developed by the students will ever exist for the public to see. Nonetheless, the class has given these Santa Clara students an opportunity to gain hands-on experience in museum exhibition. It has also provided Santa Clara's faculty and staff with insights into the complexities of **The Santa Clara Story** and the difficulties and rewards of "re-telling" it to an audience that includes alumni, current students, staff, faculty, members of the community, members of the museum, and thousands of fourth graders.

At the conclusion of the courses, my senior colleague in anthropology, Dr. George Westermark, suggested that the "Santa Clara Story" as told in these courses was a rare opportunity to hear a broad spectrum of voices and stories that situates this story beyond the boundaries of the campus and the city and into the broader Santa Clara region. In June of 2001 a proposal for this volume was made to the City of Santa Clara, Sesquicentennial Steering Committee. This committee included, Lorie Garcia, Geof Goodfellow, Harvey D. "Doug" Gross, Patricia Mahan, Jaimie Mathews, and George Wood. It was accepted as a joint undertaking between the City of Santa Clara and Santa Clara University.

During the summer and fall of 2001, participants in the Fall 2000 class revised their presentations and submitted manuscripts for this volume. I am indebted to the contributing authors for their hard work in preparing their manuscripts and to Dr. Patricia Whittier for her editorial suggestions. Special thanks are also due to Ms. JoAnne Northrup for her hard work during the classes and her encouragement regarding the creation of this volume, and to Ms. Sandra Chiaramonte of the Department of Anthropology and Sociology for her prowess in compiling the individual manuscripts into a cogent whole. I am indebted to Dr. Rose Marie Beebe of Santa Clara University and to Ms. Linda Longoria of the University of Texas at San Antonio for the final editing and proofing of the manuscript. I wish to extend my thanks to the Department of Anthropology, The Museum, and the Consortium for Archaeological Research at Michigan State University for granting me Visiting Scholar status during the fall of 2001. Furthermore, I wish to acknowledge the on-going support of my colleagues at the Smithsonian Center for Materials Research and Education, and in the Archaeology Research Lab, Department of Anthropology and Sociology, the College of Arts and Sciences, and the Office of the President at Santa Clara University. My thanks to Ken Guentert who, on a very tight deadline, gave this project the professional book design it deserved. Finally, I wish to thank Helen and Lester Skowronek of Lawrenceville, New Jersey, for the "Cougar" during this sabbatical leave, and E. Olga Skowronek and Peg Graham for their patience and support throughout this endeavor.

What is known of "The Santa Clara Story" stems from oral histories and lifetimes of devoted research by many scholars. There is no one single "correct" story, rather it is a nuanced history with a multitude of perspectives. In many ways **The Santa Clara Story** is a microcosm of the larger story of California and the Americas. I hope this volume will illuminate some of the varied voices of the past for today's and tomorrow's Santa Clarans.

R.K.S.
East Lansing, Michigan
November 2001
and
Santa Clara, California
April 2002

1. Giacomini, Jr. George F. and Gerald McKevitt, S.J. 2000. *Serving the Intellect, Touching the Heart.* Santa Clara University, Santa Clara, CA.

2. Scarborough, Caprice Murray. 2001. The Legacy of the "Glacier Priest": Bernard R. Hubbard, S.J., *Research Manuscript Series on the Cultural and Natural History of Santa Clara* No. 10, Santa Clara University, Santa Clara, CA.

3. Beyer, Ann, and Russell K. Skowronek, Compilers. 2002. *Historical Tour of Mission Santa Clara de Asís: Historical, Botanical and Archaeological Walk,* Santa Clara University, Santa Clara, CA.

SECTION I
The First Santa Clarans

Today the vast majority of people living in the City of Santa Clara are recent migrants. Whether foreign-born or from east of the Sierras California is seen as a place that is constantly changing and so, is forever new. It is a polyglot of peoples, languages, and cultures, and a place of conflict and a place of compromise. A world that must have come with the computer — or did it?

Before there were computers, or a place called Santa Clara, the valley was occupied by the first Santa Clarans. Their descendants, known today as the Ohlone, are very much part of the story of Santa Clara. The past, present, and future story of the Ohlone in the Santa Clara Valley is being written today by Ohlone and other scholars using a combination of biological, linguistic, material, documentary, and oral information. As a result of these studies, we now can say that centuries ago Santa Clara was already a home to immigrants. In these ancient times it was a crossroads for trade and a place of conflict and compromise, and a place where inhabitants of neighboring communities might not be able to completely understand the languages and customs of one another. Nonetheless, they survived and Ohlone culture is part of the Bay Area in the twenty-first century. Ohlone language, music, and arts are being revived and practiced by a growing number of people today. The future of the Ohlone is further assured in the spirituality that is a continuing part of our world.

CHAPTER 1

The First Santa Clarans

Russell K. Skowronek

We are still here!! The words reverberate across the North American continent. They are shouted by the descendants of the First Americans. In Silicon Valley, the Ohlone Indians add their voice to this cry.[1] These are modern voices of the 21st century who live in one of the most culturally diverse locations in the United States. Their story has been constructed through a combination of oral histories from beloved grandparents or the oral histories collected nearly a century ago by early ethnographers. Those have been supplemented with evidence gleaned from the study of language, ancient material culture, and biological remains to reconstruct the Ohlone world prior to the 1770s. These avenues of enquiry are all aspects of anthropology — or the study of humankind in its broadest sense. Anthropology is the most scientific of the humanities and the most humanistic of the sciences. Let us duly note that the anthropologist Alfred Kroeber once stated that the Ohlone were "extinct," a statement he would later recant. Nonetheless, it is the work of anthropologists and their Ohlone colleagues that allows all of us to understand the origins and history of the first Santa Clarans.

Information on the first Santa Clarans, the honored Ohlone ancestors, comes from a century of research conducted by Ohlone and non-Ohlone scholars associated with such organizations as the Ohlone Families Consulting Service, the Ohlone Indian Tribe, Costanoan Indian Research, the University of California, Stanford University, San Jose State University, Caltrans, Archaeological Resource Management, and Santa Clara University. Much of the information presented here is the result of collaborative projects between Santa Clara University and the honored Ohlone descendants.

Names

The indigenous peoples of the San Francisco Bay region were preliterate and what is referred to as a prehistoric society. Since "history" refers to written documents, preliterate societies are, by definition, prehistoric. When the Spanish moved among these people in the eighteenth century, they referred to them collectively as the *costaños* or "coastal dwellers." Anthropologists have transformed the Spanish name to *Costanoan* — a term that is still used today when referring to a linguistic designation for eight related languages in the Utian Family and within the Penutian stock.[2] More recently, the rubric *Ohlone* has become the most popular designation.[3] Because some modern Ohlone see the term "Costanoan" as derogatory the term "Ohlone" is the preferred designation.

Beginnings

Just as all stories must have a beginning, all cultures have creation stories to explain how they got here and their place in the cosmos. Judaism, Christianity and Islam look to the book of Genesis and the battle between "good" and "evil." This is a universal theme that is also found among the ancestral Ohlone. Here, a great flood engulfed the world following a great battle between "good" and "evil." Two islands, thought to be Mount Diablo and Mount Umannum, emerged from the waters. The only survivors were the animal-god trinity of Coyote, Eagle, and Hummingbird, who created the new people. In one story Coyote has five children who create five tribes with five different languages.

Archaeological evidence demonstrates that the Americas were populated during the last Ice Age more than 10,000 years ago. At that time, a large volume of water was trapped in continental glaciers, making sea levels as much as 300 feet lower than they are today. As the climate warmed over the past millennia, sea levels rose until about 3500 years ago (1500 B.C.), when they and the local environment became what we recognize today.

The Bay Area was first occupied in this ancient time. These

original occupants were joined and ultimately replaced by the
ancestors of the Ohlone during what archaeologists term the *Middle
Period* or the era between 900 B.C. and A.D. 900. This is based in part
upon linguistic evidence (glottochronology) and in part on changes in
material culture (artifacts). Perhaps in the future biological evidence
will be added. A number of sites dating to this era have been
identified within the limits of the City of Santa Clara near the
Guadalupe River.[4] In the Old Quad area of Santa Clara evidence for
the prehistoric Ohlone has been found on the Santa Clara University
campus. It dates from the Middle Period.

Overview

Our knowledge of life in the Ohlone region in the prehistoric and
proto-historic eras is largely based on archaeological research and the
observations of Spanish explorers and priests such as Portolá, Fages,
Crespi, and Anza who traveled in the Bay Area between 1769 and
1776.[5] In addition to these sources, a number of contemporary
illustrations made in the late eighteenth and early nineteenth
centuries aid anthropologists in the reconstruction of Ohlone life.[6]

Political and Social Organization

It has been estimated that in 1770 there were about 10,000
Ohlone living along California's central coast in some fifty separate
and politically autonomous units whose populations ranged from 50 to
500 persons. There is evidence in the archaeological and
ethnohistorical literature that in the Middle and *Late Periods* (A.D.
1100-1800) territorial boundaries were respected and defended.[7]
Although populations were small for each polity, there is evidence in
the gravegoods associated with mortuary activities of incipient social
stratification or ranking in the Late Period. The position of "chief" or
"captain" was inherited and held by either females or males. These
officials adjudicated disputes, led war parties, directed economic and
ceremonial activities, and hosted visitors.[8] Even so, the Ohlone social
hierarchy was less marked than that of the Chumash to the south and
other Native American groups with institutionalized coercive power.[9]
Fathers Magín Catalá and José Viader underscored this point when, in
1814, they wrote, "In their pagan state no superiority of any kind was

recognized."[10] Nonetheless, there is evidence that in 1790 Governor Fages negotiated with village headmen in the Santa Clara Valley to supply paid labor to work on the Monterey Presidio; thus, some coercive power must have existed.[11]

Ideology

In terms of religion, the precontact Ohlone are best considered animists, believing that all animate and inanimate objects in the world have spirits.[12] Like all animists, they also believed in generalized malevolent and benevolent spirits. These malevolent spirits made the world an uncertain and potentially dangerous place to live. People wore or carried amulets or charmstones to protect themselves and behaved in a manner prescribed by their societies to placate each of these spirits.[13] Appropriate behavior involved both solitary prayers and village-wide events. Throughout California, dancers were thought to be invested with supernatural powers. Only properly prepared individuals could touch the dancers or their feathers while they were sanctified for the ceremony. As Milliken has noted:

> Dances were seen not only as acts of veneration, but also as activities which maintained an undistorted world order. They seem to have been moments outside of sequential time, central acts of meaning as powerful to the believers as the Mass is to the believing Roman Catholic.[14]

Mortuary activities in the Late Period involved burial and occasionally cremation of special individuals with a variety of grave goods, including shell beads, charmstones, seeds and other personal belongings. Earlier Middle Period burials might contain these items, but were often bereft of any grave goods. Generally, lower status people were buried, whereas the elite, whose families could command support for preparing the funeral pyre, were cremated.[15] In 1814 Fathers Magín Catalá and José Viader of Santa Clara wrote of the pre-contact mortuary rituals of the Ohlone.

Sometimes they bury their dead, sometimes they burn them. In the time of mourning and at funerals the Indians have no other ceremony than to weep or yell until they tire. Sometimes they bury the deceased' clothes and trinkets with him.[16]

Economy and Subsistence

There is evidence that the prehistoric Ohlone were a semi-sedentary people who seasonally left their base villages of hemispheric tule reed dwellings and traveled to nearby resource procurement camps during certain seasons of the year.[17] There, following a traditional sexual division of labor, gathering, hunting, and fishing were practiced. From the Middle Period until European contact, there was a growing reliance of vegetal foods, including grass seeds, nuts, and bulbs. Evdience for these foodstuffs includes preserved charred remains and the mortars and milling stones used in their preparation. While the Bay Area is naturally rich in a wide variety of edible native plants and animals, the Ohlone insured a sustained yield of these resources through the controlled burning of extensive areas of grass and forested lands to promote the growth of seed-bearing annuals that were attractive to both humans and animals and to increase acorn productivity.[18] Women collected a number of items in these managed areas, including materials for basket-making and their most important vegetal food sources — grass seeds, acorns, and a variety of bulbs. Men hunted, fished, and collected.[19]

Clothing

Both sexes wore minimal clothing. Males usually went naked and women wore skirts of braided grass or tule and sometimes skins. In cooler weather both wore rabbit, sea-otter, deerskin, or feather robes. Both sexes wore shell necklaces and abalone pendants and were tattooed on their arms, faces, and foreheads.[20]

Prehistory in Santa Clara's Old Quad — The Three R's & D's

Since 1994 the Santa Clara University Archaeology Research Lab has worked closely with the California Native American Heritage Commission and Ohlone representatives, including the Muwekma Ohlone, the Ohlone Indian Tribe, the Rumsen-Ohlone and the Mutsun-Ohlone people, regarding the proper handling of Native American burials. Through these interactions we have developed for Santa Clara University the *"Three Rs Policy — Respect, Research, Reburial."* In this approach, all parties must respect the position of the other *and* the deceased individuals. There must be constructive discussions that will ensure that all parties are heard. As an institution of higher education committed to research that will extend our knowledge of other peoples and eras, Santa Clara wants to take advantage of such inadvertent discoveries to gain for researchers and the general public--whether of Native American descent or not — more information about Bay Area Native American lifeways. Ultimately, whether research is conducted or not, reburial will follow in a timely fashion and in a location that is agreeable to all.

Since this policy was initiated in 1994, the Santa Clara University Archaeology Research Lab has been involved in a number of projects wherein human remains were encountered. In some circumstances, the construction activities associated with these discoveries were rerouted to avoid further disturbance. In 1995 trenching for a new electric line encountered burials associated with the Santa Clara Mission cemetery. Dating from 1827-1851, they have provided the first tantalizing evidence for coffin burials in late mission period contexts. Through the *Three Rs Policy*, the Santa Clara University Archaeology Research Lab was able to analyze the grave goods and evidence for coffins associated with these burials.[21] At the conclusion of this project, a joint reburial ceremony was held by representatives of the Catholic Church and the Native American Community.

As a result of a number of construction projects, including the Alameda Mall (1994), the Arts and Sciences Building (1997) and work at Heafey Law Library (1998), the burials of more than twenty Native Americans were discovered. Although neither intact middens nor structures have been identified, we have begun to understand who these prehistoric Santa Clarans were. As a result of the *Three Rs Policy*, the Santa Clara University Archaeology Research Lab has been able to undertake the most exhaustive analysis of prehistoric Native American remains in the Bay Area.[22]

This has included a detailed osteological examination by physical anthropologist Dr. Lorna Pierce (a research affiliate of Santa Clara University, San Jose State University, and the Santa Clara County Medical Examiner's Office), the individuals have been radiographed for evidence of dietary stress and healed wounds. With the exception of a single healed broken toe the individuals (ranging in age from an adolescent to 40+) were in good physical condition.

In addition to these non-destructive analyses, we have also pursued destructive research, termed the *Three Ds — DNA, Dietary, and Dating*. This research is providing new information on the lives of the first Santa Clarans. These people, as represented in their bodily remains, provide us with one chance to let them speak through the millennia and tell us something about this place that they called, and we call, home.

For example, there is now direct evidence from Carbon 14 assay for the occupation of Santa Clara's Old Quad area by ancestral Ohlone people from 2400 to 1200 years ago. Located some ten miles from the shores of San Francisco Bay and five miles from the edge of the tidal marshlands at that time, the Old Quad area of Santa Clara was a mixture of open grasslands with stands of oaks, criss-crossed with thickly wooded streams and wet willow thickets.

In addition to Carbon 14 dating, bone samples from each of the individuals underwent nutritional stable isotope analysis. The Carbon 13 and Nitrogen 15 values, analyzed by nutritional anthropologist Dr. Margaret Graham (Santa Clara University), suggests that the individuals had diets that were terrestrially-based. Such a diet would include collected seeds and nuts and wild game; the values do not suggest a diet based on the regular exploitation of marine animals. Given the accounts of the faunal bounty of the San Francisco Bay Area at the time of contact, this observation may well point to small catchment areas in the prehistoric past.

Finally, samples were taken for DNA analysis. The prehistoric movement of Native Americans in California has been a topic for discussion for decades. One way to trace these movements will be through DNA analysis. This work has been conducted at the University of California-Davis by Dr. Fredrika Kaestle, at San Jose State University by Victoria Wu, and at Santa Clara University by Professor Angel Islas. Thus far the DNA research has allowed us to determine the sex of all of the non-adults and has revealed the presence of four lineages for a 700 year period from 2000 years ago to 1200 yers ago.

Grave goods, including abalone and olivella shell beads, were found in association with burials. These must be reburied. Nonetheless, in some cases, casts are made of the items. A set of these are given to Ohlone for their educational programs and another set are kept at Santa Clara University for teaching and future interpretive purposes.

Perhaps the most exciting aspect of this cooperative research endeavor was the facial reconstructions of four of the burials. Done by Ms. Karen Oeh, a graduate of California State University-Chico, these are the first reconstructions of prehistoric Ohlone in existence. Casts of the facial reconstructions were also provided to the Ohlone and for future interpretive displays at Santa Clara.

Conclusion

In April of 1997, Santa Clara University and the Muwekma Ohlone People joined together to rebury three of these individuals. While it was a solemn occasion for all parties, it also was a celebration of the lives of these three people and what they have told us about their lives from beyond the grave.

Yes, the Ohlone are still here, and as partners, we may all join together in uncovering this important aspect of **The Santa Clara Story.**

Acknowledgements

I am indebted to the following individuals for freely sharing their research on the Ohlone Peoples: Mark Hylkema, California Parks and Recreation; Andy Galvan, The Ohlone Indian Tribe; Linda Yamane, Rumsen Ohlone; Ann-Marie Sayers, Indian Canyon Nation of Mutsun People, Costanoan Indian Research, Inc.; Alan Leventhal, Ohlone Families Consulting Service; Robert Cartier, Archaeological Resource Management; George Westermark, Santa Clara University; Rebecca Allen, Past Forward Research; Dr. Thomas Layton, San José State University; Dr. Lorna Pierce, Santa Clara County Medical Examiner's Office; San José State and Santa Clara University; and Dr. Joseph Chartkoff, Michigan State University.

Endnotes

1. Field et al. 1992
2. Hinton 1988a:23-24; Hinton 1988b:27; Kroeber 1910; Levy 1978:485-486, 494; Milliken 1991; Shoup 1995:153.
3. Brown 1994:29-31; Margolin 1978
4. Cartier 1993; Hylkema 2002
5. Anza 1930; Crespi 1969; Font 1930
6. King 1994; Kroeber, et al. 1977; Levy 1978; Milliken 1991; Milliken 1995; Shoup 1995
7. Cartier 1993:65-67; Chartkoff and Chartkoff 1984:236

8. Levy 1978: 487-8; Milliken 1991: 58-61; Shoup 1995:16-17
9. Larson et al. 1994
10. Geiger and Meighan 1976: 127
11. Milliken 1995:104-107
12. Bean 1992: 305-308
13. Shoup 1995: 17-19
14. Milliken 1991: 51
15. Chartkoff and Chartkoff 1984: 233; Levy 1978: 489-90; Shoup 1995:19-20
16. Geiger and Meighan 1976: 99; Kroeber 1908: 26
17. Parkman 1994:48
18. Lewis 1973; Mayfield 1978
19. Blume 1994; Levy 1978; Reilly 1994; Schick 1994; Skowronek 1998
20. Levy 1978: 493-4; Shoup 1995:10
21. Wizorek 1996; Wizorek and Skowronek 1996; Skowronek and Wizorek 1997
22. Skowronek 2002

References Cited

Anza, Juan Bautista de. [1776]1930 Anza's California Expeditions. edited by Herbert Bolton, University of California Press, Berkeley.

Bean, Lowell J. 1992 Indians of California: Diverse and Complex Peoples. *California History* 71(3):302-323.

Blume, Joanna M. 1994 Grasslands--The Forgotten Resource: The Cultural Ecology of the Central California Grasslands. *Research Manuscript Series on the Cultural and Natural History of Santa Clara*, No. 1, Santa Clara University, Santa Clara, CA.

Brown, Alan K. 1994 The European Contact of 1772 and Some Later Documentation. *The Ohlone Past and Present, Native Americans of the San Francisco Bay* Region. Lowell John Bean, editor, Pps. 1-42. Ballena Press, Menlo Park, CA.

Cartier, Robert editor. 1993 *The Archaeology of the Guadalupe Corridor.* The Santa Clara County Archaeological Society and Archaeological Resource Management, Santa Clara, CA.

Chartkoff, Joseph L. and Kerry Kona Chartkoff. 1984 *The Archaeology of California.* Stanford University Press, Palo Alto.

Crespí, Juan. [1772] 1969 Excerpts from the Journal of Juan Crespí during the Fages and Crespí Exploration of 1772. *Who Discovered the Golden Gate?* edited by Frank M. Stanger and Alan K. Brown, San Mateo County Historical Association, San Mateo.

Field, Les, A. Leventhal, D. Sánchez and R. Cambra. 1992 A Contemporary Ohlone Tribal Revitalization Movement: A Perspective from the Muwekma Costanoan/Ohlone Indians of the San Francisco Bay Area. *California History* 71(3):412-432.

Font, Pedro. [1776] 1930 Font's Complete Diary of the Second Anza Expedition. *Anza's California Expeditions*, Volume 4. edited by Herbert E. Bolton, University of California Press, Berkeley.

Geiger, Maynard (O.F.M.) and Clement W. Meighan. 1976 *As the Padres Saw Them California Indian Life and Customs as Reported by the Franciscan Missionaries, 1813-1815.* Santa Barbara Mission Archive Library, Santa Barbara

Hinton, Leanne. 1988a The Ohlone Languages of the San Francisco Bay Area. *News from Native California* May/June pps. 23-24.

1988b On the Origin of California Tribal Names. *News from Native California* September/October pps. 27-28.

Hylkema, Mark G. 2002 Tidal Marsh, Oak Woodlands and Cultural Fluorescence Within the Southern San Francisco Bay Region. *Catalysts to Complexity: The Development of Late Holocene Maritime Societies of the California Coast.* T. Jones and J. Erlandson, editors, University of California Los Angeles Archaeological Institute Publication, University of California, Los Angeles.

King, Chester L. 1994 Central Ohlone Ethnohistory. *The Ohlone Past and Present, Native Americans of the San Francisco Bay Region.* Lowell J. Bean, editor, pp. 203-228.

Kroeber, Alfred. 1908 A Mission Record of the California Indians. *University of California Publications in American Archaeology and Ethnology,* edited by Frederic Ward Putnam, 8(1):1-27.

1910 *The Chumash and Costanoan Languages.* University of California Publications in American Archaeology and Ethnology, edited by Frederic Ward Putnam, 9(2):237-271.

Kroeber, Theodora, Albert B. Elsasser, Robert F. Heizer. 1977 *Drawn From Life, California Indians in Pen and Brush.* Ballena Press, Socorro, NM.

Larson, Daniel O., John R. Johnson, and Joel C. Michaelsen. 1994 Missionization among the Coastal Chumash of Central California: A Study of Risk Minimization Strategies. *American Anthropologist* 96(2): 263-299.

Levy, Richard. 1978 Costanoan. *Handbook of North American Indians,* Vol. 8 California edited by Robert F. Heizer, pp. 485-495, Smithsonian Institution, Washington, D.C..

Lewis, Henry T. 1973 *Patterns of Indian Burning in California: Ecology and Ethnohistory.* Ballena Press Anthropological Papers, Ramona, CA.

Mayfield, David W. 1978 *Ecology of the Pre-Spanish San Francisco Bay Area.* Unpublished MA thesis, San Francisco State University, San Francisco, CA.

Margolin, Malcom. 1978 *The Ohlone Way, Indian Life in the San Francisco-Monterey Bay Area.* Heyday Books, Berkeley.

Milliken, Randall Theodore. 1991 *An Ethnohistory of the Indian People of the San Francisco Bay Area from 1770-1810.* Ph.D. dissertation, Department of Anthropology, University of California, Berkeley.

1995 A Time of Little Choice, *The Disintegration of Tribal Culture in the San Francisco Bay*

Area, 1769-1810. Ballena Press, Menlo Park, CA.

Parkman, E. Breck. 1994 Bedrock Milling Stations. *The Ohlone Past and Present, Native Americans of the San Francisco Bay Region.* Lowell John Bean, editor, Pps. 43-63. Ballena Press, Menlo Park, CA.

Reilly, Erin M.1994 A River Ran Through It...The Cultural Ecology of the Santa Clara Valley Riparian Zone. *Research Manuscript Series on the Cultural and Natural History of Santa Clara,* No. 3, Santa Clara University, Santa Clara, CA.

Schick, Grant William 1994 The Ohlone and the Oak Woodlands: Cultural Adaptations in the Santa Clara Valley. *Research Manuscript Series on the Cultural and Natural History of Santa Clara,* No. 4, Santa Clara University, Santa Clara, CA.

Shoup, Laurence H. 1995 *Inigo of Rancho Posolmi: The Life and Times of A Mission Indian and His Land.* Archaeological/Historical Consultants, Oakland, CA for Tasman Corridor Archaeological Project, Santa Clara County Transportation Agency, San Jose, CA.

Skowronek, Russell K. 1998 Sifting the Evidence: Perceptions of Life at the Ohlone (Costanoan) Missions of Alta California. *Ethnohistory* 45(4):675-708.

Skowronek, Russell K., Editor. 2002 Discovering Santa Clara University's Prehistoric Past:CA-SCl-755. *Research Manuscript Series on the Cultural and Natural History of Santa Clara.* No. 12, Santa Clara University, Santa Clara, CA.

Skowronek, Russell K. and Julie C. Wizorek. 1997 Archaeology at Santa Clara de Asís: The Slow Rediscovery of a Moveable Mission. *Pacific Coast Archaeological Society Quarterly* 33(3):54-92.

Wizorek, Julie C. 1996 You Never Promised Me a Rose Garden: Santa Clara University Rose Garden Burials. Paper presented at the California Mission Studies Association Thirteenth Annual Conference, February 17, San Francisco, CA.

Wizorek, Julie C. and Russell K. Skowronek. 1996 *Rose Garden Burials.* Ms. on file Northwestern Information Center, Sonoma State University and Archaeology Research Lab, Santa Clara University.

CHAPTER 2

Today's Native Americans in the Santa Clara Area

Ann-Marie Sayers

Santa Clara is in the Costanoan/Ohlone territory, a territory that extends from San Francisco to Big Sur and as far east as the eastern side of the Diablo Mountains. Sixty miles south of Santa Clara, in the heart of the Gabilan Mountain Range, is a federally recognized "Indian Country" trust allotment called Indian Canyon. Of the 350 miles of coastal California from Santa Rosa to Santa Barbara, this is the only portion of the traditional lands that is still inhabited by descendants of its original people.

Indian Canyon was a safe haven for many native people who objected to the restrictions at the Mission of San Juan Bautista. The native people provided the labor force for the missions, and those who did not like the "new way" tried to return to their villages. They were often rounded up and returned to the mission, where one or two would be killed to set an example that would discourage runaways. Many of the people retreated or escaped to the sanctuary of Indian Canyon.

Indian Canyon today remains a safe haven for indigenous people. The original trust allotment to my great-grandfather has been opened to all native people who are in need of traditional land for ceremonies. I share my mother's belief that when ceremonies cease, so does the earth. Ceremony is crucial in the lives of native peoples as the expression and continuation of our relationship to the earth and to our history. It is also a foundation for the identities of tribes, families, and individuals.

My mother, a strong and wise woman, successfully petitioned the

U.S. government to issue her the Fee Deed to the property in 1945. Throughout her life, she maintained ties with the Mutsun families living in the canyon and with native people in outlying areas. Every weekend, she held a gathering at which she provided food. The people came with presentations of fruit, vegetables, and other foodstuffs; they sometimes left with more than they had arrived with. During these gatherings, my mother often spoke about her family's mission days and their struggles at that time. She also told stories that reinforced the spiritual values and codes of conduct of our people. She instilled in us respect for the land and its gifts. From her I learned that the proper way to pick oregano, for example, is to first thank the plant for making itself available because all natural elements are part of a whole.

The canyon is narrow and a mile long. Seven waterfalls enhance its beauty. Sycamores, bay trees, coastal live oaks, bull pines, and buckeye trees are plentiful along the creek running through the canyon. With the ceremonies that are performed here, it is a very powerful place. Sweat lodges (places for prayer), fire circles, arbors, and dancing grounds are located throughout the canyon. Tribal members and others come to the canyon for vision quests, council meetings, bear dances, moon ceremonies, purifications, talking feather circles, healing ceremonies, and many other sacred practices. On one occasion, a man from the Zuni Pueblo, in west-central New Mexico near the Arizona border, came to the canyon to perform a feather planting ceremony. He explained that he was visiting his sister in San Jose and that it was very important to him to plant a feather at the full moon. Previously, he had tried using Alum Rock Park, but people had interrupted him to ask curiously what he was doing. He would explain and then have to begin his ceremony again. The next day he found that the feather he had planted had disappeared. I said, "Say no more; that is why the canyon is here." After finishing his ceremony, he came to the cabin. His radiance and joy expressed the reason for maintaining this sacred land for native people.

The water that runs through the canyon is the blood of the earth, making many lives possible. In the Mutsun language, the word *rumme* means not just water but also the creek itself and the movement of the water. These are inseparable.

The wind that blows through the canyon is the breath of the

earth. The leaves themselves inhale and exhale. Once, many years ago, I was angry with myself and started pouring out my anger to the father of my daughter. He said, "Come outside." As I followed him out of the cabin to the lower deck, the anger was still coming from my mouth. Suddenly, from the corner of my eye, I saw a sycamore leaf wilt. When I stopped the anger flowing from my mouth, the wilting stopped. I realized that I was hurting not just myself and the man I loved but all life surrounding me — a valuable lesson about connections.

Many people find their way to the canyon. One young woman came with a fat file of papers. She said that neither her mother nor her grandmother would admit she was Indian but a great-aunt had given her the names of her ancestors. I explained the likely reason for her mother's and grandmother's reluctance to admit their heritage. In 1851 and 1852, the government signed eighteen treaties with the native people of California, but the treaties were never ratified; they simply disappeared. Finally, in 1904 they were found by a clerk in an office in Washington, D.C. In 1854 alone, the government spent over 1.4 million dollars implementing the California Indian Genocide Policy Act. Indian hunters were paid five dollars a head and fifty cents a scalp plus money for food and supplies. In such circumstances, it was suicidal to admit one was an Indian. To survive, a woman who has seen her husband and sons killed tells her daughter, "Say you are a Mexican."

The 1850 California Act for the Government and Protection of Indians had the effect of forcing a kind of slavery on the native people of the state. Among other things, this law stipulated, "In no case shall a white man be convicted of any offense upon the testimony of an Indian." Thus, native people were barred from any redress against the actions of whites. The widespread effects of the act included forcing native culture underground as a matter of survival and allowing a thriving trade in native children.

To acknowledge ones native heritage was to be marginalized and disenfranchised. A popular tenet held that there were no natives left. Not until 1924 were people who claimed their heritage permitted to vote. Even then, the families who sustained local native communities were kept "out of the loop" on important sociopolitical and land use decisions. I have to tell the young woman with the fat file that her mother and grandmother were not ashamed; they were simply acting as best they could to ensure survival.

The attitudes that produced this denial continue. As recently as 1993, my daughter came home from her first day of school in tears. She told be that a boy had said to her, "If you are an Indian, you are dead." I made her laugh and then told her, "Well, you are not dead, and you are still Indian." This made me realize the importance of educating people, of standing up and saying, "We are still here."

In 1993, we began testifying on legislation to ensure that Native American concerns are addressed and began working with the Central Coast Resource Conservation Development Council, a program sponsored by the USDA and serving six counties from Santa Clara to Santa Barbara. Our 10-year Stewardship Incentive Program has been used as a model to show how "Indian Country" can work with government. This vegetation management program incorporates traditional native practices. For example, cattails and tule have been planted in one of the local stream areas. We can harvest the green reeds to make tule dwellings and cordage. Another plant important to native culture, sedge, produces rhizomes used in making baskets.

We call ourselves Indian Canyon Nation because we are not governed by city, county, or state regulatory agencies. A major mission of Indian Canyon Nation is education. We served as host to a National Resource Conservation Service Harmony workshop, a five-day educational program for district conservationists to learn about the history of California Indians. At the workshop, Vivian Hailstone, a Karuk, Yurok, and member of the Hoopa Valley Tribe, said, "Ann-Marie, in my 85 years, this is the first time I have seen Indians talking and the government listening." This is high praise indeed from an elder.

Each year several thousand students, ranging from 4th-graders studying California Indian History to university students, come to the canyon to learn. The fee for coming here is a pledge of allegiance to the earth. We believe that when these pledges go full circle, the earth can survive a little longer.

EcoSoul, a national fuel cell education program based in Tustin, California, asked us to be a model for using hydrogen fuel cells. Indian Canyon is off the grid, so one of my questions was, "Does this mean I can have a washer and dryer?" The answer was "Yes." In the solar hydrogen cycle, electricity from photovoltaic panels and wind turbines runs an electrolyzer, a device that splits water into hydrogen and oxygen. The oxygen is released into the air and the hydrogen is pumped into storage tanks where it can be kept on site or shipped to areas with little sun. When solar energy is not available, the hydrogen can be recombined with oxygen in the air in a fuel cell. The process is analogous to the processes of nature and the only by-product is pure water. Obviously, such a program can provide for the people of Indian Canyon a source of electricity that is in keeping with our respect for nature's work and for the land itself. At our California Indian Storytelling event next year, we will not have to worry about our microphone's batteries going dead.

As part of my commitment to making the history of the California native peoples known, I was recently designated by the Native American Heritage Commission to be a Native American monitor for the Walsh/Kenna/Heafey HVAC upgrade project at Santa Clara University. As a Native American monitor, I advise and warn or caution people who move earth in archaeologically sensitive areas. I, like many Native Americans, believe that when a burial is disturbed and the remains are not ceremonially reburied, the spirit of the dead person wanders endlessly.

While I monitored the work at Santa Clara University, eight burials were exposed under the direction of Dr. Russ Skowronek, associate professor of anthropology. The assistant campus archaeologist, Linda Hylkema, worked with us. As I watched her unearth a burial using a trowel, a whisk broom, paint brushes, and dental picks, I was again impressed by the professionalism and integrity of many modern archaeologists. They work to help expose our history while, at the same time, demonstrating care and respect for the spirits of the dead. Although our history since contact has often been difficult, today is certainly the best time since contact for California Indians.

Many of the burials exposed at Santa Clara University were left in place, undisturbed and protected. The day was my birthday. To see these burials treated with such respect and reverence was the best gift I could have received. That governments and universities seek our advice and listen to us shows that we are truly still here.

SECTION II
Mission
Santa Clara

In the 1770s, the South Bay region began a transformation. New peoples, representing imperial Spain, arrived and brought with them a new social order, as well as technologies and ideologies. The center in the South Bay for these changes was Mission Santa Clara de Asís. Founded in January of 1777, it served as a nexus for Native Californians from the Bay Area and Central Valley and for peoples of African, Asian, Mexican, and Spanish descent. These new immigrants, whether priests, soldiers, or settlers, came to transform the local people and environment into a facsimile of their concept of Catholic Europe. That is, they created a New Europe in the New World. During the sixty years of its operation as a Franciscan mission, Mission Santa Clara effected profound changes in the region. The environment changed as the numbers of cattle, goats, horses, pigs, and sheep increased and denuded the countryside with their seemingly insatiable hunger. Forests were felled for fuel and building materials, and in their place, flourished orchards and agricultural fields. As the environment changed, so too did the lives of the Ohlone. As people joined the mission community, their precontact lifeways were changed. The new way of life that evolved showed a syncretism of Old World and New World experiences. By the end of Mexican rule the area had ceased to be known as the "Plain of the Oaks" ("llano de los robles") and now was simply called the Santa Clara Valley.

CHAPTER 3

The California Context

Robert M. Senkewicz

The purpose of this presentation is to offer you an overview of some of the significant happenings in California during its Spanish (1769-1821), Mexican (1821-1848), and early American/gold rush (1848-1856) periods. In this sesquicentennial series, you have already heard from others about the original Californians, the indigenous peoples who lived here for many thousands of years before 1769. While this presentation will focus on the Europeans, it is important for us to remember that prior to 1849, the overwhelming majority of California's population was comprised of these indigenous peoples, who numbered over 300,000 when the first Spanish settlement was founded at San Diego.

I would like to structure these remarks around three questions: (1) where was California; (2) what was California; and (3) who was California? I hope that these three "w's" — where, what, and who — can provide a useful context for your further study of Santa Clara University and its region.

First, where was California? For us, that question seems perhaps a bit odd. We all know that California is in the west, as far west as one can go and still remain in the contiguous 48 states. But to understand California during most of the period we are considering, we have to alter our perspective. For most of the non-indigenous people who lived in California before 1848, California was not in the west, but in the north. "California" was a mysterious place that comprised what are now three states, two of them Mexican (Baja California and Baja California Sur) and one of them American (California). It was the first place you came to when you sailed out of the ports of western Mexico, such as Acapulco or San Blas, and headed towards the north.

On that journey, you would encounter a piece of land that began at what was eventually called Cabo San Lucas and stretched north indefinitely. This land was part of a political world whose center was the palace of the viceroy located in a huge plaza built on the site of the old Aztec temple in Mexico City. In that world, this land was the far northern frontier. Like any frontier, it was almost by definition remote; also, like many frontiers, it was the subject of myth and fable.

This brings us to the second point: what was California? In the beginning, California was imaginary. It first appeared in a novel, The Great Deeds of Esplandián by Garci Rodríguez de Montalvo, which was published in Spain in 1510. In this work of fiction, "California" was an island "on the right hand side of the Indies." A place of fabulous riches, it was inhabited by a race of black women, led by a Queen named Calafia. Assisted by griffins (legendary figures with the bodies of lions and the heads and wings of eagles), they were fierce warriors whose prowess in battle was known the world over.

When Spanish sailors began sailing up the western coast of Mexico in the 1530s, they encountered land about a hundred miles to the west of Mazatlán. They assumed they had come upon an island. Would-be colonists, including Hernán Cortés, found the "island" too rugged and its inhabitants too hostile to allow the establishment of a Spanish outpost. Over the years the name of Rodríguez de Montalvo's imaginary island, California, became sardonically applied to this newly found and forbidding "island." The name stuck even after the Spanish came to realize that the island was a peninsula attached to the mainland.

But in another sense, California always remained an island. The expanse of land that connected California to the mainland of Mexico was the Sonora Desert. Then as now, this was a harsh and inhospitable terrain. Since this desert made land travel between Mexico City and California difficult, the earliest explorers all arrived by sea. The first permanent Spanish settlement in Baja California occurred in 1697, and the soldiers, missionaries, and their party traveled by ship across the Gulf of California. The Baja California outposts were always supplied from the Mexican mainland by sea, even after Jesuit Eusebio Kino mapped a land route in the early 18th century. The first permanent settlement in Alta California at San Diego resulted from a joint land-sea expedition from Baja California in 1769, but afterwards, the infant colony was always supplied by sea, not by land. The 1774 and 1775 journeys of Juan Bautista de Anza demonstrated that large colonizing parties could traverse the Sonora Desert if careful preparations were painstakingly made. But in 1781, the Quechán Indians revolted near Yuma, and they closed de Anza's land route. For the rest of the Spanish and Mexican periods, California was supplied by sea. In many respects, it might as well have been an island.

One result of this insularity was that the Spanish and Mexican settlement of California took place in areas that were accessible to the sea. Spanish and Mexican California was always a thin sliver of land, extending at most a few score miles from the coast. The settlements could never afford to venture too far from their maritime lifeline.

If California was an island in the imagination, and if the geography of northern Mexico resulted in its being treated as an island for much of its history, what was it in a political sense? It was a province of the Spanish empire until 1821. After a few years as a part of the Mexican empire, it became a territory of the Mexican republic in 1824 and remained in that general status until it was occupied by U.S. troops (who, tellingly, invaded from the sea) in 1846. It was ruled by a military government until it ratified a state constitution in 1849, although it was not formally admitted to the Union until 1850.

Third, who was in California? Again, let me emphasize that Native Americans formed the overwhelming majority of the California population until the gold rush. The approximately 400,000 indigenous inhabitants of Baja and Alta California were joined by a handful of Spaniards in 1697 at Loreto. These Spaniards were the heirs of a long tradition of Spanish expansion in the New World. For them the Spanish presence involved establishing three institutions — missions, presidios, and pueblos. These three entities had been the foundation of Spanish expansion in America since the 16th century.

Two of these three institutions were planted in Baja California. Jesuit missionaries founded 18 missions there until they were expelled by the King of Spain in 1767. After their departure, another 10 missions were founded, one by the Franciscans and nine by the Dominicans. One presidio, at Loreto, supplied the major military presence for most of the Spanish period.

Alta California grew out of Baja California, and it witnessed the development of all three of these basic institutions. From 1769 until 1822 the Franciscans founded 21 missions in this remote frontier, from San Diego in the south to San Francisco Solano (Sonoma) in the north. Santa Clara was founded in early 1777, less than a year after the establishment of a presidio and a mission at San Francisco. Exploring parties in the early 1770s had spoken very favorably of the potential of Santa Clara Valley, which the explorers dubbed "The Valley of the Oaks" in honor of a prominent natural feature. So both the Franciscans and the military were eager to establish a Spanish presence there after the founding of San Francisco.

The province was guarded by four presidios, San Diego and Santa Barbara in the south, and Monterey (the provincial capital) and San Francisco in the north. Three civil settlements, San José, Los Angeles, and Branciforte (near Santa Cruz) were also founded. While Branciforte was an ill-conceived and unsuccessful venture, the other two pueblos became relatively prosperous agricultural settlements, in which the citizens produced food for the sustenance of the soldiers in the presidios.

One objective of the entire Spanish colonial enterprise was to transform the indigenous inhabitants into productive citizens of New Spain. In the practical order, that meant making them Catholics and teaching them settled agriculture. The missions were key to both of these endeavors. Missions were far more than the church buildings that, in their restored form, are familiar to us today. They included thousands of acres of land, which was used for both agriculture and ranching. The mission crops — mainly wheat and corn, but also barley and beans and other food items — were planted, grown, and harvested by the Indians, usually under the supervision of a Spanish or indigenous mayordomo. On the large tracts of land that surrounded the farms, large numbers of animals — cattle, sheep, horses, and goat — grazed. The missions gradually developed into successful religious and agricultural communities. Their prosperity was enhanced by the outbreak of the Mexican insurgency and struggle for independence in 1810. Distracted by this conflict, the colonial authorities in Mexico City were unable to supply the California garrisons on a regular basis so the missions filled the void. They became the main source of food and other production for the province. This enhanced their power and their status within colonial society.

This new prosperity led to an increasing resentment of their power by the other Spanish settlers in California. After the achievement of Mexican independence, this resentment found support in the ascendency of a set of Enlightenment-influenced ideas hostile to the notion that it was appropriate for the church to possess landed wealth such as missions. A generation of Mexican Californians born around the turn of the 18th century strongly supported what was called the "secularization" of the missions. This was a process by which the missions would be deprived of their landed property and turned into regular (the technical term was "secular") parishes. The land would be turned back to the original owners, the Indians, with any surplus land available to be distributed to Mexican settlers.

The Mexican Congress passed such a law in 1833, and the California missions were ended. The Indians received precious little of the land. Most of it was distributed to the *Californios*, who quickly turned much of the land into a number of profitable ranchos. The major product of the ranchos in Mexican California was cattle, which were raised not for food but for their hides and fat (tallow). The hides were purchased by Anglo-American sea captains, who transported them back to the east coast of the United States. California hides became an important raw material in the development of the Massachusetts shoe industry, which was one of the first stirrings of the industrial revolution in America.

Between 1833 and 1846, over 800 land grants were made by the government of California. The land grant system was a fairly relaxed one. This was appropriate for a situation in which the availability of land far exceeded the number of potential grantees. (By 1846, there were only about 9,000 non-Indian inhabitants of California). The boundaries of the land grants tended to be imprecise: a tree, a stream, or a ridge might serve as marking the extent of a rancho. Of course, a tree could die or be cut down, and a stream could dry up or be diverted. This relaxed system worked well in Mexican California, but it proved inadequate when California became an American possession. The American system of land law, which superimposed imaginary lines in a grid pattern over a landscape, valued precision, regularity, and order. The California Land Act passed by Congress in

1851 assumed that most California land titles were invalid, and required the *Californios* to prove titles to their land in U.S. courts. Many were unable to do so. Even if they were ultimately successful in their legal contests, they found that the costs of litigation had often forced them to sell off large parts of their holdings to pay the accumulating legal bills. Within twenty years, most *Californios* had lost most of their lands to the Americans.

Americans began to come to California in significant numbers in the 1820s. The first Yankees who came to the Pacific coast were generally traders, often agents for eastern commercial firms. Since their ability to trade effectively demanded that they form good relations with the missionaries and then with the ranchers, they often made efforts to assimilate into Hispanic society. A number of them became Catholics and married *Californio* women. As men of commerce, these Yankees tended to cluster around the commercial centers of the coast: Monterey, Santa Barbara, Los Angeles, and San Diego. In the early 1840s, another group of Americans began entering California. These were people who immigrated to the territory by land on wagon trains. They generally settled in the northern part of California, often setting themselves up in the Sacramento Valley. A number of them received land grants, which they began to develop as ranchos. Often they did not interact with many of the Hispanic inhabitants of California. The overland routes they followed entered California north of most of the existing ranchos in that part of the territory where the Hispanic presence was most weak and thin.

When the armed forces of the United States conquered California in 1846-1847, things did not immediately change all that much. The U.S. military government replaced the Mexican government, but many Mexican laws remained in force. The treaty of Guadalupe Hidalgo, which ended the Mexican War in 1848, explicitly stated that property rights would be respected in all the lands that the US was taking from Mexico.

But the gold rush changed everything. In the space of a few years, hundreds of thousands of Americans swarmed into California. One result of this was that California acquired a more urban tinge. The basic settlement pattern of the gold rush was the mining camp, in which forms of government were adapted from eastern and midwestern towns and villages. Since gold was discovered in the north, San Francisco became the port of entry for both people and goods. It became an instant city, with its population exploding from a few hundred in 1846 to over 50,000 a decade later.

The gold rush introduced a number a new elements into California culture. We do not have time to develop them fully here, but let me suggest a few. First, the gold rush speeded up the pace of life. While the traditional picture of pre-US California as a blissful and pastoral Eden, a leisure-filled lotus land is certainly an overdrawn stereotype, California had never experienced anything like the frenzy that the 49ers brought. The miners staked claims on virtually every river and stream in northern California. When a claim dried up, they were quick to move on and begin the process all over again. The gold rush movement of so many people over so much land in so short a time was something that was entirely new to California, whose own Spanish and Mexican frontier past had been marked by a much less frenetic tone.

With this increased pace of life came a fundamental social instability. The institutions of government did not always take quick root in the gold country, and the rough justice of the mining camps was rarely marked by order and regularity. In addition, there was a profound psychic instability. The expectations of those who rushed for gold in 1849 and the early 1850s were rarely fulfilled, and the dream of easy riches proved a very elusive one. Californians who made money during this period did so not by directly participating in the gold rush itself, but by providing services for those who were panning for precious metals. Leland Stanford, for instance, was a grocer, not a miner, and his experience was typical. If you wanted to make money in gold rush California, the worst thing you could do was look for gold. Supplies were so limited and prices were so high, especially in the hectic early days of the rush, that any gold you discovered would soon find its way into the accounts of a Sacramento or San Francisco merchant. The gold rush did not deliver the easy wealth it promised.

Perhaps as a result of this psychic instability, racial scapegoating was a constant feature of the gold rush. While relations between Spaniards and Mexican *Californios*, on the one hand, and Indians, on the other hand, had never been placid, the racial animosity after the gold rush was both deeper and wider. In addition to continuing the struggles against the Indians, the Americans added other targets as well. In 1850 the legislature passed a Foreign Miners' Tax, which was aimed at Mexicans who were working the southern diggings below Stockton. Two of the largest vigilante movements in American history, the San Francisco Committees of Vigilance of 1851 and 1856 were aimed at Australians and Irish, respectively. Anti-Chinese acts and attitudes were also an unfortunate constant of gold rush life.

But there was one important continuity between Spanish/Mexican and American California. In the United States, when President Polk announced at the end of 1848 that gold had in fact been discovered in California, his announcement set off one of the greatest internal mass migrations in American history. The gold rush was something in which hundreds of thousands of Americans directly participated, and millions more participated vicariously through letters from families or accounts that were published in newspapers up and down the east coast. The reason for this interest was simple: California was the first place in the United States where the age-old dream that had fired explorers from all over Europe for centuries after 1492 — the dream of gold — had actually come true. This fact alone gave California a tremendous and unique place in the American imagination. Even though the gold rush did not deliver on its promise for most of those who pursued the dream, dreams and fantasies took quick root in California soil. In a real sense, California under the Americans has always been as much an imaginary place as it was in the 1510 Spanish novel in which its name had been invented.

CHAPTER 4

The Indigenous Presence in the Colonial Visual Culture of Mexico and the Southwest

Constance Cortez

Much of the art and architecture produced in the Americas shortly after European contact represents a kind of cultural discourse between Native and European populations. The presence of diverse styles found in the visual culture produced during the colonial period stands as evidence of the multiplicity of indigenous groups and of ideological and political intrusions of European colonists. At the same time, the presence of indigenous ideology and ritual in post-contact artworks attests to the conflicted nature of the encounter and, perhaps, to resistance to acculturation on the part of the indigenous population. Because of these factors, as well as the geographic distances that separate each of the diverse groups subject to Spanish rule, art forms found in Mexico and the Southwest tend to be reflective of local colonial concerns.

Despite the specificity of colonial experiences, however, it is still necessary to understand the conquest in what would become México. It was this initial encounter that functioned as an ideological and strategic template for future spiritual and military campaigns. With that in mind, I have divided the following pages into three parts. The first section offers a brief introduction to the colonial encounter in México and a discussion of Spanish strategies there. The second part addresses European arrival into New México, touching upon the actions of the Spaniards there as well as the spiritual and political agendas of Spain promoted in the arts. Finally, I will discuss indigenous communities and the reaction to the Spanish presence that is manifested in the art and architecture of the Southwest and California.

Part I. Colonial Architecture and the New Jerusalem

The conquest of Central México can divided into two phases, one of which was considerably longer than the other. The first phase took the form of a relatively brief military engagement. Landing in 1519, Hernán Cortés and his forces took only two years to conquer the Aztec Empire. In addition to his Spanish troops, Cortés was greatly aided by indigenous groups such as the Tlaxcalans, who had political axes to grind with the Aztecs, and by a Nahuatl-speaking woman named Malintzin (a.k.a. La Malinche or Doña Marina) who served as both translator and advisor.

The second part of the conquest was the conversion and assimilation of the natives of New Spain. This required strategies that were much more long-term in their scope and the responsibility rested heavily on the newly arrived Catholic priests. These mendicant friars were keenly interested in the indigenous religions of Central Mexico, and they quickly realized that a good understanding of these belief systems would aid them in the extirpation of what they viewed as idolatrous practices. Works of missionaries such as Bernardino de Sahagún and Diego Duran[1] extensively discuss indigenous ritual and daily activities of the contact period and are testaments to mendicant efforts at eradication of native religious and social customs.

Regardless of their carefully planned strategies, both conquistador and priest had difficulties comprehending their new environment. The grandeur of the Aztec capital, with its 200,000 inhabitants, was beyond anything experienced in Europe. By comparison, during the 16th century, London was the largest city in Europe with just over 50,000 people. To make sense of this New World and its inhabitants, Spaniards depended upon models that were, for the most part, based on European social paradigms and European modes of communication. For instance, readings from the popular literature of fantasy and stories from the crusades were modified to fit the situation.[2] Even classical legends were used: in labels attached to illustrations of deities from Sahagún's Florentine Codex, the Aztec god, Huitzilopochtli, is clearly to be understood as a version of "Jupiter," while another deity, Tezcatlipoca, fulfilled the role of the "other Hercules." While Sahagún was at least able to manage similes, other chroniclers borrowed wholesale beasties born and bred in the European imagination. A case in point is the depiction of Huitzilopochtli as a Bleayme,[3] a headless being with eyes in its midriff. Of course, the most important literary source that the Spaniards relied upon for their explanations was the Bible. In the sixteenth century, the prevailing Christian belief was that God had created one world and that all peoples in that world were descended from Adam and Eve. Predictably enough, speculation ran rampant as Spaniards tried to fit New World groups into a more recognizable rubric of reality. Suggestions for likely genealogical origins ranged from assignment of indigenous peoples to one of the lost tribes of Israel to their being assigned Welsh ancestry.[4]

Possibly the most important European models to be applied to the Americas were the interrelated concepts of an "earthly paradise" and the "New Jerusalem." The notion of an "earthly paradise" had its origin in medieval times[5] and was an idea primarily promoted by Franciscans. They believed that in this new Eden, the Americas, all things were possible. Furthermore, since the apex of their spiritual teaching was the image of the Apocalypse, they were therefore millennialists. They believed in the doctrine promoted by St. John in which a thousand-year rule of Christ would be made possible only after all of the world's peoples had been exposed to Christianity and given the chance to convert. In this new Eden, then, it was the Franciscans who took on the task of introducing Christianity to the Americas.

Inspired by writings such as Thomas More's *Utopia*,[6] some priests tried to set up ideal Indian communities that would protect the Indians from the Spanish conquistadors. Franciscans uniformly supported attempts at isolating the Native Americans, and Gerónimo de Mendieta actually wrote a book in which he created a new Eden based on an image of the Old World. In his *Historia Eclestiastica Indiana*,[7] he promoted a sacred vision of the Americas by creating alternative identities for some of the key players in the 16th century. Charles V, who was the emperor of much of Europe, was equated with

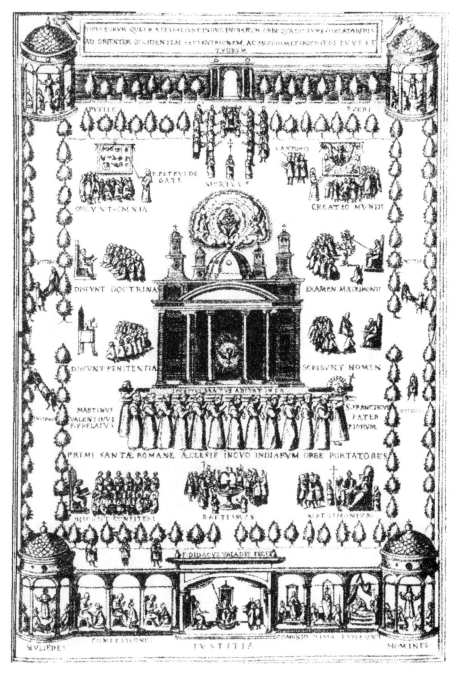

FIGURE 1: Diego Valadés. *Image of Evangelizaion from Rhetorica cristiana.* 1579.
After Cline, Howard F. *Handbook of Middle American Indians,* (Austin, University of
Texas Press, 1975) Volume 14, Figure 95.

the Messiah. Cortés took up position as a new Moses, presumably leading his band of men as well as future converts to a new Holy Land. Following the logical flow of his paradigm, Mendieta was one of the first explorers to ascribe a Hebraic origin to the indigenous population of the Americas. In his volume, he presented Native Americans as tabula raza, innocents living in their own Garden of Eden waiting for identities to be ascribed to them. Non-elite Spanish conquistadors, for their part, were presented as corrupting forces, a kind of collective serpent in the garden, ready to exploit the unsuspecting and gullible acolytes. Following all of this, it was a logical step for Mendieta to assign the Aztec capital, Tenochtitlán-Mexico, a new identity. It became the New Jerusalem.

One of the best known images of this utopian vision of the New World is by Diego Valadés, a 16th century indigenous priest who received artistic and theological training in Europe (Figure 1).[8] Here we see architecture framing Franciscan evangelization in its idealized form as a combination of the Earthly Paradise and the New Jerusalem. The first twelve Franciscans to come to the New World in 1525 are shown carrying Saint Peter's Basilica on their back. Leading the procession, is Saint Francis, raised from the dead, brandishing a cross. The numerical correspondence here between these friars and the original twelve apostles is no accident. In the 16th century, St. Francis was understood as a medieval manifestation of Christ (complete with stigmata), so it is natural that Francis's followers should mirror the apostles in their numbering. Beyond direct allusions to Christianity, Valadés's representation also offers the modern viewer a rudimentary schematic of every church built in the New World, including those that would later be built in what was to become New Mexico and California. We see an *atrio*, a large courtyard, divided into ordered spaces reserved for catechism and indoctrination. In the artist's schema, these special educational areas are clearly labeled. At the corners of the *atrio* were *posas*, chapels used for praying and in ritual in which circumambulation played a role.

What is not shown in this image by Valadés is the garden that was part of every mission. Generally speaking, such gardens were located in the cloister of the monastery and were therefore surrounded by rooms occupied by priests. Monastic private gardens functioned as places of contemplation for the priests, providing medicinal plants for their aching bodies and spiritual relief for their souls.[9] On the level of Christian symbolism, they also invoked the images of the Garden of Eden, man's fall from grace, and the possibility of redemption.

The Franciscans were among the first clergy to come to the Americas and would be the first to go to lands north of the Aztec Empire. Many of the models that had proved more or less successful in converting the indigenous peoples of México would be taken to New México and, then, on to California. There they would be tried and modified as different situations required.

Part II: On to the Southwest

In 1595, King Philip II of Spain authorized the conquest and colonization of the Kingdom of New Mexico. By January of 1598, Juan de Oñate was leading an entourage of 129 men north from Mexico. As has been noted by the scholar, Ramon Gutierrez,[10] Oñate quickly realized the historic weight of his actions. He consciously decided to recreate the Conquest of México that had occurred some eighty years previously.[11] Oñate's plan was to be accomplished by the deliberate manipulation of symbols. Under this rubric, he became the new Cortés. As in the case of the conqueror of Mexico, Oñate led his group into New México under the banner of Our Lady of the Remedies. In his retinue of conquerors, he included a group of Tlaxcalan Indians, warriors from the indigenous group who had helped Cortés to overthrow the Aztec Empire. An indigenous woman, known as Doña Inés, filled the historic slot assigned to Malinche, Cortés's translator and consort. The twelve Franciscans who accompanied Oñate were to emulate the actions of the first twelve "Apostles" who had entered México in 1525.

Linguistic difficulties were inherent in the initial contact between the Spanish forces and the indigenous populations in New Mexico. In addition to the conversion methods they had honed in Mexico, Spaniards also used a form of informal theatre to drive home a variety of points to the potential acolytes.[12] As Oñate entered each Puebloan Village, he and his men reenacted the Conquest of México, rightly reckoning that the Puebloans had received word of the victory over the Aztecs to the south. Likewise, the Franciscans were also acutely aware of the potency of mimicking earlier successful acts in México.

They built and established their churches, using much the same plan as was used in México but with some differences. For instance, as a result of the smaller populations that the Spaniards encountered in New Mexico, the *atrio*, the large courtyard that fronted churches in México, was dramatically diminished in size.

Likewise, the interiors of churches were much smaller although there was some iconic continuity to be found between the New Mexican churches and those of México. The Franciscans also created similar spatial organizations. A long central aisle was terminated by an altar screen called a reredos. Such altar screens can be understood in terms of evangelization. They were didactic devices – kinds of stages upon which connections between the spiritual realm and that of humans could be realized.[13] The former was embodied in the sculpture and painted scenes found on the reredos and the latter was realized in the celebration of the mass. The typical reredos was divided horizontally into three ascending sections, a division that was reflective of heavenly order. Saints and fathers of the church usually surrounded the most important icons, which were, in turn, generally located centrally on each tier. At the top of the screen, there was usually a reference to Christ as God, God the Father, or a reference to the holy trinity. The transition between the sacred and human realms was provided by an altar that fronted the screen. Here, priests kept objects used in

FIGURE 2: Pulpit with Solomonic Column from San José de Gracia, Las Trampas, New Mexico. 1776. After Wakeley, David. *A Sense of Mission: Historic Churches of the Southwest* (San Francisco, Chronicle Books, 1994) p. 71.

the celebration of the mass that were essential for human participation. It was in the celebration of the mass that the Christian past, with all its history, was made present in the New World.

The iconography of church interiors also spoke to notions of the New Jerusalem even in minute details of architecture. For instance, the column supporting the pulpit from San José de Gracia in Las Trampas (1776) (Figure 2) is often found in colonial architecture of the Americas. This spiraling column is referred to as a "Solomonic Column" and is a device that had been used in European architecture and sculpture for hundreds of years, most notably in the high altar of St. Peter's in the Vatican. The Solomonic column has a particular importance, however, to colonial situations.[14] The Spaniards of the 16th and 17th centuries felt that they had lost Jerusalem during the Crusades and, with the expulsion of the Moors in 1492 and the discovery of the Americas in the same year, Spain felt that the tides were turning. God was once again smiling on his people. America, with its vast stores of wealth, was seen as the "New Jerusalem" and was yet another example of the primacy of Christianity. Since the use of the Solomonic column had always been recognized as an early Christian reference to the type of column in the Temple of Solomon in Jerusalem, its placement in the architecture and sculpture of the Americas proclaimed to all the validity of the New Jerusalem. This also played to Franciscan notions of millenialism because, as it will be recalled, the conquest of Jerusalem ("new" or old) was requisite for initiating the Second Coming of Christ.

Part III: Indigenous Religion and Syncretism

Prior to the coming of the Spaniards to New México, Puebloan groups had moved south from more ancient Anasazi cities located in places such as Mesa Verde and Chaco Canyon in the four-corners area of what is today the United States. They had re-established themselves along rivers that could provide a much more reliable source of water than their northern homelands. They brought with them their architecture and their religion. Ramon Gutiérrez points out that the two main types of architecture, the home and the kiva, were both associated with religious beliefs and were each gender specific.[15] Religion and

notions of gender acted in concert to reinforce the structure of
Puebloan society.

At the time, Puebloan society was matrilineal, with descent
reckoned through the mother's line. This matrilineal reckoning had as
its basis the mythohistory associated with the Corn Mothers who gave
birth to the first humans.[16] These supernatural primordial females
functioned as archetypes and Puebloan women were therefore viewed
as generative and associated with earth and things from the earth. It
is for this reason that women owned and continue to own the houses.
They also had exclusive ownership of land that was used for
cultivation.

While women controlled the forces of earth, men controlled
elements of sky such as lightning and rain and unpredictable aspects
of nature and elements outside of the village such as hunting and war.
Men's particular sphere of power was also represented in their own
architectural complex: the kiva.[17] A kiva is a subterranean or semi-
subterranean enclosure that is covered. Its sacred interior functioned
as a site for male gatherings and a male living space where men lived
most of their lives. Rituals occurring inside were generally directed
toward the forces of nature and, often times, ceremonies beginning in
the kivas extended into public places. The latter were manifested in
dances performed on the roofs of the kivas and in public plazas.

Men invoked the energizing spirits of Hopi deities and ancestors
inside of the kivas. These deified ancestors and nature spirits were
known collectively as kachinas or katsinas. Most of the year, they
lived in mountains, but they would make annual trips, travelling
though the earth, to emerge at the sipapu, a hole in the floor near the
center of the kiva. It was through this portal in a male-controlled
architectural space that the supernatural manifested itself in the lives
of Puebloan communities.

Kachinas took on a variety of forms, but were, for the most part,
consistently associated with aspects of nature. In their non-corporeal
form, kachinas could appear as rain clouds which provided the rain
that made things grow. They could also appear as geological features,
constellations, animals, and insects. In their corporeal forms, the
kachinas physically manifested themselves as small wooden effigies
called kachina-tihus or as masks and costumes worn by human
impersonators. In all instances, men inevitably controlled the

kachinas and actually became the kachinas when they were manifested in human form.

Important societal positions were also associated with nature-controlling kachinas. Paramount among these was the position of rain chief.[18] As a rain chief, a man was believed to be able to invoke the rain that would quench and fertilize the parched earth. Hunt chiefs practiced animal magic via fetishes that they would endow with power in their kivas; this allowed the animals to be caught. Additionally, men developed warrior societies to maintain the peace within the community and to assure the community's safety from outside forces. As pointed out by Gutiérrez,[19] all of these unpredictable masculine elements — rain, war, the hunt — were balanced by the feminine generative aspects of nature. In this manner, equilibrium was maintained within the community.

After the arrival of the Europeans, it was the male aspect of indigenous religion that was consciously infused with Christianity. This was done by substituting aspects of Catholic religion for similar aspects in the Native American belief system.[20] To further gain the confidence of the indigenous people, the priests took on functions that were out of keeping with those prescribed by the Latin Church and re-created their roles to better suit indigenous expectations. The Franciscans became rain chiefs and medicine men and were, therefore, believed to be masters of the forces of nature. Proof of their abilities with animal magic was found in the priest's ability to domesticate large animals that they had brought with them. As part of their new identities, the priests became the symbolic and actual protectors of the communities, protecting Native Americans not only from natural and potentially dangerous spiritual forces, but also from the Spanish conquistadors themselves. In protecting the community from physical harm, they successfully ideologically substituted themselves for the men who had inhabited leadership positions in traditional indigenous warrior societies.

In architecture, the most significant change was the replacement of the indigenous male-run kiva by the Spanish male-run church. In many instances, the church was placed near or on top of the kiva[21] — again this was a replication of conquest protocol from Mexico. Other elements that were derived from indigenous sources or partially

FIGURE 3: Wall Murals from San Jose de Laguna, Laguna Pueblo, New Mexico. 1699. Drawing After Wakeley, David. *A Sense of Mission: Historic Churches of the Southwest* (San Francisco, Chronicle Books, 1994) p. 71

infused with indigenous meaning were also added to the church.

Although the overall plan of the churches was similar to those in Central Mexico, the frontier churches of New Mexico were made of different materials; adobe was ideal owing to its availability and its ability to retain warmth in the winter and maintain cooler temperatures in the summer.

A typical example of the syncretic treatment of architecture can be found at San José de Laguna, Laguna Pueblo, New México. This church was established in 1699 and serves indigenous people from Acoma, Zuni, Isleta and Queres.[22] Like most of the buildings of the area, this structure takes its inspiration from thousands of years of southwestern architecture. It is made of stone laid in adobe mortar with mud plaster on the inside and outside walls. Inside of the church, the nave is long (almost 105 feet) and narrow. It ends in an ornate carved and painted altar screen.

Here, the evidence of indigenous presence goes beyond the building materials (Figure 3). Murals decorating the walls of the church are not part of the standard Christian iconographic fare. Birds rest on forms that represent tombs and, according to traditional belief, they symbolize the souls of the people buried under the earth floor.[23] The *vigas*, or roof beams, had to be carried from a location at least thirty miles away and are from mountains sacred to native people. Before the church replaced the kiva, these same mountains were the source for vigas used in kiva construction. The carved and painted

FIGURE 4: Altar Screen from San Jose de Laguna, Laguna Pueblo, New Mexico. 1699. Drawing After Wakeley, David. *A Sense of Mission: Historic Churches of the Southwest* (San Francisco, Chronicle Books, 1994) p. 71

corbels that support the choir loft are flint-like in appearance, and the multicolored cedar latias above are part of the original ceiling.

The altar (Figure 4), although filled with Christian iconography, was modified to address the local concerns of the indigenous people. The artist responsible for the reredos is known simply as the *Laguna Santero* (saint maker).[24] He was an anonymous artist working in New

Mexico from 1796 till 1808, and his hand can be found in a number of altar screens located throughout New Mexico. The reredos of San José de la Laguna was created relatively late in the colonial period, sometime between 1800 and 1808. All of the saints depicted are tied directly to the concerns of the parishioners. In the center is Saint Joseph, from whom the church takes its name. He is shown in his typical pose holding the Christ child who, in turn, holds an orb and a flowering staff in his right hand. To the right is Santa Barbara, who holds a monstrance and palm. She is shown with a thundercloud and the tower in which she was imprisoned prior to her martyrdom. She is the patroness associated with thunder, lightning, firearms, and sudden death — all very appropriate for a space considered to be a new kind of kiva. To the left is Saint John of Nepomuk who wears a surplice and a biretta and holds a cross and a palm. This saint was famous for being martyred by his king after refusing to break the secrecy of the confessional. The cult of Saint John of Nepomuk is very important. It spread from Prague and Bohemia, to Mexico and then, to New Mexico where it found a ready audience in the *penitentes* who adopted the saint as a symbol of secrecy. In its New Mexican manifestation, this male society of flagellants can be understood as an outgrowth of both medieval European precursors and indigenous Native American flagellants who were associated with the Puebloan Snake Dance.[25] At the apex of the altar screen is the Holy Trinity.

Perhaps the most interesting aspect of the altar screen is the painted canopy that hangs over the altar. It is made of animal hide and decorated with symbols from the Native American tradition. Two white stars near the sun represent the morning and may reference the morning star. The eight stars located near the moon represent night. With both Christian and indigenous elements such as these

FIGURE 5: Mission Dolores, San Francisco, California. Photograph: Constance Cortez

FIGURE 6: Mission Dolores interior, San Francisco, California. Photograph: Constance Cortez.

present, it is not at all surprising that at Christmas time, the pews at Laguna are removed from the church and sacred dancing takes place there through the night.

Mission Dolores in San Francisco (Figure 5) is the sixth of twenty-one churches and the most northerly of all the missions established under the guidance of the Franciscan, Junipero Serra. Completed in 1776, it is the best preserved of all Californian missions. As is the case in earlier churches from New Mexico, Mission Dolores is made of adobe, its walls measuring 4 feet thick in places. Also like the churches in New Mexico, the mission is a single nave church with a very long aisle and indigenous architectural units (Figure 6). Here, the break between indigenous and European aspects is much clearer than at the Laguna Mission. Vigas have been brightly painted using modern materials and exactly replicate earlier layers of chevrons dyed with vegetable-based

FIGURE 7: Mission Dolore, Garden (inset, Kateri Tekakwitha). San Francisco, California. Photograph: Constance Cortez.

paints. This indigenous motif is abruptly broken in the region of the altar by triangular spandrels that contain foliage surrounding sacred monograms for Christ (IHS) and his mother (AM).

Perhaps the closest correspondence to notions of the New Jerusalem and Eden are to be found in the cemetery garden adjoining the mission (Figure 7). Here, medicinal plants continue to be grown amidst grave sculpture. As is the case in many missions throughout the Southwest, there is a sculpture dedicated to Kateri Tekakwitha, a Mohawk convert who is on the way to being canonized. As is the case in other representations of this early convert, the sculpture is an emblem of other converts to Catholicism as well as a template for correct behavior.

Conclusion

The colonial art and architecture of México, New Mexico, and California can be understood on many levels. Certainly, it is reflective of the spiritual desires and evangelization efforts of a group of churchmen. But it is also true that these art forms can and should be understood on the level of colonialism and the political motivations of foreign nations. The combination of the spiritual and political in itself is nothing new — art in Europe has functioned that way for millennia and there is ample proof that art functioned in a similar manner in the Americas prior to the coming of the Europeans. Perhaps what makes the art of colonized lands unique is the built-in bi-cultural component that visually speaks of the colonial encounter.

Endnotes

1. See for example, Diego Durán's *Book of the Gods and Rites and the Ancient Calendar* [trans. & ed. by Fernando Horcasitas and Doris Heyden] (Norman: University of Oklahoma Press, 1971) and Bernardino de Sahagún's *Florentine Codex — General History of the Things of New Spain.* 12 vols. [trans. Charles E. Dibble and Arthur J.O. Anderson] (School of American Research and the University of Utah, Monographs of the School of American Research and Museum of New Mexico, Santa Fe, New México, 1950-72).

2. See James B. Lynch, "Apocalyptic, Utopian, and Aesthetic Concepts of the Amerindian Culture in the Sixteenth Century." *Comparative Literature Studies* IV(4):363-370.

3. For a discussion of the use of the Bleayme and other misrepresentations of Huitzilopochtli, see Elizabeth Boone, *Incarnations of the Aztec Supernatural: The Image of Huitzilopochtli in Mexico and Europe.* Transactions of the American Philosophical Society, No. 79, pt. 2 (Philadelphia: American Philosophical Society, 1989).

4. Early speculations by Spaniards and later explorers are listed by John Lloyd Stephens in his *Incidents of Travel in Central America, Chiapas, and Yucatán*, Volumes I, 12th edition (New York: Harper & Brothers, Publishers, 1853) 96-97. These include, "the Jews, the Canaanites, the Phoenicians, the Carthaginians, the Greeks, the Scythians in ancient times; the Chinese, the Swedes, the Norwegians, and the Welsh."

5. For a discussion of earthly paradises and utopias see Lynch, 1967, and Donna Pierce, "The Mission: Evangelical Utopianism in the New World (1523-1600)" in *México: Splendors of 30 Centuries* (New York: Metropolitan Museum of Art ; Boston : Little, Brown, 1990).

6. Ibid.

7. Geronimo de Mendieta, *Historia eclesiastica indiana* [Estudio preliminar y edicion de

Francisco Solano y Perez-Lila] (Madrid : Atlas, 1973).

8. For a discussion of Valadés and his work see *Mario Sartor, Ars Dicendi et Excudendi: Diego Valadés incisore messicano in Italia* (Padova: Cooperativa Libraria Editrice Universitá di Padova, 1992).

9. See Chapter 6 of Jeannette Favrot Peterson, *The Paradise Garden Murals of Malinalco: Utopia and Empire in Sixteenth-Century Mexico* (Austin: University of Texas Press, 1993).

10. For Oñate's activities in New Mexico and the interaction between Spaniards and Puebloan groups, see Ramón Gutiérrez, *When Jesus Came, The Corn Mothers Went Away: Marriage, Sexuality and Power in New México, 1500-1846* (Stanford University Press, 1991).

11. Ibid., Ch. 2.

12. Ibid.

13. Ibid., 59.

14. In New Spain during the second half of the 17th century and the first quarter of the 18th, this column became the dominant architectural element represented in reredos and church facades. For the use of the Solomonic column in the Americas, see Manuel González Galván, "Barroco Salomónico," *Artes de Mexico* vol. 106 (1968): 38-31.

15. Gutiérrez, When Jesus Came, 20-24.

16. Ibid., 13-14.

17. Ibid., 21-24.

18. Ibid., 27-28.

19. Ibid., p.20.

20. For a detailed account of this Spanish-Native American interaction see, Gutiérrez, Chapter 3.

21. The placement of churches in the Southwest was in no way limited to proximity to kivas. The sanctuary of Chimayó (1813), for instance, was built over an indigenous holy site which produced mud with healing powers. These same muds are still available to visiting pilgrims.

22. Wakely, David, A Sense of Mission : Historic Churches of the Southwest. [Photography by David Wakely ; text by Thomas A. Drain; foreword by N. Scott Momaday]. (San Francisco : Chronicle Books, 1994).

23. Ibid.

24. For a recent article on the Laguna Santero see Paula B. Kornegay, "The Altar Screens of an Anonymous Artist in Northern New Spain: The Laguna Santero," *Journal of the Southwest*. V.38(1):63-77.

25. For a description of the Snake Dance ritual and self-mortification, see Gutiérrez, pp. 29-30.

26. See Wakely, *Sense of Mission*.

27. *Guide for Mission Dolores*, distributed by Mission Dolores, San Francisco.

Bibliography

Boone, Elisabeth H. 1989. *Incarnations of the Aztec Supernatural: The Image of Huitzilopochtli in Mexico and Europe*. Transactions of the American Philosophical Society, No. 79, pt. 2. Philadelphia: American Philosophical Society.

Duran, Diego. 1971. *Book of the Gods and Rites and the Ancient Calendar* [trans. & ed. by Fernando Horcasitas and Doris Heyden]. Norman: University of Oklahoma Press.

González Galván, Manuel. 1968. "Barroco Salomónico." *Artes de Mexico* 106:38-31.

Kornegay, Paula B. 1991. "The Altar Screens of an Anonymous Artist in Northern New Spain: The Laguna Santero." *Journal of the Southwest.* V.38(1):63-77.

Ramón Gutiérrez. 1992. *When Jesus Came, The Corn Mothers Went Away: Marriage, Sexuality and Power in New México, 1500-1846.* Stanford University Press.

Lynch, James B. 1967. "Apocalyptic, Utopian, and Aesthetic Concepts of Amerindian Culture in the Sixteenth Century." *Comparative Literature Studies* IV(4):363-370.

Mendieta, Geronimo de. 1973. *Historia eclesiastica indiana.* (Estudio preliminar y edicion de Francisco Solano y Perez-Lila). Madrid : Atlas.

Pierce, Donna. 1990. "The Mission: Evangelical Utopianism in the New World (1523-1600)." *In México: Splendors of 30 Centuries. New York: Metropolitan Museum of Art* ; Boston: Little, Brown.

Sahagún, Fray Bernardino de. 1993. *Florentine Codex - General History of the Things of New Spain.* 12 vols. Translated by Charles E. Dibble and Arthur J.O. Anderson. Published by the School of American Research and the University of Utah, Monographs of the School of American Research and Museum of New Mexico, Santa Fe, New Mexico.

Sartor, Mario. 1992. *Ars Dicendi et Excudendi: Diego Valadés incisore messicano in Italia.* Padova: Cooperativa Libraria Editrice Universitá di Padova.

Stephens, John Lloyd. 1853. *Incidents of Travel in Central America, Chiapas, and Yucatan.* Volumes I & II, 12th edition. New York: Harper & Brothers, Publishers.

Wakely, David. 1994. *A Sense of Mission: Historic Churches of the Southwest.* (photography by David Wakely; text by Thomas A. Drain; foreword by N. Scott Momaday). San Francisco: Chronicle Books.

CHAPTER 5

The Indians
of Mission Santa Clara

Randall Milliken

This paper describes the migration of native California Indian people to the Christian agricultural commune of Mission Santa Clara between the years 1777 and 1836. As I have argued elsewhere, this migration was not so much the result of Spanish physical or spiritual conquest as it was of Spanish psychological conquest. In the face of new diseases, environmental deterioration, and the technical power of the invading Euroamericans, the native hunter-gatherers had little choice but to join the agricultural commune, the only institution that integrated new technical training with explanation of hidden supernatural power in a rapidly changing world.[1]

First Contacts, 1769-1776

Santa Clara Valley Indian people first encountered Europeans in the fall of 1769. A Spanish exploratory expedition under Gaspar de Portolá had come up the coast from San Diego to the present Pacifica vicinity, just south of the Golden Gate, crossed the ridge overlooking San Francisco Bay, and traveled south down the Peninsula. The Portolá party camped on November 10th at the site of Palo Alto, where diarist Father Juan Crespí noted the presence of local Indian people: "At once upon our reaching here, several very well-behaved heathens, most of them well-bearded, came to the camp, giving us to understand that they were from three different villages, and I do not doubt there must be many of these, from the many smokes seen in different directions."[2]

Over the course of the next six years, from 1770 through 1775, the people of the Santa Clara Valley witnessed the passage of three

more Spanish groups through their lands. Pedro Fages passed up the
east side of the Valley and back south to Monterey in November of
1770. Fages and Crespí again explored northward through the Valley
into the East Bay in March of 1772. The Fernando Rivera-Francisco
Palóu party traveled up the west side of the Santa Clara Valley to the
Golden Gate at the end of 1774. Notes from the various expeditions
indicate that native village population sizes varied between 60 and
200 in those years. Probably about a dozen of the largest villages in
the Valley were semi-permanent central sites, while many more small
hamlets were occupied on a seasonal basis.

During 1776, a flurry of Spanish activity occurred in the San
Francisco Bay area. In the spring, a party under Juan Bautista de Anza
explored the area in search of sites for a new Presidio and missions.
Expedition chaplain Pedro Font reported two villages of "20 tule huts"
each in area just south of present San José. Passing up the west side of
the Santa Clara Valley toward the present Palo Alto area, Font noted
small groups here and there, totaling about 100 people. The party
explored northward to the Golden Gate, then returned to the Stevens
Creek area (now Mountain View), where they encountered a village
of about 100 people. Font reported: "One of the women, from the
time when she first saw us until we departed, stood at the door of her
hut making gestures like crosses and drawing lines on the ground, at
the same time talking to herself as though praying, and during her
prayer she was immobile, paying no attention to the glass beads which
the commander offered her."[3] At the Spanish camp site on the lower
Guadalupe River that day, Anza wrote, "In the place where we
camped there are three good-sized villages, each about as large as the
last one mentioned, composed of people like the foregoing, and by
whom, according to the paths and trails, the region upstream appears
to be populated."[4]

The Spaniards founded Mission San Francisco de Asís and the
San Francisco Presidio in the summer of 1776. Six months later,
on January 6, 1777, they dedicated the first site of Mission Santa
Clara.[5] Just ten months after that, settlers from Mexico founded
the town of San José three miles upstream on the small
Guadalupe River. Thus, in 1777 the local Indian people were
given an abrupt introduction to the full range of European-style

village material and social culture, livestock, house design, and daily life.

1777-1792: Era of Infant Baptisms

The year 1777 also brought new disease to the Santa Clara Valley. From January through May, the first five months of Mission Santa Clara's existence, the local Indian people visited the missionaries and presented them with gifts. In May an epidemic struck the children of the local villages around the mission. The Franciscan priests made their first baptisms on June 6, 1777. By June 23 they had baptized 54 sick and dying children. According to historian Francisco Palóu, "The Fathers were able to perform a great many baptisms by simply going through the villages."[6]

The 54 baptized children were given Spanish names and recorded in the Register of Baptisms for Mission Santa Clara. The register's contents indicates that they ranged in age from a few days to seven years old. Their home villages, also christened with Spanish names, were also indicated in the Baptismal Register. Table 1 indicates the baptisms from each village, as well as the number of the children recorded in the Mission Santa Clara Register of Burials during that summer[7] (Table 1).

The true severity of the epidemic of 1777 is unknown. The figures for deaths represent only baptized children. There is no way to know the total number of children in these villages who got sick, nor how

TABLE 1. Numbers of children baptized by Santa Clara Mission priests during June 1777, with counts of how many died during 1777.

Location	Baptized	Died
Santa Clara (northern Santa Clara)	2	1
San Francisco (southern Santa Clara)	7	3
San Francisco Solano (Agnews or Alviso)	5	3
San Juan Bautista (south San Jose)	15	10
San José Cupertino (Cupertino)	13	3
Santa Ysabel (Milpitas or N.E. San Jose)	4	2
San Bernardino (initially Mountain View)	3	0
San Antonio (initially east San Jose)	2	1

many parents chose not to bring their sick children to the foreign priests. The recovery rate of the baptized children suggests, however, that the people from the village of San José Cupertino may have had a more positive attitude toward the newcomers by the end of the summer than did the people of the village of San Juan Bautista.

The first adult convert at Mission Santa Clara, baptized on June 26, 1777, was an old man from the village of "San Francisco Solano." San Francisco Solano was a large village of approximately 200 people near the mouth of the Guadalupe River. The first Mission Santa Clara site was probably within its territory. By the end of 1777, another seven children and five teenagers joined the 54 children already listed in the baptismal register.

Baptisms averaged 104 per year over the next twelve years, 1778 through 1789. A few adult married couples were baptized in the years 1780 and1781, including most of the adults from the small hamlets of "Santa Clara" and "San Francisco," just upstream from the first Mission site (Table 2). During the 1780s, a trickle of adults from the surrounding larger villages on the Santa Clara Valley floor were baptized at the mission. The majority of converts during the 1770s and 1780s, however, were not adults, but young children and newborn infants.[8]

The meaning that Indian families attached to the ceremony of baptism is not documented. During the epidemic of 1777, baptism may have been understood as a healing ritual. Later, it may have been seen as an initiation into a religious society, an initiation that provided the convert some form of relationship to the supernatural allies of the Spaniards. It is impossible to say if the Indian families understood the Christian concept of threat and reward regarding eternal life after death, or if adults allowed their children to be baptized because of that threat and reward.

The year 1790 was the first year in which a large number of adults from a single village converted to Christianity and moved to Santa Clara Mission. In that year, 38 adults (over 20 years of age) came to the mission from "San Carlos" village or group of villages in the southern Santa Clara Valley, 20 kilometers to the south. Another 19 adults came in from the "Santa Agueda" district in the present Fremont vicinity, 15 kilometers north of the mission. The large villages of San Francisco Solano, "San Joseph Cupertino," and "Santa

TABLE 2. Yearly Baptisms between 1777 and 1810 of people from arbitrary districts designated by the Mission Santa Clara missionaries.

Year	N.M.ᵃ Santa Clara	N.P.ᵃ San Franciso	Sanᵃ José Cuperino	Sanᵇ Juan Bautista	Sanᶜ Francisco Solano	Santaᵈ Ysabel	Sanᵉ Bernadino	Sanᶠ Carlos	Santaᵍ Agueda	Sanʰ Antonio	Tayssen
1777	6	10	17	15	9	7	3			2	
1778	7	15	6	3	13	6				1	
1779	2	4	6		7		2	1			
1780	3	16	24	23	10	1	1		5	5	
1781	4	5	10	6	7	3	11	10	2		
1782			25	8	17	6	4	10		1	
1783		4	12	2	17	5	32	34	25	36	
1784		2	11	1	7	2	18	7	15	1	
1785	1	2	19	5	10	8	11	25	9	11	
1786		3	11	3	11	11	29	20	21	19	
1787	1	1	10	2	7	6	18	77	8	13	
1788		2	10	3	5	8	26	27	27	5	
1789	1	3	8	3	5	21	39	110	17	26	
1790		3	8	2	3	13	82	119	44	22	
1791		1	7	2	5	9	37	61	21	6	
1792		1	8	2	7	2	76	67	12	6	
1793	1		3		5	8	86	37	8	8	
1794			35	2	14	21	224	76	99	5	
1795			10	2	11	23	47	84	65	4	
1796			1	3		8	3	22	11	22	
1797			5		2	11	10	24	18	10	
1798				2	1	13	21	45	37	26	
1799			3	2	1	10	7	45	18	28	
1800				2	6	7	24	20	15	18	
1801			1	1		5	5	30	14	33	
1802				3		8	1	112	24	51	
1803				1		1	1	27	4	63	
1804							3	4	27	49	
1805						4		8	9	72	131
1806						5		6	2	54	95
1807						3		24	4	53	9
1808						4				53	34
1809							4		47		5
1810										62	
1811											14
Total	26	73	250	98	180	239	821	1136	561	812	274

a Nuestra Madre Santa Clara and Nuestro Padre San Francisco probably pertained to the central Santa Clara Valley Tamien group.

b San José Cupertino was probably a village of the west Santa Clara Valley Ritocsi group, also baptized under San Carlos. San Juan Bautista, too, may have been a Ritocsi village, but it may also have been a Tamien village.

c San Francisco Solano, near Alviso, was probably a village of the Alson group, also baptized under Santa Agueda.

d Santa Ysabel designated villages along Penitencia and Calaveras creeks belonging to a group whose native name was not documented.

e San Bernardino reached from Stevens Creek to the Pacific Coast, lands of the Oljon, Olpen, Partacsi, Puichon, and Quiroste groups.

f. San Carlos designated the lands of numerous groups south of San José as far as Santa Cruz, Gilroy, and Pacheco Pass.

g Santa Agueda reached from Fremont into the Livermore Valley, lands belonging to the Alson, Causen, Taunan, and Luecha groups.

h San Antonio included the hill country between the Santa Clara and San Joaquín valleys, lands of the Bolbon, Junas, and Pala groups."

Ysabel" were all closer to the mission, yet no large groups of their adults were converted until 1794. This may reflect a fear by more distant families that they would otherwise be left out of the web of newly emerging relationships that could provide local Indian families special status in the eyes of the powerful Spaniards.

During the 1790s, the Spanish missionaries proselytized heavily in the Santa Cruz mountains as well as the Santa Clara Valley. They also reached out to the Pacific coast in those years. Two children were baptized at Mission Santa Clara in early 1791 from the village of Uypi, at the mouth of the San Lorenzo River some 50 kilometers south; in October of 1791, the Franciscans established Mission Santa Cruz adjacent to Uypi.[9] Earlier, in 1786, Mission San Francisco de Asís had established the ranch and chapel of "San Pedro and San Pablo" at the present site of Pacifica on the upper San Mateo County coast. Thus, after 1791 the seashore at Point Año Nuevo was equidistant between Mission Santa Clara, Mission Santa Cruz, and the Mission San Francisco de Asís outstation. People from the Point Año Nuevo village of Mitenne were baptized at all three missions during the 1790s, the majority at Mission Santa Clara under the arbitrary regional label "San Bernardino."[10]

The English explorer George Vancouver sailed into San Francisco Bay in November of 1792. He visited Mission Santa Clara, about which he wrote an extensive commentary. Regarding the native village at Mission Santa Clara, he wrote, "Although this village did not appear so populous as that at St. Francisco, I was given to understand that there were nearly double the number of inhabitants belonging to it; and that in consequence of the many unconverted natives in the neighborhood of Santa Clara, several of the Christian Indians of good character were dispersed amongst their countrymen, for the purpose of inducing them to partake of the advantages held out to them, in which they had not been altogether unsuccessful."[11]

Vancouver described the mission village as consisting of traditional thatched huts laid out in straight rows, the paths "so abominably infested with every kind of filth and nastiness, as to be rendered not less offensive than degrading to the human species"[12]. He described the practice of separating the unmarried Christian girls from the rest of the village population:

The women and girls being the dearest objects of affection amongst these Indians, the Spaniards deem it expedient to retain constantly a certain number of females immediately within their power, as a pledge for the fidelity of the men, and as a check on any improper designs the natives might attempt to carry into execution, either against the missionaries, or the establishment in general.[13]

The Franciscans locked up unmarried women, young and old, for the night in a dormitory called the *monjerío*. Vancouver's interpretation of the purpose of the practice is open to question.

1793-1800: Resistence and Collapse in the Santa Cruz Range and East Bay

During the years 1794 and 1795, large numbers of adults finally joined Mission Santa Clara. Just prior to that, however, a number of outbreaks of resistence erupted. The first sustained resistance to Spanish encroachment around the Santa Clara Valley was carried out by Quiroste people from the Santa Cruz mountains. The initial leader of that resistance was Charquin, a 60-year-old man from the Pescadero Creek watershed. Charquin had been christened "Mateo" upon his baptism at Mission San Francisco in 1791. "He didn't even remain at the mission for eight days. Not even when the missionaries sent out messengers for him did he return. On two occasions endeavors were made to apprehend him. On one of them he retreated into the mountains and on the other he took up arms against the Christians of the mission," stated a subsequent report.[14] In February of 1793, Charquin detained two young women who had recently been baptized at Mission Santa Cruz with their husbands. Spanish troops seem to have captured Charquin that spring, although no diary of such an expedition has been found.[15]

Relations between the Spaniards and the groups of the Santa Cruz mountains deteriorated further throughout 1793. The Quirostes attacked Mission Santa Cruz in December of that year, provoked by further Spanish raids to force runaway Christians back to the missions. Missionary President Fermín Francisco Lasuén wrote on February 4, 1794: "I have found out for certain that on the night of the fourteenth of last December the pagan Indians, and some Christian Indians, from the rancherias to the northwest of that mission made assault on the guard, wounded the corporal in the head

and another soldier in the shoulder, and set fire to the old
guardhouse. The corporal fired a few shots and with that they
withdrew without serious injury to either side.... Later, a
reinforcement of troops arrived, and they have taken as prisoners to
Monterey five Christians and I do not know how many pagans. The
motive they have given is this, that the soldiers had taken away to
San Francisco various Christian Indians belonging to that place who
had been fugitives from there for some time, and they had taken a
Christian Indian woman away from a pagan man, and it was he who
was the principal instigator and leader of the disorder."[16] Eight
prisoners were taken to the Presidio of Monterey. One of them,
Ochole, was sentenced to join Charquin for an extended prison
term.[17]

A dramatic change took place during the fall of 1794. Hundreds
of adults from villages in the Santa Clara Valley, the Santa Cruz
Range, and the adjacent coast left their villages and moved to Mission
Santa Clara. But before that happened, tensions continued to mount
in the region. In March of 1794, following the arrest of some Indians
for cattle theft, Father Noboa wrote, "It is good that the present crime
has been punished, but even to go out and investigate it can lead to
terrible consequences. You see, I, who am carefully watching, see the
villages swelling in numbers, with more and more Christians. They
and the pagans are very full of themselves. If you ask me, the situation
is about to erupt, just as it did in Sonora. They are almost completely
united, and I judge, not with good will."[18] New arrests took place in
the Santa Cruz mountains, among them that of a Meve, a brother of
Charquin. In September the situation was further aggravated by the
arrival of Father Manuel Fernández at Mission Santa Clara, an
aggressive fire-and-brimstone proselytizer. "It is common knowledge
among these Indians, and verified by the reports of soldiers who
accompanied said religious, that he severely threatened the Indians
who refused to become Christians, and with some he even went
beyond threats to actual punishment," wrote military commissioner
Gabriel Moraga.

By October 29, tensions were growing. Moraga reported, "It came
to pass shortly after sunset last night that citizen Ygnacio Castro came
upon, a short distance out behind his house, a pagan Indian armed

with bow and arrows ... Castro set about interrogating him. Among other things the Indian said, as if taking pity on him, that he should get his wife and children away from the town, because the pagans were very angry. Many had gotten together, including those from very far off, and determined to come and kill all the people of the pueblo and of the mission. This man was going that night to tell the pagans whom the Father had brought in not to become Christians." Yet the next day, October 30, 1794, 45 adults representing all the major tribal village districts were baptized at Mission Santa Clara. Second Lieutenant Hermenegildo Sal arrived at Mission Santa Clara on November 1. He ordered the military escort to stop accompanying Father Fernández on his tours of harassment among the tribal villages and he met with the surrounding tribal chiefs to assure them that their people would not be forced to become Christians.[19]

Between November 12 and the end of 1794, 276 tribal adults of all ages were baptized at Mission Santa Clara. Another 2150 adults were baptized between January 1 and May 2 of 1795. The converts during those five months included the majority of the adult populations of the large and small towns of the Santa Clara Valley floor, the Santa Cruz mountains, and the San Mateo coast, as well as a significant percentage of the adults of the villages of the Fremont Plain. The negative aspects of the Spanish presence and mission life must have been clear. Christian Indians were treated by the Spanish not as ceremonial kinsmen, but as ignorant children. Traditional eating practices, sexual practices, and conflict resolution practices were not only ridiculed, but outlawed. At the mission, adult death rates were somewhat higher than previously experienced and infant mortality at least doubled the already high native rate. Yet tribal society in the Santa Clara Valley and its environs totally collapsed during the winter of 1794-1795. Overt military force was not used to achieve the conversions. The best explanation of the local people's acquiescence in the radical change in their lives is that they made a conscious choice during a period of ambivalence and psychological depression. A critical mass of people had developed a sense of futility and defeat in the face of on-going high death rates from unknown diseases, selective arrests of resistance leaders, and threats of damnation from priests such as Manuel Fernández.

New materials and manpower arrived from Mexico in 1797 for the expansion of the mission system. Construction began on the Mission San José in the present southern Alameda county in June of 1797. Approximately half of the people from the area had already become Christians at Mission Santa Clara, explaining the fact that more than 80 "Santa Agueda District" converts at Mission Santa Clara moved back north to form a founding population for Mission San José. Construction also began on Mission San Juan Bautista to the south that summer, with the aid of a seed population of Mutson people who had been baptized at Mission San Carlos Borromeo. While these events were going on, officials of the Pueblo of San José were encouraging the as-yet-unbaptized villagers of the Pala group of the San Antonio District to provide labor for a new hemp-growing enterprise. Nothing was heard of that enterprise in later years.

Also in 1797, the settlers of the town of San José de Guadalupe tried to expand their claims onto lands that Mission Santa Clara was holding in trust for the Indians. Santa Clara missionaries Magín Catalá and José Viader protested: "The King Our Lord has declared it to be his will that all the land that is estimated necessary would belong to the natives, without anyone predominating or being favored against the sovereign will. It is known that Mission Santa Clara presently maintains 1,434 Christians, and in addition to these there are more than 4,000 pagans who have their villages roundabout .... They have come to understand that the settlers are usurping the lands which God had given to their fathers. Finally, I myself can swear to having heard the pagans complain among themselves regarding the injustices and evident outrages that the settlers practice in wanting to appropriate lands that belong neither to these settlers nor anyone else." For the time being, the dispute was settled in favor of Mission Santa Clara.[20]

By the close of the eighteenth century, all autonomous native villages from the ocean shore to the eastside of the Santa Clara Valley were empty. The non-Christian villagers to the east in the inner Coast Ranges faced an unprecedented situation. Their western neighbors, from whom they had heretofore received shells and other materials from the coast, were consolidated under Franciscan direction at Mission Santa Clara. The hill people also needed these neighbors as allies to retain parity in conflict situations with people further east. Marriage had been the basis of trade and warfare alliance, and marriage with the missionized people could be arranged only by joining the mission community.

1801-1810: Eastern Hill People Move to Santa Clara

Nearly 60 adults from the San Antonio district east of the Santa Clara Valley had been converted prior to the year 1800. The nearest native group in that district, under headman Pala, had been working as paid laborers for the Spanish on various projects since the mid-1790's. Pala's group probably held the hills eastward as far as Mt. Hamilton. Pala and the rest of the adults of the group joined Mission Santa Clara in 1801and 1802.[21]

An epidemic of undocumented cause struck the Mission Santa Clara Indians in July of 1802. Only five deaths had been listed in May and four in June. Only one baptism took place at Mission Santa Clara between July and December of 1802, and that was the baptism of a dying man. In July 93 deaths were reported, 33 in August, and 37 in September. The disease spread to Mission San Francisco de Asís, where 54 people died of the "peste" in August and another 24 in September. Remarkably, no increase in monthly deaths occurred that summer at nearby Mission San José.[22]

Conversion rates at Mission Santa Clara were back to normal by January of 1803, six months after the height of the epidemic. From 1803 through 1810, an average of 50 persons a year, adults and children, came in to Mission Santa Clara from the San Antonio District to the east. They represented a number of groups, perhaps four different groups, from the hill country east of Mt. Hamilton to as far as the edge of the San Joaquín Valley. Some converts continued to come down to Santa Clara from the Santa Agueda District on the Fremont Plain in the early part of the decade, even though Mission San José had been converting local people from that area and eastward into the Livermore Valley since 1797. Some Santa Agueda individuals may have preferred to move to Mission Santa Clara because of their ties to families that had lived there since the early 1790's. Alternatively, they may have preferred to live near the town of San José.

Resistence to the expansion of Spanish control also continued into the 1800s. It proved more of an annoyance than a threat to the

Spanish, because it was always localized, the activity of a few allied
family groups along the front of the eastward wave of cultural
collapse. Resisting groups probably seldom mustered more than 50
bow-armed fighting men. One such resistance occurred in March or
April of 1804, when villagers somewhere in the hills south of the
Livermore Valley attacked a group of 20 Santa Clara Mission Indians,
killing a Christian from the San Carlos District named Jorge. Soldiers
went out twice from the San Francisco Presidio to arrest the killers, in
September and once again in October of 1804, without success.
Whatever had led to the killing of Jorge, the hill people certainly
looked upon it as an act of self defense against invading foreign
Indians. To the Spaniards, however, it was an act of civil unrest and
criminal behavior. Only temporarily frustrated by their inability to
make arrests, the Spanish awaited a more opportune moment to wield
their power.[23]

More resistance to Spanish encroachment occurred in early
January of 1805. Franciscan Father Cueva left Mission San José to
visit people reportedly sick at the Asirin village, a predominately
Mission Santa Clara group located either in the San Antonio Valley
or along Arroyo Mocho in the interior Coast Range. Cueva was
accompanied by at least five mission Indians and two soldiers. Finding
the Asirin village empty, the group proceeded into the territory of the
Luecha people, in Corral Hollow at the edge of the San Joaquín
Valley. There the missionary's party was attacked. One soldier and
three mission Indians were killed. The rest of the Spanish party,
including the wounded priest, were able to return to Mission San José.
The Spaniards retaliated for the attack immediately. Sergeant Luis
Peralta left Santa Clara Mission on January 19, 1805, with 18 soldiers
and 15 settlers. They surrounded the Luecha village, killing ten and
capturing four non-Christian men and 25 non-Christian women and
children. Peralta went out again in February to bring back two
runaway Christian men who were suspected of having deliberately led
the Cueva party into ambush.[24]

Mission register evidence suggests that the Luechas brought
themselves back into good graces with the Franciscans through
marriage alliances. On February 6, 1805, the recovering Father Cueva
baptized eight of the Luecha children at Mission San José. Five
Luecha women were baptized a month later. Six months after the

Spanish military campaign into the interior Coast Range, on August 7, 1805, a remarkable set of twelve weddings took place at Santa Clara Mission. Two of the brides, *Tasmate* and *Chauete*, were among the Luecha women who had been captured and then baptized at Mission San José in March. The men they married were two widowers who had been at Mission Santa Clara since 1791; they were from the Santa Agueda district, the same area as the three Mission San José men that the Luechas had killed in the company of Father Cueva. Within a few months of these marriages, the full Luecha group moved to Missions San José and Santa Clara for baptism. These facts suggest that the Luechas worked out their reconciliation with the Franciscans and the Mission Indian family groups through marriage alliances with long-time members of the Christian Indian community.[25]

1811-1836: San Joaquín Valley Yokuts Conversions

The native groups of the San Joaquín Valley east of the Santa Clara Valley were speakers of the Yokuts language.[26] The first Yokuts speaker baptized at Mission Santa Clara was a boy christened Melitón, baptized on April 15, 1811. The text of his baptismal entry indicated that he was from the "*ranchería de los Tugites*"; "*Los Riós*" was penned in the margin of the entry.[27] The Tugites controlled the San Joaquín River at the mouth of the Tuolumne River. Some 125 Tugites were eventually baptized at Santa Clara, most of them later in 1811 (Table 3).

Upstream from the Tugites on the San Joaquín River, at the mouth of the Stanislaus River, was a group called Josmites at Mission San José and Pitemas at Mission Santa Clara. While most of the Josmites went to Mission San José, 60 of them were baptized at Santa Clara between 1814 and 1816. Just south of the Tugites, west of present day Turlock, were the Lamames; most of them were baptized at Mission Santa Clara in 1812. Further south were the Mayemas at the confluence of the San Joaquín and Merced rivers; they went to Mission Santa Clara between 1816 and 1819, but many of them had gone to Mission Santa Cruz as early as 1810 under the name Tejey. The southernmost San Joaquín River group to go to Mission Santa Clara were the Janalames of the swamp lands between present day Merced and Los Baños; most of them were baptized at Santa Clara in

TABLE 3: Counts of Yokuts Baptisms of Mission Santa Clara, by Tribe and Year.

Year	Tugite	Lamame	Pitem	Mayem	Janalame	Lacquisemne	Apelamene	Chipayquis	Taubalame	Tonul	Atsnil	Tucusuyu	Chugea	Tinelame	Gualensemne	Totote	Sunomna	Chapaiseme	Other Named Groups	General "Tular"	General "Yndigena" or "Gentil"	TOTAL
1811	92	19																				111
1812		49																				49
1813	5	27	3	1																		36
1814	8	1	3																			12
1815	20	15	43			2																80
1816	5	5	15	75				2														102
1817				2	61		9		9													76
1818				2	40																	52
1819					1	1	37	1														72
1820	2			29		3	37	2	24	1		1			1				3			87
1821				3	3	7	6	13	41	4	11	1	29				2		7			87
1822				3	3	2	7	6	18	28	50	6	39	13	14		14		3			115
1823				1	1		1	4	6	1	13	3	14	5	45		3		13			81
1824					1	1	7	7	23	9		1	29	5	23		1		2			114
1825								3	26				19	5	14				2			63
1826									6	1				1								99
1827									20	3	3	9				8	12					118
1828									2							27	74					91
1829																	8					8
1830															11				1	1		12
1831			1												1		2			14		19
1833															1					2		2
1834				1						1			6		1				2	41	3	51
1835																			2	61	1	67
1836																		34	8	18	2	62
1837																			16	8	1	26
1838									1										1	4	3	8
1839																			4		6	11
1840																			1		5	9
1841																			2	3	19	21
1842																					5	5
1843																					34	34
1844																					8	8
1845																					3	3
1846																					9	9
1847																					13	13
1848																					12	12
1849																					7	7
Total	132	116	65	117	110	16	104	38	176	48	77	21	136	29	111	35	116	34	69	152	130	1832

1817 and 1818, but some of them went to missions Santa Cruz and San Juan Bautista into the early 1820s under the group name Notoahls.

Some of the Yokuts-speaking groups learned to appreciate the taste of horse flesh. The Franciscan missions were having trouble from San Joaquín Valley horse raiders as early as 1815. A Spanish military expedition under José Pico attempted to chastise Mayem horse raiders in the fall of that year. During the same foray, Pico also visited the Chaneches near Los Baños and the Nupchenches southeast of Los Baños, groups that soon moved to Mission San Juan Bautista. Military parties were sent against horse raiding Indians in the San Joaquín Valley at one to three year intervals from that time forward, through the beginning of the American Period in 1846.[28]

All of the San Joaquín River people were at the missions by the end of 1820, with the exception of a few individuals married in to groups further eastward on the San Joaquín Valley plain. Control of the Hispanic settlements of the San Francisco Bay area shifted in late 1821 from Spain to newly independent Mexico. Under the new Mexican government, the missionaries continued reaching eastward to Yokuts-speaking groups along the rivers that flowed westward from the Sierras into the San Joaquín. More than a thousand converts came in to Mission Santa Clara from those areas between 1820 and 1839. Many of them were merely listed in the baptismal register as being from "*Los Tulares*."

The Tauhalumnes from the present Modesto area were the largest group to move to Mission Santa Clara from the valley lands east of the San Joaquín River. They provided a total of 263 converts, 82 in 1817 alone. The Laquisemnes, on the Stanislaus River in the current Ripon area, sent some people to Mission Santa Clara, but moved predominately to Mission San José. The Apalamenes, further south on the lower Merced River were divided between Mission Santa Clara and Mission Santa Cruz (where they were identified as Huocons). The Tauhalumnes, Laquisemnes, and Apalamenes had abandoned their lands and moved to the missions by the end of 1822. Among the other Yokuts-speaking groups who moved to Santa Clara during the 1820s, most important were the Chugeas, possibly of the Riverbank vicinity along the Stanislaus River, and the Sunomnas of the present Waterford area along the Tuolumne River. Additionally, a large Sierra

Miwok-speaking group, the Gualensemnes, moved to Santa Clara from the Oakdale region along the Stanislaus River during the late 1820s.

The famous Estanislao resistance of 1828-1829 slowed the pace of Hispanic conquest of the San Joaquín Valley tribes. Estanislao was a 35 year old Laquisemne who had been baptized at Mission San José in 1821 at the age of 28. Estanislao and a number of his Stanislaus River compatriots, men, women, and children, were joined on their original Stanislaus River homelands in the fall of 1828 by some Stanislaus and Tuolumne River natives from Mission Santa Clara under Cipriano, a 38 year old Pitemas man. Cipriano and Estanislao defeated a party of 26 armed Mexicans, soldiers and citizens, together with 70 Mission San José Indian auxiliaries under José Sánchez in May of 1829. Their resistance was finally broken by Mariano Guadalupe Vallejo with 106 troops in June.[29] Among the Santa Clara converts listed at the end of 1829 as having "died afield in the Tulares and buried or cremated by their Christian and Gentile relatives" were people from Atsnil, Chipeyquis, Chugueas, Lamames, Tugites, and Laquisemnes, almost every important San Joaquín Valley group east of the Santa Clara Valley. The list proves that the Estanislao resistance was the largest multi-group cooperative resistance to Hispanic control in Central California.[30]

After the Estanislao-Cipriano revolt was suppressed, fewer tribal Indian people from the east side of the San Joaquín Valley appeared at Mission Santa Clara for baptism. In 1830, the mission population dropped below 1,300 for the first time since 1804.[31] During 1834, however, 48 people from the *tulares*, possibly refugees from a devastating malaria epidemic, were baptized.[32] Another 60 *tulares* people were baptized in 1835; they seem to have been from the edge of the foothills along the Stanislaus, Tuolumne, and Merced rivers.

Conclusion: End of the Mission System

Active mission recruitment ended with the secularization of Mission Santa Clara in 1836. At the beginning of that year there were 1,189 baptized Indians at the mission and its outlying ranches. About one-third of the them, 367 people, were Ohlone-speakers from the original villages of the Santa Clara Valley environs, or their descendants (31% of the total) . The great majority, 622 people, were native Yokuts speakers from the San Joaquín Valley, and their children (52% of the total). In addition, 37 young people were descendants of Ohlone-Yokuts mission marriages (3% of the total). Sierra Miwok-speaking migrants from the Sierra Nevada foothills totaled 104 people (9% of the total). Another 59 people from the *"tulares"* were either Miwok or Yokuts speakers (5% of the total).

With the termination of Mission Santa Clara as church-sponsored agricultural commune in 1836, Indians began to disperse to the town of San José, to private cattle ranches, and, for many Yokuts-speakers, back to old home lands in the San Joaquín Valley. Most mission lands were distributed as ranches among well-placed Hispanic citizens. Four small ranches were originally assigned to Christian Ohlone Indians. Those ranches, La Purisima Concepcíon, Los Coches, Posolmi, Ulistac, were all lost within a few short years.[33]

The full story of over 1,000 Mission Santa Clara Indian people who were alive at the end of the mission period remains to be fully researched and told. A number of Ohlone and mixed Ohlone-Yokuts Indians do speak today as descendants of eighteenth and nineteenth century migrants to Franciscan missions (see Sayers in this volume). Remarkably, however, no Indian descendants of the pre-1836 Mission Santa Clara agricultural commune are currently known to historians or anthropologists.

Endnotes

1. Early California Indian ambivalence toward the Franciscan mission system is discussed in detail by Randall Milliken, *A Time of Little Choice: the Disintegration of Tribal Culture in the San Francisco Bay Area, 1769-1810*, pp. 1-11.

2. Juan Crespí, "Excerpts from the Journal of Juan Crespí during the Portolá Expedition of 1769-1770," *Who Discovered the Golden Gate?* Frank M. Stanger and Alan K. Brown, eds., p. 105.

3. Pedro Font, *Font's Complete Diary of the Second Anza Expedition.* Herbert Bolton, ed., pp. 320, 324, 354.

4. Juan Bautista de Anza, *Anza's Diary of the Second Anza Expedition, 1775-1776.* Herbert Bolton, ed., p. 134.

5. Francisco Palóu, *The Life and Apostolic Labors of the Venerable Father Junipéro Serra.* George Wharton James, translator and editor, p. 213.

6. Ibid., p. 213.

7. During the 1980s and early 1990s the author built a computer data base of key information from each record in the three early ecclesiastical registers of Mission Santa Clara, the *Libro de Bautismos* (1778- 1863), the *Libro de Casamientos* (1778-1863), and the *Libro de Entierros* (1777-1866). References in this article which pertain to information in those

ecclesiastical registers thus derive both from the originals and from the derived computer data base.

8. The Franciscan priests at Mission Santa Clara gave Christain saints' names to the home villages of their earliest converts, and used those names to label the home places of individuals in the mission's ecclesiastical records. As the years went by, they assigned more distant villages to one of four directional districts, San Bernardino to the west, San Carlos to the south, San Antonio to the east, and Santa Agueda to the north. These arbitrary place-name assignments effectively disguised the pattern of native multi-village political territories, a pattern that probably consisted of territorial groups with two to five villages each. For a more detailed discussion of this problem, see Milliken, A Time of Little Choice, pp. 233-234.

9. Baptismal entries for the Uypi children, Lorenza and Clara, occur in Mission Santa Clara Libro de Bautismos entries # 1894 and 1907. Baptismal entries for Uypi's headman Suquel and his wife Irien are found in Mission Santa Cruz Libro de Bautismos entries #2 and 3. For more information regarding the founding of Mission Santa Cruz, see Milliken, A Time of Little Choice, pp. 108-109.

10. See Milliken, A Time of Little Choice, pp. 252 for more details about the Quirostes of Point Año Nuevo. The same page provides information about the Puichon people of the Palo Alto area, probably the first people to go to Mission Santa Clara under the arbitrary place-name "San Bernardino."

11. George Vancouver, A Voyage of Discovery to the North Pacific Ocean, and Round the World: In Which the Coast of North-West America has been Carefully Examined and Accurately Surveyed ... Performed in the Years 1790-1795 in the Discovery Sloop of War and Armed Tender Chatham, under the Command of Captain George Vancouver, p. 24.

12. Ibid., p. 13.

13. Ibid., p. 11.

14. Hermenegildo Sal, "Report to Interim Governor José Joaquín de Arrillaga, February 27, 1793," as translated by Milliken, A Time of Little Choice, pp. 276-277.

15. Charquin's resistance is documented in detail by Milliken, A Time of Little Choice, pp. 115-120. He is known to have been at the Presidio of Santa Bárbara in 1794, from which he escaped in 1795 and was recaptured. He died at the Presidio of San Diego 1798 (Mission San Francisco Libro de Difuntos, entry #1189).

16. Fermín Francisco Lasuén, The Writings of Fermín Francisco de Lasuén, pp. 298-299.

17. Milliken, A Time of Little Choice, p. 120.

18. Diego Noboa, "Informe sobre una situación muy crítica." Archives of California, volume 7, no. 54, as translated by Milliken, A Time of Little Choice, p. 122.

19. The quotes from Gabriel Moraga, "Informe al Teniente José Argüello. San Jose. October 30, 1794," Archives of California, volume 7, pp. 125-133, and from Sal, "Informe al Teniente José Argüello. San José. November 2, 1794," Archives of California, volume 7, pp. 133, are translated by Milliken, A Time of Little Choice, pp. 124-129.

20. Magín Catalá and José Viader's "Informe al Gobernador Diego de Borica," Archives of California, volume 52, p. 279, has been excerpted here in translation from Zephyrin Englehardt, The Missions and Missionaries of California. Volume 2. Upper California, p. 719. See Milliken, A Time of Little Choice, pp. 146-153 for additional contextual information..

21. Pala's baptism on April 4, 1802, as José Domingo, appears in Mission Santa Clara Libro de Bautismos, entry #4251.

22. For details regarding the epidemic of 1802 at Mission Santa Clara, including references to specific entries in the Mission Santa Clara Libro de Entierros, see Milliken, A Time of Little Choice, pp. 173-176.

23. The entry for Jorge's 1792 baptism at age 25 is found in the Mission Santa Clara Libro de Bautismos, entry #2029. His violent death in 1804 is documented in the Mission

Santa Clara *Libro de Entierros*, entry #3247. See Milliken, *A Time of Little Choice*, pp. 181-184, for additional information about the "Jorge" incident.

24. For details regarding the Luecha resistance, including excerpts from contemporary reports and citations of pertinent mission death register entries, see Milliken, *A Time of Little Choice*, pp. 185-188.

25. The Luecha marriages are noted in Santa Clara *Libro de Casamientos*, among entries #1203-1208. See Milliken, *A Time of Little Choice*, pp. 188-189, for pertinent citations of Luechas in the ecclesiastical registers of Mission San José.

26. Scholars agree that the tribal groups of the San Francisco Peninsula, Santa Clara Valley, the eastern shore of San Francisco Bay, and the west-flowing streams of the adjacent Coast Ranges spoke Ohlone (i.e. Costanoan) dialects. Disagreement exists, however, regarding the contact period language spoken along east-flowing streams of the Coast Ranges. Most texts assign it to the Yokuts, following A. L. Kroeber, *Handbook of the Indians of California*, pages 462-465. However, strong evidence that there were no contact-period Yokuts-speaking groups in the Coast Ranges is provided by Milliken, "The Costanoan-Yokuts Language Boundary in the Contact Period," in Lowell John Bean, ed., *The Ohlone: Past and Present*, pp. 99-164.

27. Melitón of the Tugite group, the first Yokuts-speaking convert, is listed in Mission Santa Clara *Libro de Bautismos* entry #5791.

28. "José Dolores Pico's Diary, 1815" is translated by Sherburne Cook, *Colonial Expeditions to the Interior of California: Central Valley, 1800-1820*, pp. 268-271. In the same volume, Cook documents numerous other Spanish expeditions against horse raiders.

29. Estanislao, whose native name was Cucunuchi, was baptized at age 28 on September 24, 1821 (Mission San José *Libro de Bautismos* entry #4471). Cipriano of the Pitemas group, native name Huhuyat, was baptized at age 25 on May 6, 1815 (Mission Santa Clara *Libro de Bautismos* entry #6297). See Sherburne Cook, *Expeditions to the Interior of California: Central Valley, 1820-1840*, pp. 168-180, for translations of historical documents pertinent to Estanislao's resistance.

30. Mission Santa Clara *Libro de Entierros* entries #6512-6525, recorded on September 25, 1829, list fourteen people who had been killed in the San Joaquín Valley over the previous months, including Cipriano (entry #6513).

31. Jacob N. Bowman, "The Resident Neophytes of the California Missions, 1769-1834." *Quarterly of the Historical Society of Southern California* 40(2):138-148.

32. Sherburne Cook, "The Epidemic of 1830-1833 in California and Oregon," *University of California Publications in American Archaeology and Ethnology* 43:316-319.

33. See Laurence Shoup and Randall Milliken, *Iñigo of Rancho Posolmi: the Life and Times of a Mission Indian*, for details regarding secularization of Mission Santa Clara, privitization of its lands, and the story of Iñigo, an Indian grantee of mission land. See also Faxon Dean Atherton, *The California Diary of Faxon Dean Atherton, 1836-1839*, p. 64, for a description of recently-converted Yokuts and other Christian Indian people at Mission Santa Clara in August of 1837.

CHAPTER 6

Telling the Mission Santa Clara de Asís Story:
A Reconstruction Based on Archaeological and Documentary Evidence
Russell K. Skowronek

Elizabeth wriggled uncomfortably in her chair as her teacher began to drone on about the missions of California. Since she was a toddler her father had dragged her from Sonoma to San Diego visiting California's missions. To her they all looked like ecclesiastical "Taco Bells." Every one of them was filled with musty displays of old books and vestments, unidentifiable rusty objects, and dusty baskets. And every story was the same — pious priests "teaching" the local Indians about agriculture, animal husbandry, clothing, and Christianity. A few talked about how the Indians had died, yet she knew from the ads on television supporting casinos that there were still Indians in California. If they were all the same, why would anyone care. In a word, it was B-O-R-I-N-G, and Elizabeth was beginning to tune-out when Ms. Bragg began asking questions. "Why were the missions built and why did people move there?" "How did peoples' lives change in the missions and how do we know it?" and "Who were the people and what was their legacy?" Elizabeth was intrigued, maybe history was not a "just-so" story after all. It could be fun and interesting too.

For most of the twentieth century, California's missions were romanticized. In the 1980s and 90s the pendulum swung the other way and they came to be reviled as monuments to Spanish imperialism. In an attempt to placate the Native American and liberal communities and yet protect their visitor base, interpreters half heartedly incorporated "politically correct" language and ideas as "add-ons" to decades-old exhibits. The results were disastrous and have served to alienate the public from mission history. At Santa Clara, we are showing that this need not be the case.[1] Archaeological, documentary, and ethnographic data can be used to create a balanced and less-biased perception of life at California's missions. This multi-faceted approach is based on a constellation of data, not on anecdotes or biased, unquestioned assumptions

Our idea of what constitutes "truth" changes through time and, as such, requires revision to reflect these changing perceptions. In mission studies, this is most evident in the broadening of the avenues of inquiry beyond the views of the Franciscans to include the accounts of local civil and military authorities, foreign travelers, and the reminiscences of Native Americans, as well as the testimony provided by archaeology and the ethnographic/historic records.

Today, the most accurate reflection of the past is a product of this interdisciplinary and multi-faceted approach. Both the documentary and material records were contemporary creations of the missions and, as such, represent primary data. While both are biased in their own ways, they are complementary and non-exclusive data sets. Since few mission-era Native Americans could write, the vast majority of documentary evidence contemporary with the mission era (1769-1837) was created by elite, Spanish-speaking males who were concerned with economics, social organization, and the ideology of the dominant system. Many of these documents have been translated and provide great detail on mission life; however, neither their authors nor their translators were unbiased in their observations.

Many of the sources referred to by scholars of the mission era should be evaluated against the fact that the authors are members of the Franciscan Order and may be interested in furthering the position of Serra's canonization or the image of their order in California history.

To attempt to balance this bias, some have turned to oral histories The integrity of the spoken word in non-literate societies is well known among anthropologists trained in the un-biased recording of these oratories. While oral histories might seem to give voice to the majority population at the missions, we must be aware of their potential shortcomings. Native American oral histories about life in the missions were recorded decades after the end of the mission era by individuals who were not trained anthropologists. Many were collected by a new generation of non-Native American political and economic elites seeking to perpetuate the "Black Legend" by demonstrating the enlightened superiority of the Protestant United States over Catholic Mexico. As oral historians will attest, the nature of the story told can be influenced by the interviewer, the context of the interview, and the questions asked.

The bias in the creation of the documentary record is further exacerbated by uneven preservation. Material data may also be biased when preservation is poor in the archaeological record. Nonetheless, material evidence is important because it represents rich and poor, male and female, young and old, European and Native American alike. Material objects are interesting to consider as simple objects, but it is their patterned physical inter-relationship in the earth that makes them useful for revealing the past. After two decades of archaeological enquiry and a century of historical research, a more complete picture of life at Mission Santa Clara is coming to light.

Background History

Mission Santa Clara de Asís is unique in California in that it has been moved and rebuilt six times. In the sixty (1777-1837) years of its existence as a Franciscan mission, the complex moved three times because of flooding and earthquakes. During this period, there were five churches. The first two (1777-1784), of wattle-and-daub construction, stood near the Guadalupe River. Later, adobe buildings (1784-1818; 1818-1867; 1822-1926) stood where Santa Clara University stands today. Floods, earthquakes, demolition, and fires combined to erase these structures. The current, and sixth, mission church stands on the site of the 1825 edifice. It was built after a 1926 fire destroyed the earlier church. Today there are few tangible reminders of Mission Santa Clara. They include: historical markers at the first, second, and third sites; the Peña or Woman's Club Adobe; the "Faculty and Staff Club" or "Adobe Lodge"; a section of the 1825 church's wall in the Saint Francis Chapel; a portion of the 1825-1851 cemetery; and, an exterior adobe wall.

Over the past thirty years, archaeologists, archivists, and historians have worked in concert to reveal evidence of each of these sites. The following reconstruction is based on the scholarship of researchers from the City of Santa Clara, the California Department of Transportation, the Santa Clara University (SCU) Archives, the SCU Department of History, the SCU Department of Anthropology and Sociology, and the SCU Archaeology Research Lab.

Ideology at the Missions

Forming a Congregation

The ultimate goal of the missions was to Hispanicize and Christianize the Ohlone, the first action being to create a congregation. Because the Ohlone were seasonal hunters and gatherers, the missions built in this area were of the *reducción* or *congregación* type. This means that rather than building a mission in an existing aboriginal town, a mission was established at a location chosen by the priests. The selection of the location was based on the presence of water, fertile soils, building materials, and an indigenous population. In the case of the Ohlone, who generally lived in groups of less than 200, the people were congregated or reduced at the new location (see Milliken, this volume). Fr. Guest argues that the first Ohlone to "come in" for conversion were attracted with gifts of glass beads, cloth, ribbons and other trade goods presented to their leaders.[2] It could also be argued that the Ohlone feared reprisals should they have resisted conversion, but the documents are mute on this topic. Nonetheless, Hylkema builds on this and argues that these early congregations should be seen as part of a larger economic relationship based on the exchange of shell beads and other commodities for labor.[3] Labor was used to construct the mission, tend livestock, and work the fields.

Recently Milliken has used an ecologically based argument to account for the Ohlone's voluntary joining of the mission community.[4] He has found that drought made their traditional subsistence base unreliable. With its combination of agriculture and animal husbandry, the mission commanded a concentrated source of food.

While many congregants "came in" to the mission, whether

because of gifts to their leaders, fear of reprisals, or for food, others were recruited by capture.[5] For all of the "good" intentions of the Franciscans, the formation of the congregation and subsequent life in the missions was often harsh and may have shortened the lives of the converts.

Evidence for Syncretism

In the Ohlone missions, priests taught Christian catechisms in the local language.[6] The fact that Catholicism became part of the lives of the Ohlone and other Californian Native Americans cannot be denied, but there was a degree of syncretism throughout the mission era, in part because of the continuing movement of new recruits into the missions.[7] For example, at Mission Santa Clara, while some "Christian Indians already sp[o]ke and underst[oo]d Spanish", Fathers Catalá and Viader admitted in their 1814 report that, after thirty-seven years of contact, their success was uneven and many "pagan" ideas still prevailed among their neophytes.[8] The following passages capture their frustrated views of their congregation.

> Among those who have come to the mission from the country in their adult age, particularly the old people, we notice a hankering after the things of paganism, idolatry and superstition. However, by the grace of God, by preaching and by labor they will be giving up these abominable evils.[9]

> The Indians are very superstitious. They worship the devils offering them seeds and they fast and dance in their honor in order to placate them. They practice vain observances. By using certain herbs, roots and feathers and other items they believe they can free themselves from their enemies and from illnesses. They practice witchcraft by means of herbs, thorns and other enchantments by means of which they attempt to injure others and obtain revenge. Finally they believe all they dream about [i.e., visions or omens]. To destroy such an accumulation of evil we know of no method more opportune than frequent preaching and instruction, time and patience.[10]

If we ignore loaded terminology, such as "pagan," "superstitious," and "idolatry," as the language of frustrated Franciscan priests whose goal was to transform or create Christians, we can see in these passages the survival of traditional Ohlone ideology in the mission setting.

The evidence for syncretism is extraordinarily clear in the continuation of community rituals in some of the missions. In 1806, Georg Heinrich, Freiherr von Langsdorff, visited missions Santa Clara and San José. He described preparations for a dance at San José. The Native Americans were "smeared with charcoal, red clay and chalk decorations all over their body. Others covered themselves with down and with shells, feathers and coral."[11] A few years later (1816, 1824) Otto von Kotzbue, a Russian sea captain, called at missions San Francisco and Santa Clara in the Ohlone area. While he was visiting San Francisco, the neophytes held a dance in front of the main entrance to the mission church.[12] The festivities were captured in watercolors and later an engraving by von Kotzbue's illustrator, Louis Choris.[13] The illustrated dancers are daubed with paint and are wearing special beaded and feathered headdresses and breechcloths— a clear indication of the continuation of the pre-contact importance of dance. It is important to note, however, that the prevalence of dancing varied from mission to mission, based on the perceptions of individual priests regarding vices. At Santa Clara, Fr. Catalá ranked dancing along with stealing, gambling, and abortion, as the most dominant vices after fornication. [14]

Even burial was not completely free of pre-contact ritual or mythology regarding the disposition of the spirit after death. Again, in their 1814 report, Catalá and Viader observed that:

> In their pagan state these Indians held and still hold a most ridiculous idea concerning the immortality of the soul. Namely, it goes out to sea to a certain point which they cannot designate, and there it is happy, etc. Concerning reward, punishment, purgatory, etc., they have no idea or explanation. At the mission they are beginning to learn these beliefs by dint of unceasing effort, teaching and preaching of the missionaries.[15]

While the priests hoped non-Christian ideas would be forgotten, they were not. Alfred Kroeber recorded fragments of these practices from Ohlone descendants in Monterey at the turn of the twentieth century.[16]

Finally, we can note that even mourning rituals contained aspects of pre-contact practices. In 1786 Jean Francois de Galaup, Comte de la Pérouse, visited the Monterey peninsula and Mission San Carlos de Borromeo (Carmel). By this time, the mission and presidio had been established for sixteen years, yet the Count noted that the Indians painted their bodies red or black when they were in mourning. According to La Pérouse, the priests compromised with them and forbid only the use of the red paint.[17] Twenty-eight years later, the priests at missions Santa Clara, Santa Cruz, and San José all reported that mourners cut their hair and the dead were buried with clothing and other grave goods.[18] Another aspect of mourning behavior that survived into the mission era was wailing. Wailing in Catholic society was a sign of grief and affection for the departed, whereas in Ohlone society the practice was meant to send the spirit of the departed away and, thus, protect the living. There is evidence that in 1812 this practice continued at Mission Santa Cruz following the assassination of Fr. Quintana, whose spirit, given his reputation, must have been greatly feared.[19]

In 1830 at Mission Santa Clara, the death of Fr. Catalá demonstrated the interweaving of Christian and Native American mourning practices. Avenzio Guzmán, a Native American born at Mission San José, witnessed the burial of Catalá. He recalled in 1884 that at the conclusion of the funeral service the congregation "burst into tears" and proceeded to strip the body for holy relics.[20] Another witness, Felis Buelna, had obtained Catalá's prayer book from an individual "who preserved it from fire, for it was customary among the Indians to burn all things that belonged to some person deceased."[21]

Archaeological Evidence for Syncretism

Recognizing beliefs or ideology in the material record is difficult for archaeologists because only the material by-products of belief systems remain in the earth. Nonetheless, there is growing archaeological evidence from the California missions of the continuation of aspects of pre-contact Native ideology. Found in both living and burial mission contexts are charmstones, bone and stone shamans' sucking tubes, rock crystals, and abalone pendants. Clam and *olivella* shell beads are ubiquitous throughout the Alta California missions.[22]

Mission cemeteries provide an excellent data set for examining syncretism. Excavations at La Purísima, San José, and Santa Clara yield the bulk of evidence on mission mortuary behavior.[23] Burials were shrouded and had an east-west orientation with arms crossed over the abdomen. At San José, it is reported that fragments of roof tiles were placed over the face. At La Purísima, in the Chumash culture area, all burials were bereft of artifacts with the exception of one which was adorned with glass beads. A very different situation existed in Santa Clara's 1781-1826 neophyte cemetery. There, the excavation of the remains of eleven individuals from some 5,000 interred, revealed over 1,900 shell and 484 glass beads in association with the burials.[24] In Mission Santa Clara's last cemetery, used from 1826 to 1851, burial with shell and glass beads continued, even though bodies were now sometimes placed in coffins.[25]

These examples, from both habitation and mortuary contexts, may indicate not only differing economic access to material items, but also conscious maintenance of ideological patterns and definitions of ethnic identity. In the case of the mission-living Ohlone, we see a blending or syncretism in public mortuary activities. The friars seem to have halted cremation and ensured the burial of the neophytes in consecrated cemeteries, but the inclusion of shell beads and pendants in burials and the occurrence of charmstones, sucking tubes and rock crystals in private living quarters demonstrate the continuation of pre-contact mortuary and healing ritual in the mission setting. The occurrence of these materials in burials and living quarters may well be a fruitful avenue of further enquiry. Their presence in these contexts may suggest a form of resistance, or simply a slow acceptance of Spanish culture caused by the constant influx of neophytes from outlying regions or different culture areas. The conversion process did not strip away life-long beliefs, but set the stage for a compromise, one in which new ideas became fused with old ones.

Social Organization at the Mission

Documentary Evidence

In addition to giving religious instruction, the missionaries attempted to teach the neophytes Spanish concepts of law and social organization. Enculturation in these areas of life served the priests by creating a familiar hierarchy of command through which orders and control could be channeled. The pre-contact hereditary elite continued to enjoy higher status at the missions even if others had "been placed over them" by the priests.[26] The "election" of *caciques* (chiefs), *alcaldes* (magistrates), and *regidores* (councilmen) by the neophytes represents the choice of known, ranked individuals from a senior lineage by the commoners of a polity. The priests clearly realized that their ability to control the Native American population existed only through the sufferance of these individuals.

Archaeological Evidence

Elites are usually recognized in the archaeological record by their greater access to exotic goods and to high-quality locally produced items and in the size, location, and construction of their homes. In the highly regulated lifeways of the mission, where housing was determined by the colonial elite, one's position in the local hierarchy would best be revealed in portable artifacts associated with the living quarters. For example, Fr. Lasuén reported in 1801 that the neophytes who lived in the tile-roofed adobe apartments at missions Dolores and Santa Clara were supplied with *manos* and *metates*, and metal and ceramic pots and pans.[27] Although the more durable items of metal and stone may have less frequently become part of the archaeological record, there is ample evidence of access to exotic goods by those who lived in the mission complex. Excavations in the neophyte housing areas of Mission Santa Clara de Asís. have yielded glass beads, bottle glass, and fragments of Mexican, English, and Asian-made ceramics, thus demonstrating these individuals access to these exotica.[28]

The importance of these very visible material correlates of status is underscored when we consider the sumptuary rules of both Ohlone and Spanish society. In traditional Ohlone society, the elite wore rabbit skin cloaks as their sign of office.[29] Whereas, two friars noted:

> At the mission [Santa Clara] the Indians clothe themselves with coarse cloth, blankets or soft tanned leather, etc., all of which is made at the said mission. All the men and women are decently dressed.[30]

The report from missions Santa Cruz and San Francisco provide more detail regarding clothing and rank. Neophyte male and female commoners wore woolen shirts (*cotón*) in addition to woolen breech cloths (*tapete*) and skirts (*pollera* or *basquina*) whereas *alcaldes* were distinctly dressed in European-style pants and shoes.[31]

The documentary and material records reveal that social inequality existed among both pre- and post-contact Ohlone. In both situations, the elite were addressed deferentially, wore items of clothing that set them apart from commoners, and had greater access to exotic goods. Thus, even if elite power was lessened in the missions, their hereditary positions continued to be recognized by both the neophytes and the Spanish.

Subsistence and Economics at the Mission

Documentary Evidence

The Spanish economic system was a radical departure from the seasonal scheduling of the pre-contact era. The local environment was altered with new plants and animals to fit the needs of the alien culture.[32] The Spanish introduced Old World livestock and a mixture of Old and New World field crops and created large-scale water control projects for power and irrigation.[33] The Spanish goal was to transform the New World into a New Europe.

The establishment of Mission Santa Clara de Asís in January of 1777 well illustrates the rapid imposition of the Spanish economic adaptation. A letter written by Junípero Serra and dated March 1, 1777, reports that the two-month-old mission was already plowing and planting corn, beans, wheat, and vegetables.[34] The *informe* penned by founders José Antonio Murguía and Tomás de la Peña in December of the same year detail their planting schedule and yields, the construction of irrigation ditches, and the livestock they brought.[35] The abundance of their yields and their attraction to the local Ohlone were noted by Francisco Palóu when writing of Serra in 1787. It is interesting to note, however, that even as Palóu wrote of the Ohlone coming for the new foods, he commented on the nearby availability of acorns, hazelnuts, strawberries, shellfish, and large trout "on which the pagans nourish themselves."[36] Fifteen years later, Fermín Francisco de Lasuén wrote a letter from Santa Clara and commented:

> For one who has not seen it, it is impossible to form an idea of the attachment of these poor creatures for the forest. There they are without a roof, without shade, without food, without medicine, and without any help. Here they have all of these things to their hearts content. Here the number who die is much less than there. They see all this, and yet they yearn for the forest.[37]

He complained in the same letter of the neophytes continuing requests to temporarily leave the mission and visit the mountains. In this passage, he reports a revealing conversation with a neophyte.

> Why, you make me think that if one were to give you a young bull, a sheep and a fanega of grain every day, you would still be yearning for your mountains and your beaches. Then the brightest of the Indians who were listening to me said, smiling and half ashamed of himself, What you say is true, Father. It's the Truth.

Neophytes at the mission had a very different pace of life from that of their non-missionized cousins. As at other missions, the day at Santa Clara was routinized around meals, work, prayers, and mass. For adults, work averaged about six hours per day. Priests [1814], visitors such as La Pérouse [1786], Vancouver [1792], and Roquefeuil [1817], and the recollections of Nasario Galindo [b. 1810] of Mission Santa Clara clearly report a sexual division of labor in the Ohlone missions. Males served as cowboys, shepherds, tanners, shoemakers, stone masons, potters, tile makers, carpenters, blacksmiths, teamsters, and butchers. They made tallow and tended fields, orchards, and irrigation ditches. Women were employed weaving, sewing, candle making, soap making, washing, making baskets, winnowing or culling wheat, grinding, sifting flour, and hoeing weeds.[38]

Communal meals served at the missions consisted of a grain-based porridge of roasted barley meal, called *atole*, or a richer vegetable stew called *pozole* made of a mixture of wheat, corn, peas and beans. At Santa Clara, these rations were supplemented with the produce of private gardens from the married neophyte quarters and, on a weekly basis, from the mission stores with fresh meat and additional rations of wheat.[39] It is said that by the 1790s the harvest of wild plant foods was more of a treat at Mission Santa Clara than a necessity.[40] In addition to locally produced foodstuffs, the priests and some neophytes had access to tea and chocolate; these were graciously shared with George Vancouver during his 1792 visit.[41] Additionally, a variety of spirits, including wine, whiskey and mescal, was consumed.[42]

Archaeological Evidence

The new economic activities and settlement system limited group mobility and required new tools. For example, a Mission Santa Clara annual *Informe* and a letter from Serra detail the tools and utensils sent to the mission.[43] These materials did not supplant but were added to Native material culture.

Native men used a variety of metal tools in their new activities at the missions, yet there is ample evidence that they continued to work stone, bone, shell, and other traditional materials. [44] They also applied the new tools to traditional purposes. For example, they continued to work shell into beads, but rather than using stone tools, they perforated the shells with iron drill bits.[45]

Native women at the missions also had new chores and learned to use new tools, but aspects of their traditional lifeway continued and were molded in this new setting. Items such as baskets continued to be made, and *metates* and other ground stone bowls, pestles, and mortars were used in their traditional forms or modified for processing newly introduced foods.[46] For example, a pestle/mano found at Santa Clara showed evidence of battering on one end, evidence of its use with a mortar in the reduction of seeds and nuts. Evidence of polishing on one side implies it was also used for grinding corn, a food introduced by the Spanish, on a metate.

The importance and continued quality of traditional female and male activities is underscored in a 1786 letter from Fr. Fermín Francisco de Lasuén to the Comte de la Pérouse in which he makes a gift to the French visitor of three items made of "rush" and one of stone "fashioned by the Indians..."[47] Thirty-one years later another Frenchman, Camille de Roquefeuil, visited San Francisco and noted "some baskets so closely woven that they hold water. These last are the remarkable product of the industry of the Californians."[48]

Archaeological data may also be used to evaluate diet when ethnohistorical data are equivocal. It must be remembered that agricultural production varied greatly from mission to mission and to draw sweeping generalizations would be erroneous. For example, Sherburne F. Cook stated in 1976 that the mission diet was inadequate to keep the neophytes productive and alive without exploiting wild resources, while Shipek suggests that not only was the diet marginal, but that the consumption of milk and cheese by lactose intolerant neophytes, already weakened by a poor diet, would have contributed to the high incidence of dysentery and other diseases.[49] These observations may also be true for the Ohlone missions.[50]

Unfortunately, archaeological evidence for diet and overall nutritional status of mission populations is lacking at this time. Such an evaluation will require a comparative analysis of contemporary mission, presidio, pueblo, and Native Californian cemeteries. These studies must search for evidence of increased or decreased dietary stress (e.g., Harris Lines of arrested growth and dental hypoplasia) and for changes in diet between the prehistoric and contact periods (e.g., changing ratios of N^{15} and C^{13}, which are indicative of the consumption of meat proteins and tropical grasses such as corn). Similar studies conducted at the Spanish seventeenth-century Mission Santa Catalina de Guale in modern Georgia indicate that such studies can lead us from speculation to fact when considering changes in historic diet and its effects on human populations.[51] Until such studies are undertaken, the analysis of archaeologically recovered floral and faunal remains will give us the best insights into what foods were available to neophytes if not their quantity in the diets.

David Huelsbeck's 1986 re-evaluation of documentary evidence, combined with current nutritional data from Mesoamerica and his baseline study of faunal remains from missions Santa Cruz and Santa Clara, suggest that the generalizations made by Cook on the adequacy of mission diets may not hold true throughout the California mission system.[52] He finds that Cook's calculations were low and that the available calories would have been more than adequate for sustaining health. At these two sites, wild species made up less than 1% of the total meat protein available, and it probably served solely to add variety to the diet. Huelsbeck's conclusions fit well with those of other researchers who have noted Santa Clara's high agricultural productivity.[53] This also matches the observations of inhabitants and visitors to mission Santa Clara. In 1792 when Vancouver visited and the population was about 1200, twenty-four cattle were slaughtered weekly.[54] The *Interrogatorio* of 1814 reports forty head killed weekly for a population of 1300, and in 1822 fifty head fed about 1400 people.[55]

Finally, archaeological data may suggest new avenues of inquiry regarding demographic collapse, health, and working conditions in the missions. Currently, documentary data suggests that at least in some of the missions where caloric intake was sufficient to maintain health, poor diet cannot be seen as primary culprit for demographic collapse. Jackson suggests that the neophytes were "grossly malnourished" and so, more prone to disease than the soldiers and settlers.[56] Additionally, it has been suggested that poor sanitation, overcrowding, and heavy labor were key factors in the demographic collapse of the mission system.[57] To date, there are only anecdotal accounts regarding burials from Mission San Diego.[58] There has been no complete scientific analysis for paleopathologies of an intact mission cemetery population in all of Alta California.[59] To evaluate the claims of a high death rate due to heavy labor and an increase in the rates of infectious disease and the spread of Old World pathogens, a comparison of skeletal remains from mission and non-mission cemeteries will be required. It will not be until skeletal populations are studied that we will have the final word on nutrition and health in each of the missions of Alta California.

A Year At Santa Clara

The continuity and change that characterized the resident Ohlone mission population was wrought in daily life. Although hundreds of pages of documents were penned during Mission Santa Clara's sixty years as a Franciscan mission, a map was never drawn and a calendar was never developed. Today, after decades of research we can reconstruct the third mission complex and the seasonal round.

The rhythm of life at Mission Santa Clara revolved around subsistence. Once chores associated with agriculture and animal husbandry were completed, emphasis shifted to activities that created the lifeways associated with the Spanish colonial frontier. Everyday tasks included maintaining irrigation canals, preparing meals, working in specific trades (weaving, smithing, potting, etc.), and attending prayers twice a day. Once a week, 25 to 50 head of cattle were slaughtered for the sustenance of the mission populace. On special occasions, such as the celebration of saints' feast days or the arrival of visitors, there would be an additional slaughter of cattle and a reduction in the work schedule.

The Mission's Legacy

When it was secularized in 1837, Mission Santa Clara de Asís became the nucleous of what would become Santa Clara University and the City of Santa Clara. Most of the former mission's lands, herds, industries, and structures were granted to Mexican families and a few Indian families.

A return to precontact lifeways was impossible because of the changes wrought by the mission on the local natural and cultural environments. The annexation of traditional homelands by the Spanish and Mexican governments meant that there were, in some cases, no unclaimed territories to which the Natives could return. In addition, life in the mission had created changes in the demographic and marriage patterns of the Native Californians. This meant that precontact polities were no longer viable. Finally, there were vast changes in the precontact natural environment that made a return to traditional lifeways all but impossible. These changes included the destruction of a broad area of grass and oak woodlands that characterized this area. From the 1790s to the 1830s, Santa Clara was home to more than a thousand people, and the oak savanna and riverine gallery forests had been destroyed.

The domesticated animals introduce by the mission also had impacts on the environment. Santa Clara had huge herds of cattle, sheep, and horses, and fewer numbers of pigs and goats, which outcompeted non-domesticated species (e.g., antelope, deer, and elk) for native bunch grasses and acorns. The transformed environment was hostile to traditional subsistence strategies. Those who tried, such as the followers of Yozcolo, fell afoul of the Mexican authorities. With little wild game for hunting, they rustled cattle, horses, and sheep instead. As a direct threat to the *rancho* economy, they were forcibly suppressed by the military[60].

For the vast majority of the now land and homeless Spanish-speaking Christian Indian residents of the mission, there was no choice but to become part of the households of these new *ranchos*. As laborers, they continued participating in the activities of agriculture and ranching that they had become dependent on at the mission. The stage was set for the transformation of Santa Clara and its environs into the "Golden Triangle" in the Valley of Heart's Delight.

Acknowledgments

I am indebted to my colleagues, the Assistant Campus Archaeologist, from the Santa Clara University Archaeology Research Lab, Linda Hylkema and her predecessor, Julie Wizorek for their insights into the archaeology of Mission Santa Clara. This work has further benefitted from the earlier research of Mark Hylkema, California Department of Parks and Recreation; and from Santa Clara University Dave Huelsbeck, and the late B. Mark Lynch.

Endnotes

1. Skowronek 1998
2. Guest 1985: 25-6; 1989: 1-2
3. Hylkema 1995: 33-34, 79
4. Milliken 1995:135-136
5. Phillips 1993
6. Spearman 1963: 131-151
7. Guest 1989: 6
8. Geiger and Meighan 1976: 41
9. Geiger and Meighan 1976: 60
10. Geiger and Meighan 1976: 50-51
11. Weber 1991: 52-54
12. Weber 1991: 58-60
13. Kroeber et al. 1977: 95
14. Englehardt 1909: 26; Geiger and Meighan 1976: 106
15. Geiger and Meighan 1976: 145
16. Kroeber 1906: 169-250
17. Weber 1991: 17
18. Geiger and Meighan 1976: 99
19. Castillo 1989: 123
20. Archdiocese of San Francisco Archives, Catalá Beatification Documents, No.. 41, p.80
21. Archdiocese of San Francisco Archives, Catalá Beatification Documents, No. 51, p.100
22. La Purísima—Deetz 1963: 180; San Luís Rey—Soto 1961: 34-6; Soledad—Farnsworth 1987: 398,415; San Antonio—Hoover and Costello 1985: 74-83;Santa Inés—Costello 1989: 145-7; San José—Dietz 1983; Santa Clara—Cambra et al. 1995; Hylkema 1995; Wizorek and Skowronek 1996; Skowronek and Wizorek 1997:81-85
23. Humphrey 1965; Galvan 1993; Hylkema 1995; Wizorek and Skowronek 1996
24. Hylkema 1995:67-85
25. Wizorek and Skowronek 1996; Skowronek and Wizorek 1997
26. Shoup 1995: 49-50
27. Kenneally 1965: 206
28. Cambra et al. 1995; Hylkema and Skowronek 2000; Skowronek and Wizorek 1997
29. Geiger and Meighan 1976: 126-7
30. Geiger and Meighan 1976:147
31. Geiger and Meighan 1976: 151-3
32. Czosek 1994
33. Milliken 1995:149; Shoup 1995: 46-47; Webb 1952: 67
34. Tibesar 1955 v.3: 119
35. Santa Clara 1777: 13-14
36. Geiger 1955: 196-200
37. Guest 1973: 281
38. Chapman 1959: 102-104, 109; Geiger and Meighan 1976: 131-132; Guest 1973: 300-306; Milliken 1995:86-88; Weber 1991: 14, 28-29, 65-66
39. Milliken 1995: 87
40. Milliken 1995: 88
41. Weber 1991: 27
42. Geiger and Meighan 1976: 90
43. Santa Clara 1777: 11-12; Tibesar 1955, vol. 3: 141

44. Cambra et al. 1995; Hylkema and Skowronek 2000
45. Hylkema 1995:79; Skowronek and Wizorek 1997:82
46. Costello 1989: 139; Deetz 1963: 180, 186; Farris 1992: 2; Hoover and Costello 1985: 77-83; Soto 1961: 36
47. Kenneally 1965: 143
48. Weber 1991: 65
49. Cook 1976 : 34-55; Shipek 1985: 490
50. Geiger and Meighan 1976: 78-80; Jackson 1992
51. Larsen, 1990
52. Huelsbeck 1986
53. Guest 1973: 336-342; Jackson 1991: 393-396
54. Weber 1991: 3
55. Geiger and Meighan 1976: 85; Chapman 1959: 103; Jackson 1992: 147
56. Jackson 1992: 153
57. Jackson 1994:117-143; Jackson and Castillo 1995:48-50; Shoup 1995: 63- 64
58. Margolin citing Shipek 1990:38; Trafzer 1992:72
59. Humphrey 1965; Mitchell et al. 1993
60. (Holterman 1970: 22-23)

References Cited

Archdiocese of San Francisco Archives. 1883-1884. Catalá Beatification Documents. Copy on file. Santa Clara University Archives, Santa Clara, CA.

Cambra, Rosemary, N. Sánchez, Alan Leventhal, Elena Reese. 1995 *Results of a Phase I Presence/Absence Subsurface Archaeological Testing Program and Archival Literature Search on the Vanguard Parcel Located on the Southeastern Corner of Benton and Sherman Streets, City of Santa Clara, Santa Clara County, California.* Report to Mark Robson Santa Clara Development, Ohlone Families Consulting Service, San Jose. Ms. on file City of Santa Clara Planning Department.

Castillo, Edward D. 1989. The Assassination of Padre Andrés Quintana by the Indians of Mission Santa Cruz in 1812:The Narrative of Lorenzo Asisara. *California History* 68(3):116-126.

Chapman, Cristina Alviso. 1959 Early days at Mission Santa Clara. *California Historical Society Quarterly* 38(2):101-111.

Cook, Sherburne F. 1976. *The Conflict Between The California Indian and White Civilization.* University of California Press, Berkeley.

Costello, Julia G. 1989. Santa Inés Mission Excavations:1986-1988. *California Historical Archaeology* No. 1. Coyote Press, Salinas.

Czosek, Virginia C. 1994. Blessed with Orchards, Cheered with Vine: Ideologies of Agriculture in the Transformation of Alta California. *Research Manuscript Series on the Cultural and Natural History of Santa Clara.*

Deetz, James J. F. 1963 *Archaeological Investigations at La Purísima Mission.* Annual Report, Archaeological Survey, Department of Anthropology, Univ. of California, Los Angeles, CA.

Dietz, Stephen A. 1983 *Final Report of Archaeological Investigations at Mission San Jose (CA-Ala-1)*. Archaeological Consulting and Research Services, Inc., Santa Cruz.

Engelhardt, Zephyrin, O.F.M. 1909 *The Holy man of Santa Clara or Life, Virtues, and Miracles of Fr. Magín Catalá, O.F.M.* The James H. Barry Company, San Francisco.

Farnsworth, Paul. 1987. *The Economics of Acculturation in the California Missions: A Historical and Archaeological Study of Mission Nuestra Señora de la Soledad.* unpublished Ph.D. dissertation, Department of Anthropology, University of California, Los Angeles.

Farris, Glenn. 1992 Finding the Mission Indian Housing at San Juan Bautista SHP. *California Mission Studies Association Newsletter* 9(1):2.

Galvan, Andrew. 1993 *A History of the Ohlone Indian Cemetery*. Paper presented at the California Mission Studies Association Annual Meeting, Mission San Antonio, February.

Geiger, Maynard J., O.F.M. 1955 *Palou's Life of Fray Junípero Serra*. Academy of American Franciscan History, Washington, D.C..

Geiger, Maynard (O.F.M.) and Clement W. Meighan. 1976 *As the Padres Saw Them California Indian Life and Customs as Reported by the Franciscan Missionaries, 1813-1815.* Santa Barbara Mission Archive Library, Santa Barbara.

Guest, Francis F., O.F.M. 1973. *Fermín Francisco de Lasuén (1736-1803)*. Academy of American Franciscan History, Washington, D.C.

1985 New Look at the California's Missions. *Some Reminiscences about Fray Junípero Serra.* edited by Francis J. Weber, pp. 77-87. Knights of Columbus, Santa Barbara.

1989 An Inquiry into the Role of the Discipline in California Mission Life. *Southern California Quarterly* 71(Spring):1-68.

Holterman, Jack, 1970. "The revolt of Yozcolo: Indian warrior in the fight for freedom." *The Indian Historian* 3(2):19-23.

Hoover, Robert L. and Julia G. Costello, editors. 1985. *Excavations at Mission San Antonio, 1976-1978.* Institute of Archaeology, University of California, Los Angeles.

Huelsbeck, David R. 1986 Wild Animals in the Mission Diet: Luxury or Necessity? Paper presented at the Society for Historical Archaeology Annual Meeting, Sacramento, CA.

Humphrey, Richard. 1965 The La Purísima Mission Cemetery. *Annual Reports of the University of California(Los Angeles) Archaeological Survey* 7:179- 192.

Hylkema, Linda, and Russell K. Skowronek. 2000 Diving into the Past. *California Mission Studies Association Newsletter* 17(2):3-5.

Hylkema, Mark. 1995 *Archaeological Investigation at Mission Santa Clara (CA-SCL-30) for the Re-Alignment of Route 82.* California Department of Transportation, District 4, Oakland.

Jackson, Robert H. 1991 Population and the Economic Dimension of Colonization in Alta California: Four Mission Communities. *Journal of the Southwest* 33(3):387-439.

1992 The Dynamics of Indian Demographic Collapse in the San Francisco Bay Missions, Alta California, 1776-1840. *American Indian Quarterly* Spring 141-156.

1994 *Indian Population Decline, The Missions of Northwestern New Spain, 1687-1840*. University of New Mexico Press, Albuquerque.

Jackson, Robert H. and Edward Castillo. 1995. *Indians, Franciscans, and Spanish Colonization, The Impact of the Mission System on California Indians*. University of New Mexico Press, Albuquerque.

Kenneally, Finbar, O.F.M. 1965 *Writings of Fermín Francisco de Lasuén*. Academy of American Franciscan History, Washington, D.C..

Kroeber, Alfred L. 1906. Indian Myths of South Central California. *University of California Publications in American Archaeology and Ethnology*, edited by Frederic Ward Putnam, 4(4):169-250.

Kroeber, Theodora, Albert B. Elsasser, Robert F. Heizer, 1977 *Drawn From Life, California Indians in Pen and Brush*. Ballena Press, Socorro, NM.

Larsen, Clark Spenser, Editor, 1990. the Archaeology of Mission Santa Catalina de Guale: Biocultural Interpretations of a Population in Transition. *Anthropological Papers of the American Museum of Natural History*. No. 68, New Yor.

Margolin, Malcom. 1990. Spanish Missions and California Indians Conference. News from Native California. Heyday Books, Berkeley.

Milliken, Randall Theodore. 1995 *A Time of Little Choice, The Disintegration of Tribal Culture in the San Francisco Bay Area, 1769-1810*. Ballena Press, Menlo Park, CA.

Mitchell, Patricia, Rose Tyson and Brad Holderman. 1993. Summary of Findings for a Portion of the Human Remains from the 1989 Excavation at San Diego Mission de Acalá. Poster Session #1 Abstract *Southwestern Anthropological Association* annual meeting, San Diego.

Phillips, George H.1993. *Indians and Intruders in Central California, 1769-1849*. University of Oklahoma Press, Norman.

Santa Clara. 1777. Santa Clara Mission *Informes*. Ms. on file, Santa Clara University Archives, Santa Clara, CA.

Shipek, Florence C. 1985 California Indian Reactions to the Franciscans. *The Americas*, XLI(4):480-493.

Shoup, Laurence H. 1995. *Iñigo of Rancho Posolmi: The Life and Times of A Mission Indian and His Land*. Archaeological/Historical Consultants, Oakland, CA for Tasman Corridor Archaeological Project, Santa Clara County Transportation Agency, San Jose, CA.

Skowronek, Russell K. 1998. Sifting the Evidence: Perceptions of Life at the Ohlone (Costanoan) Missions of Alta California. *Ethnohistory* 45(4):675-708.

Skowronek, Russell K. and Julie C. Wizorek. 1997 Archaeology at Santa Clara de Asís: The Slow Rediscovery of a Moveable Mission. *Pacific Coast Archaeological Society Quarterly* 33(3):54-92.

Soto, Anthony, O.F.M. 1961. Mission San Luis Rey, California—Excavations in the Sunken Gardens. *Kiva* 26;34-43.

Spearman, Arthur Dunning, S.J. 1963 *The Five Franciscan Churches of Mission Santa Clara, 1777-1825*. The National Press, Palo Alto.

Tibesar, Antonine, O.F.M. 1955 *Writings of Junípero Serra*. Academy of American Franciscan History, Washington, D.C..

Trafzer, Clifford E. 1992. Serra's Legacy: The Desecration of American Indian Burials at Mission San Diego. *American Indian Culture and Research Journal* 16(2):57-75.

Webb, Edith Buckland. 1952. *Indian Life at the Old Missions*. University of Nebraska Press, Lincoln.

Weber, Francis J. 1991. *Prominent Visitors to the California Missions*. The Archival Center, Mission Hills California.

Wizorek, Julie C. and Russell K. Skowronek. 1996 *Rose Garden Burials*. Ms. on file Northwestern Information Center, Sonoma State University and Archaeology Research Lab, Santa Clara University.

CHAPTER 7

Demographic Patterns
at Santa Clara Mission, 1777-1840
Robert H. Jackson

In 1777, the Franciscans established Santa Clara mission on the banks of the Guadalupe River near the southern end of San Francisco Bay. Missions were complex colonial institutions that had evolved over several centuries along the northern frontier of New Spain (colonial Mexico). The goal was to create communities of sedentary indigenous citizens of the Spanish empire who eventually would assume the obligations expected of all other native peoples of Spanish America. These obligations included paying tribute (a poll tax) and providing labor when needed by the Spanish government or Spanish entrepreneurs. The indigenous villagers were also to be integrated into the economy of colonial Mexico as producers and consumers. Missions administered by members of a number of missionary orders proved to be a cost effective way of bringing native peoples on the fringes of New Spain under the sway of Spanish control.

The indigenous population of central Mexico lived sedentary lives based on agriculture prior to the arrival of the Spaniards. The Ohlone/Costanoan of the southern San Francisco Bay region also lived in permanent village sites occupied over long periods of time, but their villages did not appear to be "real" towns to the Spanish. Therefore, the Franciscans oversaw the creation of new communities from scratch. The mission was to be not only a center of religious worship, but also a functioning indigenous community. To form the new indigenous community, the Franciscans congregated native peoples at the mission.

The Franciscans stationed at all twenty-one California missions pursued similar goals, but patterns of congregation or the formation of indigenous communities at the missions varied from establishment to establishment. The pattern of congregation at Santa Clara was somewhat different from patterns at other California missions, because the Franciscans continued to congregate new converts to the mission community as late as the 1820s and 1830s.[1] Congregation occurred in two phases. During the first phase, which lasted until the first years of the nineteenth century, the Franciscans congregated villagers from the southern part of the San Francisco Bay region and southward towards the modern city of Morgan Hill (Table 1).[2] The population reached a recorded high of 1,514 in 1795, but the numbers also fluctuated over the next three decades.[3] Between 1805 and 1832, the Franciscans congregated some 1,832 *tularenos* (generic Spanish term for native peoples from the Central Valley), mostly Yokuts from the San Joaquin Valley. In 1827, at the peak of resettlement of Yokuts to the mission, the population of Santa Clara totaled 1,462. The numbers dropped to 800 by 1834 as the number of new recruits decreased.[4]

The pattern of building construction at Santa Clara was similar to that at other California missions (Table 2), with an emphasis on the construction of the central complex or *casco* from 1779 through the mid-1790s. This entailed the construction first of temporary wattle and daub structures, followed by more permanent adobe buildings.

TABLE 1: Baptism by district to Santa Clara Mission, 1777-1815

íDistrict	Years	Numbers of Baptisms
Santa Clara	1777-1793	25
San Francisco	1777-1796	71
San José Cupertino	1777-1801	250
San Juan Bautista	1777-1803	98
San Francisco Solano	1777-1800	178
Santa Ysabel	1777-1808	238
San Bernardino	1777-1804	821
San Carlos	1779-1817	1158
Santa Agueda	1780-1807	561
San Antonio	1777-1815	805

SOURCE: Mark G. Hylkema, "Archaeological Investigations at the Third Location of Mission Santa Clara de Asís: The Murguía Mission, 1781-1818," Caltrans District 4, Oakland, California, 1995, 35.

TABLE 2: Building construction at Santa Clara Mission.

1777-1779: Two structures of palizada built. The first was a chapel, and the second contained ten rooms including quarters for the missionaries, quarters for the servants, offices, and a granary. An irrigation ditch opened.

1779: A flood on January 23, 1779 destroyed the buildings erected in the previous years, and the Franciscans relocated the mission to a new higher site. During the winter a new temporary chapel and quarters for the missionaries and some Indians built. Beginning in the spring following the rainy season an irrigation ditch was opened. New buildings of palizada were built including a church, residence for the missionaries, granary, kitchen, office, and three corrals.

1780: An adobe structure with eight rooms built. Its uses included a new residence for the missionaries, offices, and granary.

1781-1784: A new adobe church built 40 ½ varas in length.

1781: A granary and a second structure built, both of adobe.

1783: One of the palizada buildings erected in 1780 burned.

1787: An adobe wing 40 varas long built to complete the mission quadrangle. It contained a reception room, four other rooms, and a zaguan (a covered passage way). A store room for fire wood built, and a new irrigation ditch opened.

1788: Fire destroyed the tule roofs of four buildings which had to be replaced. An adobe wall built, and a retaining wall of stakes erected along one of the five planting fields.

1789: A two story adobe structure with an overhanging balcony built near the sacristy. The walls of the residence of the missionaries raised.

1790: Two adobe structures and an adobe corral built. One building served as the residence for the mayordomo (overseer).

1791: A granary and tile kiln built.

1792: A granary and eight houses for Indian families built.

1793: Fourteen houses for Indian families built. An adobe corral renovated, as well as the quarters of the missionaries.

1794: Nine houses for Indian families built.

1795: Two wings of the quadrangle roofed with tiles. The church enlarged. A retaining wall built along one of the planting fields.

1796: The other buildings of the mission complex received tile roofs, and a soldiers barracks built.

1797: Four rows of Indian houses received tile roofs.

1798: One hundred and sixty houses built for Indian families. Each had an enclosed patio.

1799-1809: No annual reports are available for these years.

1813: A new soldiers barracks built.

1815: An adobe corral built for cattle.

1818-1819: A new church built to replace the structure completed in 1784.

1822: The quadrangle built in the 1780s abandoned, and relocated to a new site a short distance away. Two wings of the new quadrangle were built. However, the Indian house built in the 1790s continued to be used.

1823: Two adobe wings and a new soldiers barracks built.

1824-1825: A new adobe church built.

SOURCE: Annual Reports, Archivo General de la Nacion, Mexico, D.F., Santa Barbara Mission Archive-Library, Santa Barbara, California.

FIGURE 1: c. 1809 map of a section of the *casco* at the second site of the Santa Clara Mission.

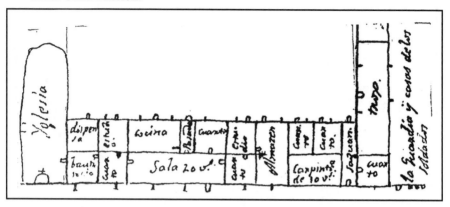

The first adobe church was completed in 1784, and by the early 1790s the main *casco* was largely complete (Figure 1). Neophytes continued to live in traditional conical grass huts, except for single women and older girls. This changed in the 1790s. Between 1793 and 1798, the Franciscans directed the construction of 183 adobe houses with tile roofs for neophyte families.[5] In the 1820s, the Franciscans moved the *casco* a short distance and built a new church and adjoining buildings (Figure 2), but the neophyte housing continued to be used.

The transition in Indian housing occurred when the mission population was still relatively large. The construction of European-style housing was part of a larger crown-sponsored initiative to promote more rapid assimilation of the indigenous population. The annual reports from most of the other missions also record the construction of European-style housing.[6] This transition contributed to the poor health of the indigenous population, since a large number of people lived in close proximity with poor sanitation.

A conjunction of factors contributed to the demographic collapse of the neophytes congregated at Santa Clara mission. Epidemics and chronic ailments culled the mission population, and disease was particularly devastating among young children born at the mission. The Franciscans continued to bring new converts to live at the mission, but at the same time the number of deaths was consistently higher than the number of births (Figure 3). Life expectancy was low, and on average children born at Santa Clara lived only 3.2 years.[7]

How important was the congregation of large numbers of people

FIGURE 2: 1854 Black map showing the two building complexes at Santa Clara Mission.

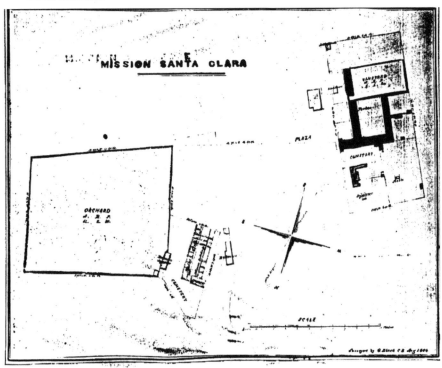

at the missions? A useful comparison can be made between Santa Clara and the two southernmost California missions San Diego and San Luis Rey. The Franciscans at these two missions also baptized thousands of Indians, but only congregated a small percentage of the neophytes at the mission itself. The indigenous population continued to live in a more dispersed pattern. Mean life expectancy at birth at San Diego and Luis Rey, for example, was much higher than at Santa Clara.Mean life expectancy at San Diego was 6.4 years, twice that of Santa Clara, and for San Luis Rey it was 19.1 years.[8]

Medical care was rudimentary at best, and some medicines used, such as mercury pills used to treat syphilis, could be worse than the disease itself. Poor quality medical care also played a role in high infant mortality and high death rates among women of childbearing age. Pregnant women did not receive adequate pre-natal care from celibate (more or less) Franciscans who had little or no practical knowledge of how to care for pregnant women. Moreover, the

FIGURE 3: Births and burials recorded at Santa Clara Mission, 1777-1840

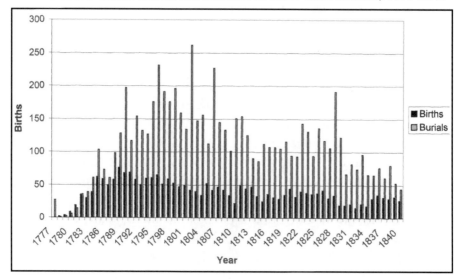

Franciscans systematically persecuted the traditional indigenous practitioners who specialized in caring women and young children. Many babies were born with low birth weights or chronic ailments including congenital syphilis, and did not survive long. Moreover, poor sanitation and unprotected water supplies in the mission village contributed to high mortality rates among children. It was all too easy for young children living at the mission to contract potentially fatal infections or diarrhea, which if not properly treated, can cause dehydration and death.

Mortality patterns at Santa Clara mission are unbalanced in age and gender structure. During the first phase of congregation at the mission, the population of baptized Indians consisted primarily of young children. The conversion of adults lagged behind that of children. Moreover, during the early period of the history of the mission, the Franciscans kept large numbers of children at the *casco* for indoctrination while adults continued to live in their traditional villages. The insecurity of the food supply was one reason for this practice. By the end of the 1790s, however, the Franciscans had largely completed the conversion and congregation of the local adult population, and in subsequent decades, the number of young children (*parvulos*-children under age 9) and females declined in relation to the total population. A gender balanced population would roughly have equal numbers of males and females. By the late 1820s, however, females constituted less than forty percent of the total population. In the same years, *parvulos* constituted less than ten percent of the total population (Figure 4). Pre-contact indigenous populations most likely were high fertility high, mortality populations, but at the same time the age and gender structure was more balanced than it was at Santa Clara by the late 1820s. At the end of the mission period, the majority of neophytes were males, which was another indication of the inability of the indigenous population living at the mission to reproduce itself.

The final and most controversial conclusion is that conditions at Santa Clara and the other missions in general played an important role in demographic collapse. A comparison of demographic patterns at San Carlos and the populations of the four military garrisons established in California (San Diego, Monterey, San Francisco, Santa Barbara) highlight the importance of conditions in the missions. An analysis of baptisms and burials at Monterey presidio shows that, unlike Santa Clara, baptisms/births usually outnumbered burials.[9] Mean life expectancy at birth for children born at the four presidios was considerably higher than for the indigenous population of Santa Clara. On average, these children lived to between 25 and 40, a

FIGURE 4: The population of parvulos and females as a percentage of the total population of Santa Clara Mission.

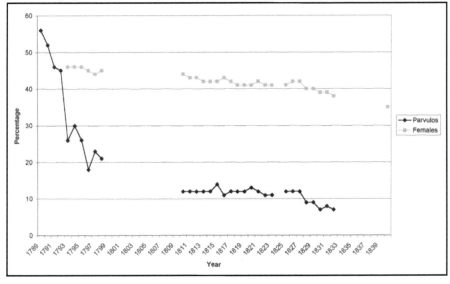

pattern more in line with contemporary European populations.[10] The populations of the presidios lived in environments like those of the missions (the same climate, diseases, diet, etc.), but did not experience the same high mortality as did the indigenous population of Santa Clara. Even with the medical care of the day, the population of Monterey and the other three presidios did much better than the indigenous population of Santa Clara. This difference may be accounted for by the different labor regimes and social policies implemented at the missions: extensive corporal punishment, the use of European style clothing that harbored germs, European-style housing which was difficult to keep clean, and particularly the practice of incarcerating females at nigh in cold, damp, unsanitary dormitories.

The indigenous population of Santa Clara mission declined rapidly following the secularization of the missions, which entailed the legal emancipation of the Indians and the civil administration of the mission estates. Secularization of the missions and the transformation of the missions into politically autonomous indigenous communities was a planned outcome of the mission system. There was a general dispersal of the surviving indigenous populations living at the missions, and many former neophytes went to work on the ranches being granted to prominent and politically connected settlers or in the towns emerging in the province. Others settled in *rancherias* located in the vicinity of the ex-missions. In 1839, according to a report prepared for the provincial government by William Hartnell, 400 Indians continued to live at Santa Clara. The decline resulted from out-migration as well as heavy mortality during an 1838 smallpox outbreak. In 1842, there were still 300 natives at the mission, and 130 in 1845.[11] The demise of the indigenous population continued in the decades following the conquest of California by the United States.

Notes

1. Santa Clara Mission Baptismal Registers, Archive of the University of Santa Clara, Santa Clara, California.

2. For a discussion of the location of the villages the Franciscans congregated Indians to Santa Clara mission from see Mark G. Hylkema, "Archaeological Investigations at the Third Location of Mission Santa Clara de Asís: The Murguía Mission, 1781-1818," unpublished manuscript on file with Caltrans District 4, Oakland, California, 1995, 32-38.

3. Jackson, Indian Population Decline, 173-174.

4. Santa Clara Mission Baptismal Registers, Santa Clara Univesity Archives.

5. The Women's Club Adobe is an example of the houses the indigenous population lived in.

6. For building construction at the other missions see Robert H. Jackson and Edward Castillo, Indians, Franciscans, and Spanish Colonization: The Impact of the Mission System on California Indians (Albuquerque, 1995), 137-168.

7. Jackson, Indian Population Decline, 104-105.

8. Ibid., 89-90.

9. San Carlos Mission Annual Reports: Archivo General de la Nacion, Mexico, D.F.: Santa Barbara Mission Archive-Library, Santa Barbara, California.

10. Jackson, Indian Population Decline, 173-174.

11. Ibid., 174.

References Cited

Hylkema, Mark G., "Archaeological Investigations at the Third Location of Mission Santa Clara de Asís: The Murguia Mission, 1781-1818," Caltrans District 4, Oakland, California.

Jackson, Robert H., Indian Population Decline: The Missions of Northwestern New Spain, 1687-1840. Albuquerque: University of New Mexico Press, 1994.

Jackson, Robert H. and Edward Castillo, Indians, Franciscans, and Spanish Colonization: The Impact of the Mission System on California Indians. Albuquerque: University of New Mexico Press, 1995.

SECTION III
Nineteenth Century Santa Clara

The legacy of Mission Santa Clara is seen in the city and university that today bear its name. At the mission, disparate peoples were brought together to learn a new way of life based on new ideas, technologies, and values. In the 1830s and 40s, when the mission was transformed into a parish, new immigrants from Mexico and the United States came to call Santa Clara home. By the end of the century, they would be joined by Irish, Germans, Italians, Portuguese, Chinese, Japanese, and Slavic peoples. Within the City of Santa Clara, these different ethnicities lived harmoniously side-by-side with earlier peoples of Ohlone and Mexican descent. These new immigrants further transformed the cultural and natural environment of the Santa Clara Valley, turning it into the world's fruit bowl, the "Valley of Heart's Delight."[1]

Into this melting pot and into the rubble of the mission came the Society of Jesus in 1851 to establish the first institution of higher education in California-Santa Clara College. Within the walls of this nascent university, a polyglot of students, like their mission-era predecessors, came together to learn a new way of life based on new ideas, technologies, and values. The philosophy they learned sought to balance curricular competence with compassion for the other members of their community. It is a conscious realization that people depend on each other to survive.

1. Czosek, Virginia C.. 1994. Blessed with Orchards, Cheered with Vine:Ideologies of Agriculture in the Transformation of Alta California. *Research Manuscript Series on the Cultural and Natural History of Santa Clara.* No. 2, Santa Clara University, Santa Clara, CA.

CHAPTER 8

The Immigrants Who Built Santa Clara

Lorie Garcia

S anta Clara is considered a workingman's city and owes its unique identity today to the various waves of the immigrant ethnic groups from Europe and Asia who settled here and whose labor contributed to its formation and growth. The backgrounds of these immigrants varied, but they came for similar reasons, to build new and better lives. In accomplishing their personal goals, they built Santa Clara.

1775-76 Anza Expedition

Eight years after the discovery of San Francisco Bay in 1769 by Spanish explorers, the first immigrants of European extraction arrived in the Santa Clara area. The Juan Bautista de Anza 1775-76 expedition brought almost 200 people to California, both military and civilian. The establishment of Mission Santa Clara de Asís in January 1777 and the founding of the Pueblo de San José adjacent to the mission site eleven months later saw the first appearance of non-native people to settle the area. The contributions of members of this expedition and their descendants, Galindo, Bernal, Alviso and Berryessa, built the early foundation on which the City of Santa Clara would later grow. Besides their involvement in pueblo and mission life, after secularization several of their children became grantees of the ranchos carved from previous mission-owned land.

Juan Chrisóstomo Galindo, who was born in 1783 the son of expedition member Private Nicolás Galindo, served during the 1840s as the *majordomo* of Mission Santa Clara, entrusted with complete oversight of the mission lands and buildings. He married Ana Maria

Jacoba Bernal y Sanchez, a daughter of Private Juan Francisco Bernal, a member of Anza's expedition. One of their daughters, Juana Francisco, married José María de Jesus Alviso, grantee of *Rancho Milpitas*. Their other daughter, María Anna, married James Alexander Forbes, British Vice-Consul during the 1840s and grantee of *Rancho El Potrero de Santa Clara*. When he died in 1877, aged 94, Juan Chrisóstómo had spent his life in Santa Clara, contributing to both the Mission and American periods, the latter as a citizen of the new Town.

María Zacharías Bernal y Berryessa (Berreyesa), the sister of Ana María Jacoba, married José de los Reyes Berryessa y Peralta in 1805; he was the son of Nicolás Berreyesa, who came with Anza not as part of the military but as a *pobladore* or settler. Their history is intimately connected with that of the New Almaden quicksilver mines (Rancho San Vincente). In August 1861, following the sale of the family interest in *Rancho San Vincente*, María Zacharías purchased the "Berryessa Adobe" from the Galindo family for one of her younger sons, José Guadalupe Fernando Berreyesa y Bernal (nicknamed Fernando) and his wife María Vincente Catalina Rodriguez (Catarina). In 1868 she also deeded another adobe in the Town of Santa Clara to her daughter Carmen, widow of Lorenzo Pinedo, grantee of *Rancho Las Uvas*, which had been patented by the United States Land Commission to Martin Murphy in 1860. María died in 1869 and Fernando in 1875, but his wife Catarina lived until 1938, and died just a few weeks short of her 104th birthday.

In the mid 1840s, Lorenzo Pinedo built the first frame house constructed in Santa Clara, which stood until the beginning of the 20th century. One of his daughters, Dolores, married William Fitts, an American immigrant, who gained renown as the last stage driver and first horse-car driver on the horse car trolley line constructed on the Alameda. The other daughter of Lorenzo and Carmen was Encarnacíon. She never married and became an author, credited with writing the first cookbook printed in California and recollections of life in Santa Clara during the mission days.

American Immigrants of 1846

In the fall of 1846, just a few months after the Bear Flag Rebellion in Sonoma, approximately 175 men, women, and children arrived at Mission Santa Clara as part of the first large overland American immigration to California and Oregon.

Among these were William Campbell and his family, who arrived in October, settling into one of the adobe buildings belonging to the mission. The following two years would see William playing an active roll in changing the face of the Santa Clara area. In November his wife died and the following month he enlisted in Captain Charles Weber's company of California Riflemen, participating in the Battle of Santa Clara on January 2, 1847. That same year he pre-empted a claim to 160 acres two miles south of Santa Clara and established a wheat farm on the land. After he had surveyed 70 blocks of land for the Alcalde of San José that April, in October 1847, Fr. Suárez del Real, the Mission Priest, hired him to survey land near the mission complex on mission land and draw up a town plat. A little less than five years later, this land, with its blocks and streets located as he placed them, became the Town of Santa Clara. In late 1847, William and his two oldest sons established a sawmill near present day Saratoga, but due to the discovery of gold it would be the fall of 1848 before it was in operation. In July 1849, William married his second wife, Kisiah McCutchen, who had also arrived as part of the "Great Migration" of 1846, and in the fall he helped establish the Methodist Episcopal Church in the Santa Clara Valley, with his son preaching at the home of Samuel Young (co-leader of the 1846 Harlan-Young Party).

Kisiah McCutchen, her husband John and their two children William and Amanda, were part of the last party to make it over the Sierras before the crossing became impassible due to the arrival of the winter snowfall. Due to a disagreement between John and his brother William at Fort Bridger, William and his family separated from John and joined the Donner Party, with the resultant tragedy. John and Kisiah, however, arrived safely at Sutter's Fort on October 25, 1846, and the family proceeded to Mission Santa Clara, sailing down the Sacramento River to San Francisco Bay and thence to Alviso, a trip that took 10 days. On March 30, 1847, Kisiah gave birth to a daughter, Margeline, the second American child born in Santa Clara County. About a year later, John left his family for Oregon and was never seen again. For six generations, descendants of Kisiah have lived in Santa Clara, with her great-great-great grandson, Jamie Matthews, currently serving as a member of the Santa Clara City Council.

Gold Rush Immigration

The years following the discovery of gold in 1848 brought an overwhelming rush of both American and European immigrants to the area. One of these was Antonio Fatjo. Born in Spain in 1828, at the age of 15, he went to South America on a tour for his health. When the ship reached Santiago, Chile, he was hired to work in the wholesale dry goods house of Infanta Brothers and abandoned his voyage. After he had been in Santiago six years, married and had two children, reports of the fabulous gold finds in California reached Santiago, and Antonio left to seek his fortune. Upon reaching California, however, he met José Arques, another Spaniard from Chile, and went into business with him, establishing a wholesale and general merchandise store in San Francisco. In the fall of 1849, Antonio moved to Santa Clara and opened a general store called the Farmers Store, becoming one of the first merchants in Santa Clara. This store was located in the Arques Block on Franklin Street. Antonio continued his business relationship with José Arques for many years, associating with him in both cattle dealing and the mercantile business. Like their father, his sons made important contributions to Santa Clara's economic life. The eldest, Antonio V. became a banker, instrumental in the re-organization of the Santa Clara Valley Bank and later organization of the Mission Bank. His son Robert A. was a philanthropic man, who, when he became Town Treasurer, donated his entire salary to worthy local organizations. After Antonio decided to sell his store, his son John bought it and ran it under the name of John Fatjo and Son. For many decades, this store would provide food staples to the residents of San Clara, in particular to the newly arrived immigrants from Spain and Portugal in the first part of the twentieth century.

The German Colony

Towards the middle of the nineteenth century, unrest in the German states led to a large immigration of Germanic peoples to the United States. From the 1850s through the 1880s, several of these immigrants settled in Santa Clara and they became known as the German Colony.

Frederick Christian Franck was born in Waschbascherhof, Bavaria, on December 23, 1828, and at age fifteen left school to learn the harness and saddle making trade. Two years later, he immigrated to the United States, working in New York City, making saddles for the US government to use in the Mexican-American War. In 1848 he left New York, finding work in Cleveland, Buffalo, Cincinnati, Louisville, and New Orleans before starting to California in 1851, where he arrived in San Francisco in February 1852.

Franck set out for the gold mines, but by the end of the following year, he decided that gold mining was not as fruitful as he had hoped and established a shop in San Francisco for the manufacture of saddles and harnesses. In 1855, at age 27, he moved to Santa Clara where he permanently established his saddle and harness business, acquiring a partial ownership in the Santa Clara Tannery. Franck was eminently successful, invested wisely and acquired substantial property holdings. He was a member of the Town Board of Trustees for eight years and promoted projects for the Town's development. He helped organize the fire department and held the position of Chief for six years during the 1870s. He was also one of the incorporators of the Bank of Santa Clara. In 1871, Franck was elected to the state legislature and re-elected two years later for a second term. From 1894-95, he served as a state senator, representing the 30th District of the state, which encompassed most of Santa Clara County. F. C. Franck died in 1902, two years after the death of his wife of forty years, Caroline.

Jacob Eberhard was born in Kork, in the Grand Duchy of Baden, Germany, and immigrated with his family to America when he was fifteen. They settled in Galena, Illinois, where Jacob worked as a tanner and saddle maker, learning the trade from Ulysses S. Grant. In 1858, Jacob came to Sacramento, obtained employment as a laborer, gold miner, and harness maker, and opened his own harness shop there in 1862. While in Sacramento, he met Mary Glein, who had emigrated with her parents from Cassel, Germany, and whose father, Philip, owned the Santa Clara Tannery, which he had purchased in 1858 from John Henry Messing, who had married Mary's sister Louisa. On November 1, 1864, Jacob and Mary were wed, shortly thereafter moving to Santa Clara where, in 1867, Jacob bought the Santa Clara Tannery from Philip Glein.

By the time of the Santa Clara Tannery's incorporation in 1892 as the Eberhard Tanning Company, it had gained worldwide prominence providing leather goods to such places as the Royal House of Great Britain. By 1915, the Eberhard Tanning Company occupied eleven acres, one of the largest tanneries in the world. Its greatest boom occurred in 1925 when there were one hundred men employed, turning out two hundred hides per day, in addition to processing wool. Each month, $25,000 worth of leather went to one Minnesota company alone.

Like F. C. Franck, Jacob was involved both socially and politically in Santa Clara's growth. He was a founding member of the Odd Fellows and the Santa Clara Verein, and served as a member of the Town Board of Trustees. Both his son, John Jacob, and his son-in-law, Delos Druffel, would serve several terms as both Town Trustees and President of the Town Board.

Abram Block, born in Bohemia in 1830, immigrated to Missouri in 1844 and then came to San Francisco in 1856, where he established a mercantile business. In 1874, after meeting with reverses because of the depreciation of mining stocks, he moved to Santa Clara where he invested the money he had left in a 96-acre fruit ranch, long known as the Gould Fruit ranch. Within ten years, he was widely known as a pear culturist, ranking among the prominent horticulturists in California and employing hundreds of people, shipping hundreds of thousands of dollars of fruit annually.

No German community was complete without a brewery, and by the 1880s, Santa Clara had two breweries. The largest was that of George Lauck, located at the corner of Alviso and Benton Streets, where the fire station exists today. It was in existence until 1958, but by then was only a warehouse and distribution center for out-of-town brews.

As the number of German settlers in Santa Clara rose

dramatically in the 1860s through the 1880s, they became very influential. They established the Santa Clara Verein in 1868, and four years later, the charter members, who included C. W. Werner, F. C. Franck, C. Liebe, John Hetty, August Habrich, Leopold Hart, William and August Gabriel, Henry Uhrbroock and Henry Albert, in addition to Jacob Eberhard, purchased a piece of land where they erected their club building. This became the center of the German community's social, cultural, and physical fitness activities; gymnastic exercises were staged regularly, along with dramatic and musical events. When The German Association for Home Protection was organized on December 1, 1885, with F. C. Franck as president, the meetings were held at the club building. By 1881, there were forty-five members representing the most important people, economically and politically, in Santa Clara.

Prior to WWI membership dwindled as many Germans moved away. The war brought anti-German feelings, and after the War there were only five members after the war; the name was changed to the Santa Clara Club.

The Chinese

A few Chinese had appeared in the Santa Clara area after the gold rush, such as Sing Kee, cook, laundryman, and weather prognosticator, employed by Dr. Saxe in 1860. The first Chinese immigrants to arrive as a group entered Santa Clara Valley as workers on the construction of the San Francisco and San José Railroad in 1863-64. While most of these early Chinese immigrants found employment with the railroad and as land clearers and domestics, they were quickly found to be highly desirable as farm laborers, because they worked harder for less money than comparable white help. During the era of grain growing, the requirement for field hands was minimal, but as the orchards began to be planted, the need for inexpensive labor was a key element in the establishment of an orchard and vineyard economy.

The Chinese remained dominant in orchard work until the turn of the century. In addition, they packed all the fruit in the valley until 1903, when Portuguese and Italian women began packing fruit and their husbands and brothers and sons worked as laborers for the various packinghouses. In 1860, there were twenty-two Chinese in Santa Clara County and by 1870 there were 104 Chinese farm workers. The numbers continued to rise, and by 1880, there were 689 Chinese farm workers, representing 48 percent of the agricultural workers in the country. A high was reached in 1890 with 2,723 Chinese, mostly men. The Chinese Exclusion Acts of the 1880s resulted in a decline of the Chinese workforce, and by 1908, farmers hired very few Chinese workers to harvest their crops. The jobs were filled by Japanese.

Unlike the situation in larger towns, in the Town of Santa Clara, there was no Chinatown proper. Providing laundry service, however, proved to be the most prevalent business opportunity for the Chinese immigrants, and the 1886 Sanborn Map showed half of the block on Franklin Street between Jackson and Main Streets occupied by Chinese "wash houses." The businesses were located on ground floor with living space above.[1]

The Portuguese Immigrants

In the later part of the 19th century, the King of Hawaii went to Madeira and the Azores Islands, Portugal, making arrangements to contract and transport families to work on the sugarcane and pineapple plantations in Hawaii. Work on these plantations promised a better life than economic conditions at home could provide, and many made the decision to immigrate. As early as 1880, they were being transported to Hawaii and by 1896 there were 4,000 Portuguese living in Honolulu. By 1902 there were 6,000 with 5,500 more Portuguese immigrants living on plantations. After discovering the harsh conditions of life on the plantations, many Portuguese immigrants came on to California after spending a decade in Hawaii; several settled in Santa Clara as the climate was similar to that at home.

During the first part of the 20th century, others came to join family members who had arrived previously. The Portuguese immigrants worked harvesting the orchard fruits and cutting apricots for drying. They also established the first dairies in the Santa Clara area, one of the first being that of the Semas family located on Lawrence Station Road, now Lawrence Expressway.

Unlike most of the early Portuguese who immigrated to Santa Clara, Manuel Enos did not come via Hawaii. He left his home on the Azores Islands as a cabin boy on a whaling ship when he was ten years old. As he matured, Manuel became a harpooner and finally left the sea, settling in Gloucester, Massachusetts. In the late 1890s, he came west, married Annie, and settled first in Watsonville and then in Santa Clara. Manuel found work at the Pacific Manufacturing Company, which was the beginning of the Enos family's involvement in the lumber business. In 1924 Manuel's son, Manuel Jr., founded the Santa Clara Lumber Company on Lincoln and Clay streets, with another son, Eugene, working for the business. From 1929-32, Manuel Jr., served as a Town Trustee and, during the rough years of the depression, helped many farmers by providing them with the lumber they needed, letting them pay for it when they could. Today Santa Clara Lumber exists in its original location, still owned by the Enos family, although the lumberyard no longer covers half of a city block.

The Freitas family's arrival in Santa Clara followed the more traditional pattern of Portuguese immigration. Born on December 2, 1882, in Santa Serra, Madeira Island, in the early 1900s, Manuel Joaquin Freitas left home to join his brothers who had immigrated earlier to Hawaii. There he met Augusta Pacheco Vierra, who had been born in Hilo Hawaii. They married in 1911 and shortly thereafter moved to the island of Kauai. There their first four children were born. The Freitas family came to California in 1925, first settling in Oakland and two years later moving to Santa Clara, where Manuel's brother "Jack" lived. During the 1920s, most of the arriving Portuguese immigrants found work as laborers on farms and in canneries. Manuel Freitas, Sr. was no different. Life was not easy for this hardworking family of seven. Money was scarce and there were no luxuries, but the family had plenty to eat, growing their own vegetables, walnuts, plums, and grapes and raising chickens and rabbits. While it would take a long time before their home was paid for, the family was "happy because they felt secure." Everyone had their chores and took care of each other.

As with the vast majority of the immigrant families of that time, earning their citizenship was very important to the Freitas family. While Augusta had a fourth-grade education, could read and write, and was fluent in English, Manuel Sr., did not. After working all day to support his family, Manuel studied English by attending classes at Santa Clara High School and became an American citizen. All the children graduated from high school, the two boys served in WWII and the girls married, starting married life at home before moving into their own homes.

The early Portuguese immigrants in Santa Clara, following an old tradition in Portugal, founded the *Societad Espiritu Santo,* the Society of the Holy Ghost, which maintained their cultural heritage and provided assistance to the members of the Portuguese community. Santa Clara's SES Hall was dedicated in 1896 and has continued in use since then, numerous festivals being celebrated there during the year.

The immigrants, who came to Santa Clara, were not only responsible for the existence of the town but for the growth and success of the fruit industry and other businesses that brought renown to it. Their contributions, economically, politically and socially, made Santa Clara the place described in the 1904 "Progressive Santa Clara" as "an abode where fruit and flowers lend enchantment to the eye, and where health and plenty are the portions of her people." This pattern continues today as the newest ethnic groups arrive and make their contributions to the ever-evolving story of Santa Clara.

Endnote

1. While the European and American immigrants are well documented and can be represented by selected individuals, the Chinese immigrants were rarely recognized as individuals but generally referred to simply as the "Chinese." Although they provided the workforce essential to the development of an agricultural economy, both as agricultural workers and in the construction of the railroad system necessary to transport the harvest, and accounted for a large proportion of those employed in the provision of domestic services, their contribution was largely ignored. When a specific person was mentioned a name such as "China Johnny" (proprietor of a "wash house" in Santa Clara) was more often than not used, rather than the person's actual Chinese name. In large part this was due to the way in which these immigrants were viewed, a prejudice that led to such actions as The Chinese Exclusion Acts, which prohibited the immigration of Chinese to the United States.

References Consulted

Campbell, Ronald. 1995. Freelove Eberhard: An Oral History Interview Conducted by Ronald Campbell on June 24, 1974. Santa Clara City Library, Santa Clara, CA.

Garcia, Lorie. 1997. Santa Clara: from Mission to Municipality. *Research Manuscript Series on the Cultural and Natural History of Santa Clara*, No.8, Santa Clara University, Santa Clara, CA.

1999. Historical Background of the Fernando Berryessa Adobe, 373 Jefferson Street, City of Santa Clara, Santa Clara County, California. Report. Written for Gil Sanchez, Architect Inc. Report on file City of Santa Clara Planning Department, Santa Clara, CA.

Harris, Samantha, Jennifer Geddes, Kate Hahn, Diane Chonette, and Russell K. Skowronek. 1995. The Eberhard Privy: Archaeological and Historical Insights into Santa Clara History. *Research Manuscript Series on the Cultural and Natural History of Santa Clara*, No. 7, Santa Clara University, Santa Clara, CA.

Hylkema, Mark G. 1996. *Archaeological Investigations at the Third Location of Mission Santa Clara De Asís: The Murguiá Mission, 1781-1818* (CA-SCL-30/H). California Department of Transportation, District 4, Oakland, CA.

Lick, Sue F. 2000. *Stories Grandma Never Told: Portuguese Women in California.* Heyday Books, Berkeley, CA.

Payne, Stephen M. 1987. Santa Clara County: Harvest of Change. 1st ed. Windsor, Northridge, CA.

CHAPTER 9

Santa Clara University and the Jesuit Tradition of Education

Paul J. Fitzgerald, S. J.

This article treats three interrelated subjects: the life and spirit of Ignatius of Loyola, founder of the Jesuits; the Ignatian philosophy of education; and Santa Clara University as an heir and an example of this tradition of education.

I.

Iñigo López de Oñaz y Loyola, later known as Ignatius of Loyola (1491-1556), was a contemporary of Teresa of Avila and John of the Cross, and like them he was a great Spanish mystic.[1] Like them and many others of his generation, he was also a cross-over figure from the late Middle Ages into the Early Modern era. In him we find a marvelous example of the expansive spirit of the Renaissance: a thirst for knowledge old and new, a love for all that is human and noble, a comfort with psychological complexity, and a desire to see all things in the light of a God always greater than we can hope for or imagine. But for the grace of God, he might have remained an obscure and ultimately forgotten figure in the sweep of history. As it is, he gave birth to an institution (the Jesuits) and to a spirituality that have profoundly marked the course of Christianity for nearly five centuries.

Iñigo was the last of eleven children in a family of the minor nobility in the Basque province of Guipuzcoa in Northern Spain. He later chose for himself the name Ignacio out of devotion to St. Ignatius of Antioch, a martyr bishop from the second century known for his courage in the face of danger, his faithful care for his people, and his undying love for Christ Jesus.

Ignatius received an early education as a scriptor and soldier from a friend of his father, a certain Juan Velazquez de Cuellar, chief treasurer of the Royal Court at Madrid. His early ambition was to make a name for himself through military exploit, then find employment at the royal court where he would live a life of vanity, ease and luxury. At the start of a minor war between the Spanish Hapsburgs and the French Valois, in the Pyrenees' mountain passes of Navarre, Ignatius seized his opportunity and enlisted. He took command of the garrison soldiers of a small fortress in the defensive works around the city of Pamplona. In a French attack, Ignatius was hit by a cannon ball. His leg was shattered and with it his dreams of vainglory.

The French victors admired him for his foolish bravery — Ignatius had convinced his fellow soldiers to hold the indefensible position to the last man — so they allowed the half dead officer to be carried home on a litter to the castle of Loyola. Ignatius spent the next six months in slow recovery. During this convalescence, his religious conversion began. There were only two books in the castle: a "Lives of the Saints" and a "Life of Christ," the latter being a synopsis of the four Gospels. Some days, Ignatius would spend hours day-dreaming about future battles, heroic exploits, and a certain lovely lady at court, after which he would feel only sadness and emptiness. On other days, he would daydream about becoming another Benedict, or Francis, or Dominic, about doing great and heroic things for God, and casting in his lot with Christ, after which he would feel lastingly happy and filled with enthusiasm and peace.

Paying attention to these "inner movements of the Holy Spirit," as he would later come to call them, Ignatius slowly abandoned his martial dreams, and adopted a new life plan — to be a pilgrim in search of God's grace. When he was able to walk again, he left his home after having laid his sword on an altar to the Virgin and after having exchanged his fine clothes with those of a poor man. He spent the next several years of his life wandering, begging alms, eating poorly, searching for God's grace. He prayed constantly, experimenting with various forms of prayer, seeking the advice of priests, monks, religious and lay people. Ignatius also listened to his own heart and to the promptings of God in his own imagination. And as he had learned to do during his months of recovery, Ignatius payed attention to his experiences of inner consolation and desolation.

The more he entrusted himself to God in prayer, the more clearly he came to see that God loved him, sustained him, and desired his service for the spread of the Gospel. Ignatius slowly systematized these experiences of grace into a program of prayers, readings from scripture and reflections upon God's goodness. He wrote these down, and he shared both the evolving text and method with whomever God placed in his path. Over time, Ignatius' program of prayers took on a definitive structure; he called them "Spiritual Exercises". He explained the title by a comparison: "just as taking a walk, traveling on foot, and running are physical exercises, so is the name of 'spiritual exercises' given to any means of preparing and disposing our soul to rid itself of all its disordered affections and then, after their removal, of seeking and finding God's will in the ordering of our life for the salvation of our soul."[2] The Spiritual Exercises allowed others to experience grace as Ignatius had, i.e., as a movement towards freedom, a liberation of the self from sin and for love, and a means of gaining greater intimacy with God in Christ Jesus. Centuries later, the Exercises, both in the form of a structured retreat program and in the looser structure of a daily spiritual practice, continue to make available Ignatius' hard won insights into the practice of prayer. The Exercises found Ignatian Spirituality, a world-view and a set of criteria for seeking and finding God in all things. This remains the guiding spirit of the Jesuit Order. It is also alive and well in the many congregations of women religious who have adopted and adapted Ignatian Spirituality to their own life and work. And there are millions of lay persons who, over the centuries, have chosen to avail themselves of this school of prayer.

Basically, Ignatius constructed a fourfold retreat program, to be done over the course of thirty days, in silence, in peace, and in prayer. During the first "week",[3] the retreatant should consider his/her own sins in the light of God's gracious pardon, and in so doing gain greater faith, hope and love. The second week of the retreat considers the public ministry of Jesus, affording the retreatant the opportunity to deepen familiarity and friendship with Jesus. The third week asks the retreatant to accompany Jesus through his passion and death, placing the believer at the foot of the cross with Mary and the Beloved Disciple. Finally, the fourth week allows the retreatant to experience anew the resurrection of Christ and to feel, taste, sense the power of divine love unleashed by this saving event. From these four weeks of prayer come a new-found inner peace, a heightened sense of one's inestimable worth in God's eyes, and a deep desire to place oneself at the service God and neighbor in whatever way God sees fit to call the person, whether as a priest, as a religious, as a virgin or as a sacramentally married person. No matter what state of life one should adopt, no matter what honest work one elects to do, the retreatant is led to accept that hers is a vocation, a calling from God to a life of holiness and service, for the glory of God and the good of souls.

After his early pilgrim years of introspection and self-discovery, Ignatius began to shift his focus from the inward journey to public ministry, though he never stopped praying. A "contemplative in action", he preached publicly about the goodness of God, the beauty of the world, and the virtue of faith. He also began to share his methods of prayer with anyone who asked. Ironically, this landed him in trouble with Church authorities. After all, this street preacher was a layman, trained as a soldier and as an accountant. In Salamanca, Ignatius was arrested by the Inquisition and his teachings were carefully examined during a month-long stay in jail. In the end, they found nothing against sound doctrine in his program, but he resolved to get a proper theological education, both to avoid future trouble with the Inquisition and also to better equip himself intellectually so that he could preach the Catholic faith.

After a few years studying Latin, Ignatius went to the University of Paris where he eventually earned a Master's degree in Sacred Theology. While in Paris, he also made friends, with whom he shared his Spiritual Exercises. In 1534, with several other students and one professor, Ignatius pronounced vows in a little chapel on the slopes of Montmartre. They promised God that they would embrace perpetual poverty and chastity. They also pledged to attempt a voyage to Jerusalem to preach Christianity to the Muslims. Fate would have it that the way to Jerusalem was barred to them because of a war with the Turks. So after a year of living in Venice, serving the poor in hospitals, Ignatius and his little band went to Rome to place themselves at the service of the Vicar of Christ, who was Paul III at the time. With the Holy Father's blessing, they chose to become a new type of religious order, distinctly different from the existing orders and congregations.

The heart of their corporate ministry was preaching and giving the Exercises, which meant that their chief task was to help all persons, in body and soul, such that they might experience the consolation of God's grace. The first Jesuits (more than one thousand by the time of Ignatius' death) were to be poor, chaste and obedient, yet they were monks without cloister, without a distinctive habit, and without the obligation to gather together throughout the day to sing the liturgy of the hours. They were to be at home in the world — the marketplace, the prison, the court, the slums — wherever the Spirit led them to preach the consolation of God. By word and deed, the Jesuits were to give witness to God's gracious desire to save all people. Concretely, this meant that Jesuits should help people in every spiritual and practical way to escape slavery to sin and gain the graced freedom of their true status as children of God.[4]

Ignatius did not mean to found a teaching order but rather an order of mendicant preachers. So why are more than half the 23,000 Jesuits in the world today teaching in grammar schools, mission schools, technical schools, college preparatories, colleges and universities?

II.

The entrance of Jesuits into the field of education began quite logically in the need to form the young men who were asking to join the Order. To systematize their training and to prepare them well for the tasks of ministry, a *ratio studiorum* (a systematic curriculum) was composed. With it came the birth of the modern academy. To educate the steady influx of novices, Ignatius directed in 1545 that a college be opened in the Spanish city of Gandia. Money was begged from wealthy Catholics (some things never change!) who in return asked if their sons could study along side the young Jesuits in formation. An affirmative response opened up a whole new means for Jesuits to help souls and help society. Colleges were opened in Germany, Portugal, Sicily, everywhere that young men were entering the Society of Jesus (this was the name that Ignatius and the others had chosen for their brotherhood — the founder didn't want his companions to be called 'Ignatians'). The truly decisive step came in 1548 in Messina;

responding to the initiative of a delegation of prominent lay persons, Ignatius sent ten hand-picked Jesuits to open Europe's first modern school dedicated primarily to the education of young laymen.

In these first Jesuit colleges, there was a structured curriculum with a set pattern of classes, subjects and years. What is now the standard pattern in all high schools and colleges was largely invented by the Jesuits — a course of studies that was ordered, progressive, and internally cohesive. Before this, education had been like apprenticeship — one found a master and learned from him, until such time as he thought the candidate was ready for his final exams. The Jesuit schools were to have an academic calendar and 'grades', starting with introductory and general courses and then moving toward more specialized and more advanced areas of study. At the heart of the curriculum were the humanities, especially the great books of the classical world. The basic idea was simple: reading good books teaches good morals and makes good people. By reading the classics of Greek and Latin literature, the students would learn the great lessons of the ancients about human freedom and slavery, about wisdom and folly, about virtue and vice, with their concomitant good and bad consequences in the social order. As well, there was the clear conviction that these authors laid an intellectual foundation to support the reasonableness of faith in God and love for one's neighbor, just as the Hebrew Scriptures laid an inspired foundation for passionate belief in the Messiah and in his Gospel. In a word, the Jesuits would first teach both Aristotle and Isaiah so that the boys would later be able to read St. Thomas Aquinas. Quite literally, the graduate of a Jesuit school would truly be a Renaissance man, for this was indeed the age of the rebirth of Western Society at the dawn of the modern era.

These new colleges were meant from the outset to be more than simply for the good of the students who attended them. Ignatius hoped that by sending well educated and morally good people out into society, they would act as a leaven, raising the whole mass: *puerilis institutio renovatio mundi* — the education of youth for the renewal of the world. Schools such as the Roman College (1551), today known as the Gregorian University, were to be platforms for ministry to the whole city. The boys put on plays and pageants and musicals; the Fathers wrote the scripts, composed the music, and designed the mechanics for the spectacles, all in order to attract the crowds so that the Gospel could be preached — much as Jesus preached — by telling stories, by intriguing people to wonder about the beauty of creation, by cajoling people into new insights into their own lives, and by encouraging people to acts of courage, prudence and magnanimity.

There was also an emphasis, from the very beginning, on the study of science and mathematics. Because Ignatius was a mystic, a stargazer, and a Christian, he believed very strongly in the medieval notion that the *Vestigia Dei*, the traces of God, are still discernable in the dust of the garden of Eden; they can be discovered through the study of physics, biology, chemistry, even astronomy. It is estimated that, at one point during the 18th century, one-half of all the telescopes in Europe were in Jesuit colleges. Today, there are 32 craters or "seas" on the lunar surface that still carry Jesuit names.[5]

Two of Ignatius' favorite mottos were "seek and find God in all things"and "do everything for the greater glory of God". These capture well the integration of reason and faith in Ignatian spirituality. By holding the two in tension, one can avoid the danger of amoral scientism on the one hand and blind obscurantism on the other. By valuing both faith and reason, the Jesuits contributed to the early modern rebirth of intellectual life where all scientific pursuits could have both internal rigor and a moral compass. As well, Jesuits taught that scientific advances praised God and brought humanity closer to the Creator of all.

Rhetoric was an integral part of the curriculum. The young should learn how to construct an argument, engage in a debate, and listen attentively to opposing points of view. In 1545, when Pope Paul III convened the Council of Trent, he asked Ignatius to send him three Jesuits who would serve as the Pope's personal theologians at the council. Diego Laínez, Alfonso Salmerón, and Pierre Favre were sent, but the latter died en route from Spain and was replaced by Claude Le Jay. Ignatius instructed them to be "slow and amiable of speech. . . listen closely, the better to understand the speaker's point of view. . . give countervailing reasons [to your own propositions] in order not to appear partial or to inconvenience anyone. . ."[6] In a word, Ignatius wanted his men to listen attentively to others, be sensitive to their ideas and opinions, and to put forth their own positions in a spirit of true humility. This appreciation of the art of conversation meant that all the students of the Jesuits would learn the art of persuasive public speaking. All studied logic and epistemology, to better understand what we know and how we know it. These mental skills would prepare the students for lives of public usefulness in commerce, in government, in the law. They would also provide one of the most valuable of life skills — the ability to think.

Classical languages, both Greek and Latin, were taught. Latin was not only a key to the ancients, to Virgil and Cicero and Horace, but it was also the international language of the day. Knowing Latin allowing the educated young person to enter into nuanced and far-ranging conversation with people from quite different cultures. Ignatius experienced this himself when he lived in Paris in the Latin Quarter, named so because Latin was the spoken language in the streets of this crossroads of the youth of Europe. Poetry and literature, as I mentioned, were taught in a "great books" approach to education. The young were led on a great voyage of discovery; their minds were expanded beyond the provincial attitudes of their particular town or city. They were shown the whole expanse of the known world, a world only recently quadrupled in size with the opening of communication with the Americas, with Africa and with Asia. And always, the moral dimensions of these new contacts were held up for rigorous examination.

European Jesuits followed the European conquest of distant lands and opened up schools among the newly encountered peoples, yet the Jesuits often had an appreciative regard for the newly met cultures. For example, the indigenous peoples of the region that came to be known as Paraguay were organized into *reducciones*, inland settlements far removed from the slavers and from the evils of the plantation system. For a century and a half the Jesuits worked with the Guarani to build colossal churches, symphonic orchestras and peaceful communities that resisted the cultures of death. The mission to the Guarani was both an educational and an evangelical enterprise, for indeed these were merely two sides of a single coin — one seeks to understand what one believes, and one believes in order to understand.

Francis Xavier, one of the first Jesuits and Ignatius' best friend, went half way around the world, baptizing and preaching the Gospel to a million people from India, Malaysia, to Japan. He was followed by thousands of Jesuits who carried Western science, literature, law and philosophy, all that was considered to be useful to human beings and human communities, all that was seen as a means of approaching the really important human questions. Certainly errors were made; new and different cultures were not always understood, and a certain European sense of superiority (which was true in matters military but seldom true in matters moral or aesthetic) was invariably inmixed with Jesuit missionary efforts. Today, Jesuits are able and willing to confess our sins and to acknowledge our mistakes; one would expect nothing less of Christians. Nor should we be proud of our accomplishments, though there have been many. The sins are ours; the successes are God's.

In fact, great things were accomplished — Alexander de Rhodes devised the phonetic alphabet for the Vietnamese language and wrote the very first book in modern Vietnamese, a catechism which was very sensitive to the Confucian background of many of his converts. High literacy rates in Vietnam followed upon this orthographic innovation. This was only one example of Jesuit intellectual service to culture. In Japan, Jesuit Missionaries opened the first academy of painting to introduce Western techniques (e.g., vanishing point perspective), all the while searching to integrate a Japanese aesthetic sense. The paintings that were produced by the young Japanese converts depicted Gospel scenes in Japanese costumes, architecture and sensibilities.

Certainly, in many of the missionary endeavors, Jesuits showed themselves to be as pig-headed and as culturally insensitive as other Christian missionaries out of early modern Europe, but at times, they were brilliant in their openness to finding God already present and at work in new and foreign cultures. These Jesuits saw themselves as instruments of Christ who writes straight with crooked lines and pours new wine out of old wineskins.

Dancing, fencing, singing, painting, musical composition — all the arts were taught, for the Creator was to be praised by human beings in every language, including that of the brush, the cello and the grace of athletic exploit. The human being as artist, as scientist, as moral agent in society is called upon to act "in God's eyes what in God's eyes he is — / Christ — for Christ plays in ten thousand places, / Lovely in limbs, and lovely in eyes not his / To the Father through the features of men's faces."[8] In all our educational and missionary efforts, the person of Jesus Christ was and remains the standard against which all is measured. Mateo Ricci, Frans Verbiest and Johan Adam Schall went to China, to the court of the emperor, and they brought mathematics and mechanical engineering as their calling card. They offered to redo the Chinese calendar and to introduce almanacs for better flood control, better harvests and general human thriving in the Middle Kingdom. In return, they asked only for the freedom to share their faith in Christ Jesus, through whom were made the heavens and the earth. Some of the Chinese were hard pressed to understand the reasons behind the magnanimity of the Jesuits' service, yet they came to appreciate the service as a gift, and as an object lesson in grace, done in order to broach the subject of God's graciousness — for love shows itself in deeds over and above words.

This then was the *ratio studiorum* of the early Society of Jesus: to explore the divine in all that was human, to expand scientific and social knowledge, to educate the mind, body and soul so that the whole person, rooted in faith and grounded with virtue, could serve God by serving the common good. This has remained the central insight of Jesuit education for 450 years: everything that is human is a venue for the encounter with the Divine, and all that draws the human being to full stature as a moral person in community is an opening to grace.

III.

The first of the Jesuit colleges and universities in North America was founded in 1789 by John Carroll, a former Jesuit[8] and the first Bishop of Baltimore. At the time, there were only 30,000 Catholics in the USA, mostly in Maryland. Carroll wanted them to have a college so that an educated Catholic laity could guide and protect the small flock in the Protestant-dominated republic. Georgetown was followed by a college in St. Louis, then the College of the Holy Cross in Worcester, Massachusetts, then St. Joseph's in Philadelphia, then Loyola in Baltimore. Today, there are 28 colleges and universities, ranging from the small Spring Hill in Mobile to the large Loyola Chicago. There are also 49 high schools, and a rapidly growing number of middle schools. Each in its own way, adapting to the exigencies of the local situation, attempts to give flesh and blood to the founding vision of Jesuit education.

Santa Clara University was founded in 1851, in the wake of the Gold Rush and the conquest of California from Mexico. For much of its history, it was a small school in a bucolic valley known mostly for its plums and apricots. Jesuit Father Bernard Hubbard, the "Glacier Priest", is exemplary of the work of many professors who combined teaching and research, always seeking to wed the life of the mind with that of the soul.[9] More recently, the "Valley of the Heart's Delight" has been renamed "Silicon Valley", and with this evolution, the place of science and technology in society has become ever more important subject of research and discussion at SCU. The university began as a boarding school, serving the children of both the *Californios* and new Catholic immigrants. Today the university has become far more culturally diverse, and this cultural richness has vastly improved the university's ability to offer an integrated education in the best light of the Jesuit tradition.

Fr. Peter-Hans Kolvenbach, the Superior General of the Society of Jesus, was a recent visitor to campus. In October of 2000, he gave the keynote address at the major academic conference of the university's sesquicentennial year, "The Commitment to Justice in Jesuit Higher Education." He challenged educators at Jesuit universities to "form each student into a whole person of solidarity who will take responsibility for the real world."[10] For this to happen, students must be afforded the opportunity to come into contact with the "gritty reality" of the world, especially the world of the poor and the disenfranchised. Students at Jesuit universities today must learn to think and to feel, to analyze and to understand, in the light of faith and in the light of the Gospels, so that they may respond to the problems of our world and offer constructive, creative solutions to social problems. Not that Catholicism should be imposed upon our students, yet certainly the person of Jesus Christ must be proposed as the measure of our actions and as the goal of our hoping.

An integrated education must have some undergirding principle of integration, a *norma non normata*, that guides the updating of any educational tradition. Fr. Kolvenbach's call for educating the whole person in solidarity with the real world is such a principle. It allows for the reformulation of a core curriculum in which the values and the goals of the *ratio studiorum* are maintained even as they are made new: to lead students to good knowledge, good morals and to the possibility of reasonable and passionate faith in God and service of humanity. The core curriculum does this by exposing all students to a breadth of knowledge, both in letters and in the sciences, giving them the tools to 'seek and find God' in all things human and in all of God's creation, so that their education not only sharpens their minds and gives them marketable job skills but also inspires them to help build more just and humane communities.

Higher education can be integrated in the interplay between three basic questions, repeatedly examined under the rubrics of many different academic disciplines. The first is the question of identity: "Who am I?" and "Who are we?" A variety of courses pose these questions in light of what we know, how we know it, what we ought to do, and what we may hope for. The consideration of these questions invites the students to rise above utilitarian individualism and to reach toward the beautiful, the meaningful and the communal. In this regard, the centrality on campus of the de Saisset Museum and the Mission Church are telling, for the beautiful and the holy, the artistic and the sacramental, complement each other. All those earthly creatures and creations which point us towards beauty, truth and goodness are sacramental, symbols in the deepest sense that point towards the infinite, portraying the grace that they convey.

The second basic question asks, "What kind of world is it in which we live?" The pursuit of knowledge and understanding about the diversity of human ways of being embodies the perennial Jesuit quest for contact with, respect for, and appreciation of all human cultures. As students move beyond mere tolerance to true appreciation of diversity, they also often come to embrace more deeply the cherished values of their own particular traditions.

The third line of questioning leads students to consider their own willingness and readiness to commit themselves to the construction a better world. Students are invited to consider their future professional and personal contributions to the common good. Can these be rooted in a sense that God invites us and accompanies us as we seek to foster the thriving of all human beings in justice and peace? Building on this threefold interrogation, the specializations of majors and minors equip students with specialized knowledge and skills that will enable them to make positive contributions to the common good through a life of professional competence and expertise.

And as was the case four centuries ago with the first Jesuit schools, so too is SCU a platform for an apostolic reach into the surrounding community. Santa Clara Community Action Program (SCCAP) is a long standing, student-run community service program that sends students to a wide variety of social agencies in the valley and beyond. On a different level, the Arrupe Center for Community-based Learning structures student interaction with social agencies within the context of academic courses and disciplines. The liturgical life of the Mission Church, the exhibits at the de Saisset Museum, the plays and music and dance programs in the Performing Arts Complex, and the great number of public lectures bring large numbers of guests onto campus throughout the year. These events entertain, intrigue and subtly challenge audiences to imagine a better, more just and more human world. Faculty, staff and student reflectors, under the auspices of the Markkula Center for Applied Ethics, lead ethical discussions for local business leaders, health care workers and other professionals.

The forty Jesuit Priests and Brothers at SCU do not carry on this mission alone. Indeed, the lion's share of the work in making SCU a modern embodiment of a Renaissance idea is done by the 650 (mostly lay) members of the teaching faculty and the 800 staff persons. The creative participation of the 7,600 students in the undergraduate and graduate programs gives the educational enterprise its dynamism. And many of the 58,350 living alumni/ae remain passionately committed to helping and guiding the university. SCU remains a Jesuit institution within the Roman Catholic Church's tradition of offering pastoral care and educational service to Catholics and non-Catholics alike. The pursuit of scholarly dialogue within and across academic disciplines, within the broad university community, and with the larger social world beyond the boundaries of the campus have furthered progress in, and hunger for, truly integrated education. There is a palpable atmosphere on campus of mutual respect, of cooperative learning, and of reverence for the human person. Perhaps this above all is the clearest sign that SCU is and remains an articulation of Ignatius' founding vision of education: a community of inquiry into the wonders of creation and the weight of social responsibility as essential expressions of our gratitude to, and search for, God.

Endnotes

1. For a good general biography of Ignatius and his first companions, see Jean La Couture's *Jesuits, a Multibiography*, translated by Jeremy Leggatt. Washington, D.C.: Counterpoint, 1995.

2. Spiritual Exercises, [1], in *Ignatius of Loyola — The Spiritual Exercises and selected works*, George Ganss, S.J., ed., New York: Paulist Press, 1991, p. 121; Fr. Ganss' general introduction is quite rich and helpful. By "disordered affections", Ignatius refers to the human tendency (temptation) to want something in the wrong way. Ignatius saw all creation as thoroughly good; we simply need to come to know our deepest desire — the love of God — and then to desire all things within the context of this one great love. A thorough description of Ignatius' theology can be found in Hugo Rahner's *Ignatius the Theologian*, Michael Barry, trans., New York: Herder and Herder, 1968.

3. While he called the four phases of the retreat "weeks", Ignatius had a keen insight into human psychology and spirituality, and so he would tailor the number of days of each of the weeks in response to the progress of the particular person. One would stay in a week until s/he had received the graces and the insights that were essential to that phase of the retreat.

4. On the apostolic strategy of Ignatius and his early companions, see John W. O'Malley, S.J., *The First Jesuits*. Cambridge, Mass: Harvard University Press, 1993. On the importance of social settings for early Jesuit ministries, see Thomas M. Lucas, *Landmarking: City, Church & Jesuit Urban Strategy*. Chicago: Loyola Press, 1997.

5. William Bangert, S.J., *A History of the Society of Jesus*. St. Louis: The Institute of Jesuit Sources, 1972, p 188.

6. Quoted by Jean Lacouture, p. 80.

7. Gerard Manley Hopkins, S.J., "As kingfishers catch fire" in *Poems and Prose of Gerard Manley Hopkins*, ed. W. H. Gardner, New York: Penguin Books, 1963, p. 51.

8. For a variety of reasons, some political and some theological, the Society of Jesus was suppressed, i.e., suspended, in most parts of the world in 1773 and was restored again in 1814.

9. See Gerald McKevitt, S.J., *The University of Santa Clara, a History*. Stanford University Press, 1979, pp. 245-248.

10. Peter-Hans Kolvenbach, S.J., "American Jesuit Higher Education for Faith and Justice" in *explore*, Spring 2001, p. 18. The entire text of Father General's address is available online at www.scu.edu/bannaninstitute.

Recommended Further Reading

The Catholic University As Promise and Project: Reflections in a Jesuit Idiom by Michael J. Buckley, S.J., Georgetown University Press, 1999.

Your Word, O Lord: Meditations for College Students and Everyone Else by Cornelius M. Buckley S.J., Ignatius Press, 1987.

A Pilgrim's Journey : The Autobiography of St. Ignatius of Loyola, Ignatius Press, 2001.

Thirty Days : On Retreat with the Exercises of St. Ignatius by Paul Mariani, Viking Press, 2002.

CHAPTER 10

"A Very Happy Group"
19th-Century Student Life at Santa Clara
George F. Giacomini, Jr.

The French writer Voltaire once commented that history doesn't repeat itself, but men do. That aphorism could well be applied to any study of university student life. The case can be made that the attitudes and activities of traditional-aged college students have not changed much from the late 19th to the early 21st centuries. But the environment and the society in which they find themselves has changed dramatically. Twenty-first century California, heavily populated, largely urbanized, technologically sophisticated, is not the California of 1851 when Santa Clara University was founded.

1851 California was a raw and turbulent frontier. The impact of the discovery of gold in California, almost co-eval with its acquisition by the United States, brought an influx of population to capitalize on the instant riches that gold and its associated activities promised. Joining the established Hispanic population, the *Californios*, and recent American settlers were men and some women from the United States, South America, Europe and Asia. The population of the new state exploded from around 15,000 non-Native Americans to some 150,000 in only a few years.

One of the more settled areas was the Santa Clara Valley, anchored by the Mission Santa Clara de Asís and the pueblo of San José, the oldest civil settlement in California. The established residents, both *Californio* and American, wanted a more formal educational structure for their children than home tutoring could provide. Thus they importuned the Jesuit missionaries in the Oregon Territory to come to California and open a college.

Despite discouragement by their Roman leadership, Fathers

Michael Accolti, S.J., and John Nobili, S.J., came to California, surveyed the situation, and decided that Santa Clara would be the best place to open a school. In March 1851, at the request of the bishop, Nobili took possession of Mission Santa Clara and in May began the first classes at Santa Clara College.[1]

The attraction of the college was immediate and, although finances remained precarious, it quickly achieved a reputation as "the first educational establishment in the state."[2] It was a classic European college with students ranging in age from grade school through college age divided into two divisions, one for the younger students and the other for the older students. The student body from the beginning was a diverse one. There were offspring of the established *Californio* families like the Alvisos, Berryessas and Vallejos, sons of the older American families like the Murphys and Burnetts; children of Gold Rush immigrants and an international mix from the San Francisco consular corps. For almost 20 years, the college bulletin was printed in both Spanish and English and the college's appeal cut across denominational lines with half of its early student body other than Roman Catholic. A graduate of 1859 looked back fifty years later: "They were of all ages and nationalities and opposite creeds. But they were Santa Clara boys. . ."[3]

Life on Campus

What Santa Clara provided and what the parents of its students sought, beyond educational instruction, was an orderly and structured program to offset the disorderly rough-and-tumble environment that was California in the 1850s. The 300-year-old Society of Jesus had established an outstanding educational reputation, particularly in Europe. The Italian Jesuits who established the college were accustomed to operating a tightly structured, highly organized operation. Their approach met the desires of California parents perfectly.

For over fifty years, Santa Clara was noted for its regimented life both in the academic and social spheres. Its co-founder, Michael Accolti, once commented unfavorably about the "unlimited liberty" found at other California colleges while extolling Santa Clara's discipline. But he noted that Santa Clara's order was "not so stringent as that enforced at West Point."4 Students frequently commented about the strictness of Santa Clara life. In 1858, a student wrote: "You must not urge it on me to remain here next year dear Ma because I cannot stand it."5 The wit and playwright Wilson Mizner recalled his days at Santa Clara forty years later:

> The only difference between Santa Clara and any other prison was that classes instead of a stone quarry brought a student out of his cell for a considerable period of each day. . . . The college prohibited everything but study and, once enrolled, the festive young student might as well have been waiting for the chair."6

What gave the college such a reputation? Partially it was the academic rigor, partly the social restrictions. The curriculum left little room for student choice and the organization of the academic day ensured a kind of dulling routine. For the older students, the day began with a bell around 5:30 a.m., washing outside at the pump and later in a detached washroom, followed by dressing and morning mass. A short time to prepare for class preceded breakfast. Classes were held six days a week with half days on Wednesdays (later Thursdays) and Saturdays. The classes began at 9:00 a.m. and continued until noon. After lunch, classes resumed at 2:00 p.m. until 5:00 p.m. Dinner was a 5:30 p.m. followed by study hall and lights out by 9:00 p.m. There were, of course, moments of conversation and brief recreation during the day, but the regimen, especially in the early years, was unrelenting.

Classical languages — a challenge for many - were required of all students studying for a degree. Examinations, conducted at the end of each semester, were both written and oral for each course. The anxiety they caused seems even greater than in the present-day. One student wrote his mother:

> We pased (sic) through the trying order of Natural Philosophy, Mathematics, and Latin to day, that is a written examination in each, and on Monday we will have written examinations in Elementary Chemistry and Rhetoric. After that oral examinations commence and will last until Saturday next . . .

The following week he reported: "during the examinations which ended today I have not eaten enough to support a baby. . ."7 The oral examinations were especially trying. Students being examined went to the front of the room before the assembled class and were quizzed by their instructor. The routine practice of exacting oral examinations lasted into the mid-20th century.

Living at the college, especially in the early years was a challenging experience. The first students slept where they could, frequently in lofts above their classrooms. Faculty were no more favored. Two Jesuit professors were described as sleeping "wherever they could find a place, rolling up their mattress every morning, not knowing where they would unroll it at night." Classes were held in the old adobe buildings around the Mission and then in the remodeled California Hotel adjacent to the Mission. The initial scarcity of classrooms caused one Jesuit to teach seated on a trunk in a corner of the garden, "his pupils seated on trunks around him."[8]

The California Hotel provided the college with its first real dormitory although the building also provided space for eight classrooms. Then in the 1860s and early 70s, the college added two buildings that provided more dormitory space. The Scientific Building provided dormitory space for younger students on its top floor with classrooms and laboratories on its lower floors. A few years later, the College Hall, later known colloquially as "the Ship," housed 130 students in a first floor dormitory and had a 3000 seat auditorium on the second floor.

A perennial topic of conversation, then as now, was the food. The first cook was renowned for being able to prepare all his meals using "one single kettle, in which he used to make the soup, boil the meat, and cook the vegetables." Moreover, he was able to prepare food without lard or butter because it was too expensive. He claimed that on feast days he would use tallow candles "to make the food more palatable."[9] One of the early students complained to his father that bread at breakfast was "sour as vinegar" and that while "they are very willing to give some meat such meat as it is and some bread, but nothing to drink at all and no soup."[10] Others provided a different perspective. On holy days and other special occasions students reported "the tables were bounteously provided with inviting viands and even the 'generous wine' was not wanting. . . Turkeys, chickens, etc., disappeared with edifying rapidity."[11] In retrospect, students commented favorably about the food. "Yes, they fed us well – good, substantial, nourishing food; not fancy trimmings and side-dishes that appeal to the eye, but the coarse fare that builds up the growing boy."[12]

The twice-weekly free afternoons provided opportunities to escape the confines of the fenced-in campus. Students were permitted to go out with a chaperone and larger excursions were sometimes planned. On the first Saturday of each month, students could go out to visit parents or friends as long as they were able to return by evening. Nobili believed that students should "be exposed to as few as possible distractions calculated to wean them from their books. . ."[13] One of the first students, W.H. Menton recollected:

> We were actually walled in, and there was only one entrance, serving at the time as an exit but inevitably, a watchful padre stood sentinel. We got out by special permissions from the "folks at home," or when a picnic took us to Murphy's ranch near Sunnyvale. And upon our return we had to stand search for contraband goods in the form of cigarettes and love letters.[14]

The sense of confinement perhaps contributed to the tension that occasionally developed between the boarding students and the "day dog." The day scholar came in the morning and went home and into the world in the late afternoon. It appears the boarding students resented this semblance of freedom. One former student remembered, among other encounters, the "Battle of the Oranges":

> [T]here were no boarders in sight until we were well inside the gate, and then how the yard was literally filled with boarders well supplied with small oranges, which they refused to eat at their breakfast; and coming from behind trees, benches, the old handball court, and the old chapel steps, they began the bombardment. I dare say there was not a day scholar escaped the barrage.[15]

Such outbursts were generally not met with a "boys will be boys" attitude, but with a resolution to insure that the expected discipline be maintained at all times. But, in fact, boys will be boys and the boys seemed to take special delight in frustrating efforts to keep them in line. Picking on the "lowly day scholars" was too obvious and flagrant a violation as were food fights in the dining hall. Night time was better for boyish pranks.

The eight foot fence that surrounded the campus, keeping students in and the world out, was a challenge that could not be ignored. Frequent attempts were made to scale its height and avoid the ever-present Jesuit prefects on patrol. In later years, a watchman patrolled the grounds with two dogs to ensure students did not leave the campus confines. He was not as vigilant as the Jesuits and brief escapes over the wall became more common. Such stories are like those told by Santa Clarans of the 1930s to 1950s who evaded curfew by devising all sorts of stratagems to sneak out of their residence halls for similar brief tastes of freedom.

Dormitories were more susceptible to successful capers. Each dormitory had a faculty "prefect" assigned to sleep there. These men were usually young Jesuits — who, it was believed, could better withstand the rigors of sleep-deprivation than the older priests. Although it was rumored that prefects slept with one eye open, it was possible around midnight to create sounds of rumbling thunder by rolling a 16 lb. shot down the aisle or even worse scatter bb pellets along the floor thereby insuring the disruption of everyone's sleep. One graduate boasted of getting up in the middle of the night and swapping articles of clothing among all the sleepers — a shoe here, a sock there, a shirt elsewhere — so that chaos ensued in the morning as sleepy residents scrambled to find their clothes and get out of the dormitory in a timely fashion so as not to get demerits. The culprit cleverly exchanged some of his own clothing to avoid suspicion.[16]

Since most minor offenders sooner or later were caught, the standard penalty was the awarding of demerits that, when they reached a certain number, resulted in sterner measures. Some offenses like drunkenness and unauthorized overnight absences were deemed serious enough for dismissal. Ultimately, the most common form of discipline was "Letter A." The name came from the room in which the penalty was worked off. Students reported to Room A where they were assigned "lines" either to memorize or write out. "Letter A" was held on Thursday and Sunday afternoons, thus depriving the offending students of their free time. Some students thought the worst part of "Letter A" was listening to their fellow students playing baseball just outside of the door. Corporal punishment, though common in 19th-century schools, was unusual at Santa Clara. Prefects were urged by the president to teach by example and to remember that "no matter how repulsive they may seem to you, boys are entitled to respect."[17]

One disciplinary episode became very public and reinforced the image of Santa Clara as a proper and disciplined institution. In 1875 students seized two of the dormitory prefects and tied them to their beds in a "skillful and well-laid plot of a few malcontents." The students then "climbed through the window to liberty and license." After identifying the guilty parties, President Varsi expelled twenty of them. He noted that "it has done us a great good for never have students conducted themselves as well as they do now." He then sagely observed: "Pruning the tree at the proper season ensures the physical as well as the moral health of the body." Reporting on this story, a newspaper praised Varsi and the college claiming that its disciplinary philosophy "is the true cause of the success of this noble college."[18]

Activities

Clearly, the confines of a tightly regimented, all boys' school needed some approved outlets for youthful exuberance. They were found in a wide variety of informal and organized activities. General recreation, though confined to specific parts of "the Yard" which separated day students from boarders and younger students from collegians, was a regular occurrence. Daily there was the casual conversation and distractions that happened between classes and over the lunch hour and on Thursday afternoons and on weekends. Among the older students, hunting became a popular Thursday afternoon sport. While weapons were required to be deposited in the gun room, they could be withdrawn and used for duck hunting in the marshy area along the Alameda or along the Guadalupe River.[19] Weekends lent themselves to day-long picnics at Stephens' Creek in Sunnyvale, horse-drawn and later electric trolley rides into San José, and special excursions by train to Manresa Beach near Santa Cruz.

President Robert Kenna, S.J., in the mid-1880s decided that the older boys should be able to leave the walled confines of the campus unaccompanied by prefects. This provided a degree of independence previously unknown but was soon stopped when Kenna was ordered by his superiors in Rome not to allow such freedom. When he became president again in 1901, Kenna successfully ended the practice of requiring chaperones when students left campus.

National holidays, feast days and the president's birthday were anticipated with excitement because they always meant a suspension of the regular routine, a special menu in the dining room, and a variety of kinds of entertainment. Thanksgiving and Washington's Birthday, for example, always engendered a formal program by the students in the college auditorium. Typically, there was a musical performance by one of the many music groups. Always, there was a formal speech appropriate to the occasion, the recitation of fitting poetry or prose, and a humorous theatrical production described as "a farce." Feast days had similar celebrations. The feast of St. Joseph on March 19, also the anniversary of the founding of the college, was observed as a holiday with a procession to St. Joseph's shrine and music by the brass band, the college orchestra or the choral society. The afternoon was usually filled with a variety of competitions, some serious like the 75-yard dash, others less so like the three-legged race or the greased pole climb.[20] The president's birthday was an even more special holiday at which the president feted the student body. On his birthday in 1872, President Aloysius Varsi, S.J., rented horse carts to transport the students into San José to a specially reserved rink for a day of skating, followed by a special dinner with a printed bill of fare. The day concluded with a round of student toasts to the president's health and, after an urgent and rousing request from the assembled students, general absolution for those students who had yet performed their punishments. It was described as "a day long remembered by our students."[21]

A hallmark of Jesuit education from its earliest years was the ability of Jesuit-educated students to speak and write with clarity and style — the *eloquentia perfecta*. One way to develop this skill was through public speaking and virtually from the beginning debate played a major educational and recreational role in the life of Santa Clara students. In 1856 a debating society was founded by Fr. Accolti. Five years later, Fr. Edmund Young, S.J., arrived at Santa Clara and for the next thirty years supervised the college's rhetorical endeavors. He reorganized the debating society's structure to reflect the organization of the American Congress, an organizational structure later imitated by many schools. In this Literary Congress, lower classmen formed the House, upper classmen the Senate. Topics of current political and economic interest were vigorously argued between the two, capped by the annual Ryland debate always held in a packed auditorium before an appreciative audience of fellow-students and townsfolk.[22] Debate became the popular extracurricular activity for many students and caused one alumnus to observe that debate and public speaking "made the sons of Santa Clara stand forth pre-eminent in the public life of our State."[23]

Drama was another facet in the development of the articulate and poised graduate of Jesuit education. When President Varsi built the College Hall in 1870, it was with an eye toward having an appropriate venue for both debate and dramatic productions. The 3,000-seat auditorium, described in the *Alta California* as "larger and handsomer than any thespian temple in San Francisco," spurred the progress of theatrical productions. Shakespeare's plays were always popular offerings and tickets were sold in both Santa Clara town and San José. In 1881, a $0.50 adult ticket for Macbeth bought in San José included "car fare both ways."[24]

Many of the student productions had a patriotic or spiritual theme. Professor Charles D. South wrote "Santiago" shortly after the Spanish-American war and, with Santa Clara students as the cast, saw it performed in both San José and San Francisco. His play "Constantine," dealing with the Roman Emperor's conversion to Christianity, brought special trains from San Francisco that provided capacity audiences. Former student and Broadway playwright, Clay M. Greene, wrote the "Passion Play of Santa Clara" for the college's golden anniversary in 1901. This elaborate production required a large cast and gave many students a chance to strut the stage. Martin Merle, another successful playwright, wrote and produced several popular plays before he graduated. His most successful, "The Light Eternal," was first performed at Santa Clara. With a professional cast, it then toured the West Coast and ultimately was produced in New York. All of these campus productions gave ample opportunity for interested undergraduates to develop the *eloquentia perfecta*.

Another activity that permitted students to develop their reasoning and expressive talents was the monthly literary magazine. *The Owl*, begun in 1869, was one of the earliest examples of this type of endeavor. It aimed at "mental improvement" and to reflect the "intense classical studies" that characterized Santa Clara.[25] Although it was printed for only six years, until revived in 1931, its issues were full of reflections on the topics of the day, ranging from discussions of Darwin's theory of evolution and papal infallibility to criticisms of the treatment of Native Americans and of the arguments of "female

suffrage agitators."[26] At the turn of the century, *The Redwood* appeared
and for some twenty years chronicled campus events — such as the
visits of Theodore Roosevelt and Irish poet, William Butler Yeats — as
well as national and international issues. Both *The Owl* and *The
Redwood,* combined with debate and drama, provided Santa Clara
students with major intellectual, oratorical and imaginative outlets to
help ease the academic routine and social restrictions that so
characterized Santa Clara.

Athletics

While Santa Clara strove to impart a structured, classical
education to its students, it did so in the larger context of the Jesuit
philosophy of education that stressed the education of the "whole
man." This meant that physical as well as intellectual and moral
faculties should be developed. Over the years, various forms of athletic
activities became part of the life of the Santa Clara student. By 1856
the college could boast of having a large outdoor swimming pool, 160
by 120 feet, created in a hollowed out part of the orchard on the east
side of the Alameda. The following year a building was constructed
that served as both a gymnasium and theater. As an athletic arena, it
was the location for boxing matches (some authorized and some not)
and fencing lessons. By the 1870s the Yard was the site for numerous
intramural baseball games. A few years later, a handball court was
constructed in the Yard next to the student chapel, while an athletic
field suitable for both track and field events and baseball games was
constructed roughly where Kenna Hall stands today.

Intercollegiate athletics began with the creation of a baseball team
by the early 1870s and baseball quickly became a favorite sport. At first
all games were required to be played on campus, and on Thursdays
and Sundays crowds of the local citizenry would come to campus to
cheer on the collegians as they played against semi-professional teams.
In time, major and minor league professional teams would make
regular appearances in the springtime and an intercollegiate schedule
developed. *The Owl* faithfully recorded those early games in great
detail. It noted in 1874 that "Baseball is really alive again, and we
rejoice to see it." The story went on to describe a game with the
College of the Pacific.[27] By 1890 exceptions were made to the rule

requiring games to be played only on-campus. Sunday afternoon games were allowed in San José, and large contingents of students went into town to cheer on the team. As off-campus games became more common, students were exempted from afternoon study hall and the time for the evening meal became more flexible. Students took their baseball seriously and when a fight broke out between fans, students and players in a St. Mary's game, athletic relations between the two schools were suspended for a number of years.

The introduction of football raised a controversial issue on campus setting students against administration. The faculty was particularly skeptical and saw the sport as "a game full of dangers."[28] Nonetheless, the students prevailed, and in 1895 football was given "qualified recognition" to be played intramurally as long as students received "written permission from parents to play on the college eleven."[29] Within a year, they had cajoled the president, a supporter of athletics, to permit the team to play an outside opponent. Although football escalated in popularity, the program was abruptly terminated in 1905 after a national outcry for its abolition because of the number of injuries and fatalities it caused. The president explained the decision as a necessary one "until we can conscientiously allow the children, who have been confided to our care by loving parents, to enter into it without such fearful danger to life and limb."[30] It would not be resumed until after the end of World War I.

To fill the void caused by the loss of football, two other sports developed on campus. Basketball, a "safer and less strenuous game," was offered as a substitute for football but it did not catch on with students as either a participation or spectator sport until the 1920s.[31] A more popular substitute was rugby. With rugby, Santa Clara resumed the competition it had in football with Stanford and California and expanded its intercollegiate schedule to include schools like the University of Southern California. Games with local rivals attracted large crowds and as a result of its growing athletic prominence, Santa Clara began to be seen as a "big time" school, like its larger rivals. Success in rugby led to a number of Santa Clarans playing on All-American teams in international competition and in the Olympic games.

The expanding athletic program at Santa Clara seems to have had two dramatically different effects on the college. On the one hand, it reinforced one of the hallmarks of Jesuit education. Every aspect of a person, the intellectual and the physical, the spiritual and the emotional, was to be developed. Organized athletics played a significant role in the education of the whole person in the classical Roman model of a sound mind in a sound body. On the other hand, athletics can be seen as having a subversive effect on the maintenance of the regimen and strict order that characterized a Santa Clara education. The scheduling of games away from the campus, permitting teams to be gone overnight, allowing students to travel to San José and San Francisco, undermined the regular routine of campus life. The time for the evening meal was no longer firmly fixed. Afternoon and evening study halls were disrupted by excused absences or dismissed altogether. The time for "lights out" was ignored when train loads of students were late in returning from games. And so, while the physical activity that comes with athletics was an integral part of Jesuit education and athletic competition helped bring Santa Clara increased public recognition, at the same time intercollegiate athletics began to undermine the bases of the social and academic structure and order upon which Santa Clara had established its reputation.

During its first fifty or so years, students at Santa Clara lived in European-style college environment characterized by strict rules and regimentation. But it was not an altogether stifling experience. One student fondly remembered it as "a little world of our own."[32] In this world, young men were encouraged to develop the habits of intellectual and social discipline in an atmosphere of unambiguous expectations. But it was an environment lightened by a wide variety of activities, most of which supported the intellectual and social goals of Jesuit education. Certainly forensics and drama, literary endeavors and team-building fit in well. Perhaps a case can even be made that the imagination and inventiveness students showed in their efforts to evade or frustrate various regulations was consonant with the development of the whole man. As we reflect on a period that seems so unlike the present, let a turn-of-the-century student sum up his experience. "Our joys were simple . . . the college spirit ran high . . . and for all of us Santa Clara possessed something that was worth living and fighting for. . . All in all, I think we were a very happy group."[33] I hope that in fifty years time, today's Santa Clara students will be able to say the same.

References

1. Gerald McKevitt, S.J., *The University of Santa Clara: A History*, p. 27.

2. *Daily Alta California*, July 17, 1855 cited in George Giacomini and Gerald McKevitt, *Serving the Intellect, Touching the Heart: A Portrait of Santa Clara University*. p. 44.

3. Recollections of A.D. Splivalo '59, *The Redwood*, October 1908. Archives of Santa Clara University (hereafter cited as ASCU)

4. McKevitt, p. 80.

5. Ibid., 46.

6. Edward D. Sullivan, *The Fabulous Wilson Mizner*, p. 67.

7. Charles R. Barry, Dec. 15, Dec. 23, 1877, cited in Giacomini and McKevitt, p. 98.

8. McKevitt, p. 44-45.

9. The Owl, May 1870. p. 156. ASCU

10. McKevitt, p.46.

11. *The Owl*, January 1872. ASCU

12. *The Redwood*, March 1919. p. 112. ASCU

13. McKevitt, p. 45.

14. *The Redwood*, March 1919. p.111. ASCU

15. *The Monthly Santa Claran*, January 1937. p. 2. ASCU

16. *The Monthly Santa Claran*, February 1936. p. 3. ASCU

17. McKevitt, p. 89.

18. McKevitt, p. 87-88.

19. *The Owl*, February 1875. ASCU

20. Giacomini and McKevitt, p. 93.

21. *The Owl*, April 1872, p. 272-3. ASCU

22. *The Owl*, February 1936. p. 3. ASCU

23. McKevitt, p. 102.

24. McKevitt, p. 96; Giacomini and McKevitt, p. 93.

25. McKevitt, p. 105.

26. Giacomini and McKevitt, p. 46.

27. The Owl, November 1874. P. 114. ASCU

28. McKevitt, p. 144.

29. Giacomini and McKevitt, p. 92.

30. San José Daily Mercury, November 7, 1905 "SCU Clipping Scrapbook," Microfilm 1. ASCU

31. San José Mercury, December 14, 1905. "SCC Clipping Scrapbook, 1902-06." ASCU

32. The Monthly Santa Claran, February 1934, 1. ASCU

33. The Monthly Santa Claran, September 1936. p. 3. ASCU

SECTION IV
Twentieth Century Santa Clara

Santa Clara continued to transform itself during the twentieth century. In a single lifetime, Santa Clara has moved from growing and packing fruit to growing silicon chips and developing computer technology. Today the Valley of Heart's Delight is Silicon Valley, and some would say the center of the economic world. Its capital is Santa Clara. The changes have brought new people, ideas, and technologies into the community. Old ways have been abandoned in favor of the new. And with these changes, the world of Santa Clara was turned upside down, not unlike the world of the first Santa Clarans, the Ohlone, two hundred years earlier. Solace for many in these changing times was often found in "their" school — Santa Clara University.

In the twentieth century, Santa Clara University educated generations of students to help others and to be part of the new emerging world that is Santa Clara today. As the community changed, so did the University. Since 1950 people of color and women have come to make-up a significant portion of the faculty, administration, and student body. Faculty and students have served their country and their community with selfless devotion. Many have made exciting discoveries that have shaped the lives of the people of Santa Clara, the nation, and the world.

CHAPTER 11

Early History of Science at Santa Clara

Carl H. Hayn, S.J.

When Santa Clara College began in 1851, one year after the statehood of California, the academic scene was much different than it is today, especially in the sciences. The Newtonian laws, Maxwell's equations, and other fundamental laws were known, but experimental science, as we know it today, was in its infancy. There were no telegraphs, telephones, radios, house lighting, automobiles, etc. It was the period of the famous Gold Rush and people lived a frontier life.

Santa Clara was founded by Italian Jesuits who, for the most part, had been educated at prestigious universities in Italy, France and England. They established a liberal arts curriculum with a very strong emphasis on Latin and Greek, together with Philosophy, English, History and a smattering of Natural Science. These they judged to be essential for a good liberal education. During the first year forty students were enrolled, and Santa Clara became The first institution of higher learning in California.

On April 28, 1865, Fr. John Nobili, S.J. obtained a charter from the State, which empowered the College to grant degrees. At first only the B.A. degree was conferred. Vocational training such as business and experimental science were not included. Later however, yielding to pressure from both parents and students, the school introduced a commercial program giving students the opportunity of learning business skills. Four years later, the administration added a science curriculum but continued to require the inclusion of liberal arts courses. The new programs led to the Bachelor of Science degree, which soon became more popular than the arts degree.

By 1858 a considerable amount of new scientific apparatus had arrived from manufacturers in Paris. The school catalogue stated that the college possessed "complete philosophical"[1] (i.e. physical) and chemical apparatus. The cost to the institution was nearly ten thousand dollars. Also purchased was "a large collection of biological specimens and an impressive collection of minerals." Each year additional purchases were made to "keep pace with the progress of science."[2] Ten thousand dollars was an enormous sum of money at that time when $5.00 was a typical weekly wage for workmen in San Francisco.

The "philosophical" apparatus included:

> 28 instruments for experiments in mechanics
> 25 for hydraulics
> 52 for pneumatics (properties of air and other gases)
> 66 for heat experiments
> 50 devices for electrical measurements
> 1 large glass-disk electrostatic generator
> 69 optical instruments, and
> 1 complete Daguerreotype apparatus (for producing photographic pictures on silver coated copper plates).

In 1871 the College Catalogue announced the introduction of several vocational courses such as telegraphy, photography, surveying and printing.

The students' daily schedule began at half-past five in the morning. After dressing, the students assembled in the chapel for the celebration of Mass. Breakfast at 8:00 a.m. was followed by an hour-and-a-half to prepare the day's lessons. Morning classes ran from nine o'clock until noon. After a two-hour break for lunch and recreation, the rest of the day, until 5:00 p.m., was again spent in the classroom. Wednesday and Saturday afternoons were free.

Santa Clara College soon gained an enviable reputation as an excellent academic institution. One historian stated that Santa Clara was unequalled in California "for scholarship both literary and scientific."[3] At that time, Santa Clara had the largest number of professors and tutors of any institution on the Pacific Coast. It was also said to have the best equipped laboratories in the West. These facts, mentioned by the press, subsequently brought an increase in applications for admission to the school.

A visitor from Scotland was impressed by the five hundred chemical reagents and by the most recent inventions from Europe, including electrical instruments and a Duboscq telescope. Another visitor, from San Francisco, was surprised to find what he said was "the only copy in America of a famous European apparatus for the liquefaction of gases."[4] He also was struck by the collection of Geissler discharge tubes that contained gases such as hydrogen, helium, mercury and neon, each exhibiting its own characteristic spectral lines. According to him there was only one other such collection in the United States. The early directors of Santa Clara were convinced that their college was "easily first" in California.

Some of the better known scientists, mostly Jesuits, who contributed to the academic life of Santa Clara were the following:

Fr. Charles Messea, an Italian, established the first science department. A professor of chemistry and natural sciences, he supervised the purchase of an impressive list of scientific instruments that were manufactured in France. Today the de Saisset Museum houses some of these instruments. Many of the minerals are displayed in cabinets that line the corridor of the physics building. Additional mineral specimens are in storage in the Ricard Observatory and also in the de Saisset Museum.

In the 1860s Fr. Messea was joined by three other Jesuits. One was Fr. Anthony Cichi "whose reputation as a chemist and mineral analyst led to his being frequently consulted by mining firms"[5] during the gold rush days. Incidentally, Fr. Cichi had a parrot which he kept in an outdoor cage. The story is told that some students taught his parrot to say: "Go to hell Cichi; Go to hell Cichi." Obviously, Fr. Cichi did not appreciate their prank.

A second Jesuit to join Fr. Messea was Fr. Aloysius Varsi in whose honor Varsi Hall received its name. He had studied physics and higher mathematics at the University of Paris. At Santa Clara he taught both physics and chemistry.

The third Jesuit to join Fr. Messea was Fr. Joseph Neri, who was trained as a chemist and became a well-known specialist in spectroscopy and electricity. He constructed the first storage battery in San Francisco, a peroxide of lead combination containing about thirty plates. He became famous as the first person to introduce electric lighting on Market Street in San Francisco, the first ever seen in California. To make the beam of his arc lamp unidirectional he used a spherical mirror and a Fresnel lens. Fr. Neri was also a mineral analyst. While he headed the chemistry department, he supported it with the income from chemical assays that he performed for the miners in the gold country. One historian mentioned that the name Neri became a byword in "science in California" during the latter part of the 19th century.

Another well-known Jesuit was Fr. Joseph Bayma, who was a mathematician, a philosopher and theoretical physicist. He wrote a book "Elements of Molecular Mechanics" and was recognized as a pioneer in stereochemistry.[6] He also published five mathematics textbooks.

Little is known of Fr. Francis Veyret. In a speech given by Archbishop Riordan of San Francisco, he was referred to as a "genius"[7] in mathematics and physical science. One of his students in "higher mathematics" was Fr. Jerome Ricard who later became the famous "Padre of the Rains."

One of the best known scientists at Santa Clara was John Montgomery, a lay professor who taught physics. His principal research interest lay in the field of aeronautics. He studied birds in flight and concentrated on the lifting ability of a curved wing. Montgomery was the first person ever to achieve a controlled flight in a glider whose wings were designed in imitation of a sea gull. He accomplished this feat in 1883, two full decades before the Wright Brothers' first engine propelled flight in 1903 at Kitty Hawk in North Carolina.

Mr. Cornelius Reinhardt, his mechanic, constructed a wind tunnel so that he could study the airflow of flour dust over various wing designs. Reinhardt also built a "merry-go-round," ten feet in diameter, so that Montgomery could (1) use models with different wing curvatures to study their lifting ability and (2) observe the thrust of propeller blades having different pitches and shapes. It was his intention eventually to employ such propellers to supply thrust for his gliders. Baby carriage wheels on the gliders and a wooden runway placed on the slope of a hill in the Evergreen area in San José were used to get his gliders air-borne.

In 1905 Montgomery hired a balloonist to lift his glider four thousand feet into the air. It was then cut loose and, after some maneuvering, was guided back to the spot from where it left the ground. Mr. Victor Lougheed, the half-brother of Allen Lockheed, the founder of Lockheed Aircraft Corporation, said it was "the greatest single advance"[8] in the history of aviation.

During a period of two weeks, Montgomery and an associate, Joseph Vierra, made fifty-five flights in the Evergreen area, circling about and eventually returning to the starting point. Descriptions and results of his flights were presented in a paper that he gave at the aeronautical conference during the 1893 World's Fair held in Chicago. It was Montgomery who coined the word "aeroplane" while others still called it a flying machine.

During his years as professor at Santa Clara University, Montgomery was also engaged in other research work. He made a rectifier that changed alternating current to direct current. He also made a rheostat to increase or dim the stage lighting for the Passion Play enacted by the students at Santa Clara. Together with Cornelius Reinhardt, he produced a teletype system for which he held a patent. Another of his patents, pertaining to one of his glider designs, was helpful to the Wright brothers as they worked on their aircraft at Kitty Hawk.[9]

The researches of Montgomery are narrated in a book, written by Fr. Arthur Spearman, S.J., entitled "John Joseph Montgomery, Father of Basic Flying." In collecting material for this book, Fr. Spearman interviewed Cornelius Reinhardt who, as mentioned above, had been Montgomery's mechanic. At that time he lived in New Almaden and was 89 years of age. It was my good fortune to accompany Fr. Spearman and serve as a witness to this interview. Mr. Reinhardt told us that Montgomery used twenty-four stove bolts to attach the wings to the fuselage. The bolts were located immediately above the head of the pilot of the glider. Since the bolts were three inches long, Reinhardt tried to convince Montgomery to shorten them because they presented a serious danger to the head of the pilot. Montgomery refused because he wanted to use those bolts again to test other wings.

In the interview, Reinhardt related how Montgomery's fatal accident occurred. During a flight with a new set of wings,

Montgomery, attempting to adjust the wing's angle of attack while in flight, pulled the elevator controls too hard thereby causing the glider to turn upwards at an angle of about sixty degrees. The glider stalled and side-slipped throwing Montgomery's head against one of the bolts that penetrated his skull. Reinhardt saw blood and gray matter oozing from behind Montgomery's right ear. Wishing to spare his wife an additional shock as she approached the damaged glider, he pinched off the part of the brain that was protruding from his skull. "For forty-five cents worth of bolts," said Reinhardt, "Montgomery could have prevented his death."[10]

An obelisk monument, commemorating Montgomery's balloon assisted flight, is situated on the Santa Clara campus just south of Varsi Hall. Another monument stands at the entrance of Evergreen College on Yerba Buena Road in San José, and an historical marker is located nearby at the foot of the hill where his death occurred.

The elementary school in that region bears the name Montgomery as also does a school in Chula Vista near the airport at San Diego where a number of Montgomery's flights were made. The former engineering building on the Santa Clara campus bore the name Montgomery Laboratories.

Columbia Studios produced a full-length film of Montgomery's life and entitled it "Gallant Journey." State Senator John F. Thompson, in a speech, said that Montgomery's flights gave California the distinction of being the birthplace of modern aviation. Alexander Graham Bell stated that "All subsequent attempts in aviation must begin with the Montgomery machine."[11]

Fr. Richard Bell was an American Jesuit. He did pioneering work in radio broadcasting. Becoming interested in Guglielmo Marconi's wireless telegraphy he duplicated that work at Santa Clara. In 1933 Marconi visited Fr. Bell and was shown through his laboratory. Bell's research lasted more than four decades, during which time he was credited with several inventions and held a patent for a radio-signaling device. According to the recollections of a workman who assisted him, Fr. Bell sent his first voice message by radio in 1904. He communicated frequently with Mr. Charles D. Herrold, a San José radio pioneer, and also lectured to packed houses on the subject of wireless transmission.

Fr. Jerome Ricard, another Jesuit, was born in France. He was an astronomer and developed a sun spot theory by which he predicted the weather. He had remarkable success, being correct about 82% of the time![12] Fr. Ricard compared disturbances on the surface of the sun with the climatic conditions on the earth and concluded that there was a causal relationship between sunspots and terrestrial weather. According to Dr. Douglas O'Handley, a NASA space scientist, this connection between the earth's weather and sun spot activity is accepted as a fact today although it initially had a number of adversaries. Orange growers in southern California, athletic promoters and also the Hollywood motion picture industry consulted Fr. Ricard's weather predictions when scheduling their activities. In 1915 Ricard began a periodical called "Sunspot" in which he published his weekly and, later, monthly predictions. For more than thirty years he carried on his work. At the height of his popularity the Knights of Columbus raised $50,000 for the construction of the Ricard Observatory for the "Padre of the Rains."

In purchasing a telescope Ricard had a costly and embarrassing experience. Eager to have the biggest and best telescope, he decided to purchase a giant five-foot reflector and commissioned a man in Vancouver to make the 60-inch mirror. After three years of delays, promises and exchange of letters, and the expenditure of thousands of dollars on the material to be used, a large crate finally arrived. On opening the packing crate Ricard found a very large slab of concrete but no mirror!

In 1895 he obtained an eight-inch refracting telescope from an abandoned Methodist college at Napa. He also purchased several expensive seismographs to record motions of the earth. At his death in 1930, Dr. Robert Sproul, president of the University of California, said that Ricard's death "is a great loss to the scientific world." (For more on Ricard, see Kesten and McKay — this volume.)

A very colorful personality was Fr. Bernard Hubbard, the "Glacier Priest." He received that name while studying in Austria and climbing the Tyrolese Alps at every opportunity. He was listed in the Santa Clara University Bulletin as a member of the geology department but his heart was in Alaska. Each summer he traveled there with several stalwart university athletes to explore its craters and glaciers. An account of his expedition to the biggest active volcano in the world, Aniakchak, was described in the *National Geographic* Magazine.[12]

Hubbard was also interested in the language, life and culture of the people. During the year 1937 he lived with the "King Islanders," the Inupiat Alaskans who dwelt on steep cliffs that rise precipitously above the waters of the Bering Sea. He recorded on film their ethnic traits, rituals, social life, games and customs.

At the end of each summer, he returned to the Santa Clara campus to edit the many roles of film and to prepare his popular nationwide lectures. Within one five-month period, he delivered 275 lectures across the nation. Over 200,000 ft. of his films and 50 film shorts are stored in the Smithsonian Museum of Natural History in Washington, D.C. Among his more important writings were two books: "Cradle of the Storms" and "Mush, You Malemutes." He published many articles and press releases and produced a dozen travelogues for Fox Movietone. Anthropologists have described his King Island pictures as being "of enormous ethnographic and historical significance."[14]

Such is the proud early history of science at Santa Clara University spanning its first hundred and ten years from 1851 to 1961.

Endnotes

1. Gerald McKevitt, *The University of Santa Clara: A History* (Stanford, 1979) p. 71

2. Ibid., p. 71

3. Brian J. Clinch, "The Jesuits in American California," *Records of the American Catholic Historical Society*, vol. 17 p.139

4. McKevitt, p. 72

5. Ibid.

6. Stereochemistry deals with the spatial arrangement of atoms and groups of molecules responsible for the properties of substances.

7. Archives of Santa Clara University, Santa Clara, California

8. Victor Lougheed, *Vehicles of the Air, a Popular Exposition of Modern Aeronautics with Working Drawings* (Chicago, 1911), p. 138.

9. Arthur Spearman, S.J. *John Joseph Montgomery, Father of Basic Flying*, Santa Clara University, 1977, p. 249.

10. Ibid., p.245

11. Ibid., p. 249

12. McKevitt, p. 228

13. Bernard R. Hubbard, S.J., 1931. "Aniakchak the New Volcanic Wonderland of the Alaskan Peninsula Is Explored," *National Geographic*. Vol. 60 (September) pps. 319-345.

14. Caprice Murray Scarborough, "The Legacy of the 'Glacier Priest': Bernard R. Hubbard, S.J., *Research Manuscript Series on the Cultural and Natural History of Santa Clara*, No. 10, Santa Clara University, Santa Clara California.

References Consulted

McGinty, Brian. 1979. "Luminous Century," Westways (Sept.) Sept. 1979, p.18ff

McKevitt, Gerald, S.J. 1979. *The University of Santa Clara, A History 1851-1977.* Stanford University Press, Stanford, CA.

Scarborough, Caprice Muray. 2001. "The Legacy of the 'Glacier Priest': Bernard R. Hubbard, S.J., *Research Manuscript Series on the Cultural and Natural History of Santa Clara,* No. 10. Santa Clara University, Santa Clara, CA

Spearman, Arthur Dunning, S.J. 1967. *John Joseph Montgomery, Father of Basic Flying.* University of Santa Clara.

National Geographic, vol. 60 (Sept. 1931) pp. 319-345.

National Geographic, vol. 65 (May 1934) pp. 625-626.

Archives of Santa Clara University

1987. *The Alaskan Shepherd* (May-June), vol. 25, No. 3.

1931. The Redwood, Santa Clara Yearbook.

2001. The Santa Clara Magazine (Spring) , vol. 12, pp. 16-21.

CHAPTER 12

The Great Depression and World War II
Recollections of Santa Clara University
Leonard McKay

In August of 2000, JoAnne Northrup, the Curator of Exhibits and Collections at the DeSaisset museum asked me to do a lecture for a sesquicentennial course titled "Telling the Santa Clara Story". She called me because I had been at Santa Clara during the war years of 1940 through 1947. I was at first taken aback as I was not the typical student of that time. I was neither Catholic, a scholarship athlete, a scholarship academic, nor from a financially well off family. Instead, I had gone to a non-Catholic high school, and my family was faced with financial difficulties, so I had to work at various jobs before and after school. In the question period after my lecture, one student asked, "Facing financial difficulties and being a non-Catholic, why did you attend Santa Clara? Why didn't you go to San José State?" My answer was immediate, "Because of my great respect for the Jesuits." At the time, there were many outstanding Jesuit scientists at Santa Clara and then as now the reputation of a Santa Clara University education was excellent. In answer to Ms. Northrup's request, I asked that the subject be broadened from "The War Years," to "The Great Depression of the 1930s and the War Years of the 1940s.

Santa Clara University

Santa Clara University, the oldest college in California, celebrates its 150th anniversary, and I'd like to explain a little of what I know about the campus during the 1930s and 1940s. As a Jesuit-run institution, it has always had a very high reputation, but this is written from a personal view about its most difficult times. The campus was much smaller during the 1930s when I first walked on the site bordered by Lafayette, Franklin, and Santa Clara Streets and the Alameda. It was entirely a men's college and the priests were easily identified by their black cassocks and small three cornered bireta hats. Most Jesuit brothers, who attended the beautiful gardens and the buildings, also wore clerical garb. The campus was always colorful, and the Mission had been rebuilt after the disastrous fire of 1925. In 1930, the king of Spain sent a replacement bell for the rebuilt mission. That bell rings the Angelus to this day. The old Alameda was the eastern border of the campus and has since been closed to traffic. The engineering buildings and the Orradre Library are now on the eastern side of the Alameda, with a lovely, tree shaded parkway where the old road once was. This was once the major road connecting the old Mission of Santa Clara to the Pueblo de San José, and the early San José Spanish settlers came from the Pueblo by horse and ox cart to attend mass at the mission. During my school days, it was the site of the Eberhard Tannery, which emitted a foul odor when processing leather. There was no football stadium, but only Ryan Field, a baseball diamond. The ROTC (Reserved Officer Training Corps) installation was where the new athletic compound is now. Fr. Jerome Ricard, S.J., conducted his experiments on his frequently derided sun-spot theory. His theory today is frequently revived as "sun flares." In 1927, Fr. Hubbard was making his first of many trips to the then remote and uncharted Alaska. The faculty consisted of 34 Jesuit priests and lay professors; all were male. Among them were Fr. Gianera, Fr. O'Connell, Fr. Boland, Fr. Ricard, and Fr. Hubbard.

Fr. McCoy was the president when the great Depression hit in 1929. Although the country was reeling from the stock market crash, Santa Clara was still afloat financially and was planning a new building program. The four story Nobili Hall was to cost $220,000, plans were laid to build Varsi Library and the Engineering School's Montgomery Lab was to get a second story. These were the last buildings to be built until after World War II.

By 1932 the depression really hit. Unemployment in the United States hit a record 25%, Franklin Delano Roosevelt was elected president, and Fr. Lyons was named president of Santa Clara, with Fr. Zach Maher as the Jesuit Provincial. By 1934 SCU had serious

financial problems, as did all of
the Jesuit institutions. Fr. Lyons
felt it was his job to keep Santa
Clara afloat while the Provincial
wanted SCU to share the
burden of other, less fortunate
colleges and to provide support
for the young Jesuit
seminarians. (Partially because
of the seriousness of the
depression and unemployment,
many young men chose to join
the Jesuit order.) Enrollment at
the university fell to under 400.

Fr. Maher, the Provincial,
was having major problems
supporting less fortunate
schools, and he expected Santa
Clara's president to share the
burden, which Lyons refused. He
was replaced before the

FR. RICARD, S.J., and instrument in the
SCU observatory. (McKay Collection)

completion of his term of five years, a great rarity if health was not a
consideration.

In November of 1933, a popular graduate of SCU, Brooke Hart,
was kidnapped and murdered; his body was found in San Francisco
Bay some weeks later. Two San José men, Holmes and Thurmond,
were suspected of the murder, but before they could be tried, a lynch
mob was formed and they were hanged in St. James Park in San José.
Some reports claimed that Santa Clara students were the ring leaders,
but I don't believe this to be true. Fr. Gianera was then Dean of
Faculties, and he would not have allowed such a thing to happen.
One of the alleged leaders was a respected attorney in the Louis
Oneal law offices. Oneal was one of the two political bosses in Santa
Clara County and a friend of the very popular California Governor,
Sunny Jim Rolph. Rolph stated that if any of the lynch mob was
arrested, he would personally pardon them.

Fr. Gianera was a most remarkable man for he knew the name of
every student that attended the school, and he could recall each and

every one years later. Gianera first came to Santa Clara as a student in 1903, entered the Jesuit order in 1907, and returned to Santa Clara as a teacher. He served as vice president, as dean of faculties, and in 1945, was named president.

Communism was a real threat and the dictators, Hitler in Germany and Mussolini in Italy, were starting to flex their muscles. Japan was launching its "Greater Co-prosperity sphere" in which Japan would dominate all of Asia and Australia. Hitler wrote *Mein Kampf*, advising the world exactly what he planned to do, but no one believed him. Isn't it strange that China is now telling us that their 200 million-man army is going to take Taiwan, and we choose not to believe them?

It is hard for us today to know what life was like during the depression. My family was fortunate in that we never went hungry. But money was scarce, and barter was rampant. If anyone had any excess and it wasn't saleable, you gave it to your neighbor or friend, and when they had an excess, they shared with your family.

In Santa Clara Valley there was a rich fruit and vegetable harvest. Most women canned peaches, pears, apricots and fresh vegetables. It was a big deal to have chicken on Sunday. For many depression, years I wore shoes that had holes in the soles; once the soles wore out, a replacement sole could be bought for 25 cents. The purchase included a packet of glue that let go after a few days, and I learned to walk heel-down first so that the sole wouldn't fall off.

Of course, there were no televisions, no computers, no calculators and no cell phones. Most houses had an ice box, not a refrigerator. If you had a telephone, it was usually on a party line.

We were well off, however, compared to the people coming from the America's dust bowl, the Okies, Arkies and Texans. Many people in California resented these immigrants because they were taking jobs from Californians and were living desperate lives just trying to exist. When I interviewed John Steinbeck in 1939, he was resented by the people of Los Gatos and Salinas because he championed the cause of the "Okies" in his book "Grapes of Wrath." Steinbeck had been born in Salinas and was then living in the mountains above Los Gatos.

Because jobs were scarce, most women were expected to stay at home so that men could have what jobs were available. Fruit pickers were paid five cents a box for prunes and about the same for cutting apricots. Emergency measures were passed under the Roosevelt Administration to offer government employment in a host of assistance programs, WPA, NRA, NYA, and CCC. New government programs helped, but those employed on government make-work projects weren't expected to work very hard. In these bleak days, I was hired by the NYA (National Youth Administration) as a clerk in the California Employment Office at 25 cents per hour.

Escape in these bleak days was provided by the movies. Talking movies were new, and Busbee Berkeley extravaganzas, westerns, and lavish productions provided a few hours away from one's troubles. At home people huddled around their radios (housed in wood cabinets and given pride of place in the living room) to hear Jack Benny, Ed Wynn, Eddie Cantor, and the Lone Ranger.

At Santa Clara, President Fr. Lyons was having great success with the Passion Plays, and the football teams were earning revenue. Santa Clara, under Coach Clipper Smith, played to crowds of 60,000 against the rival St. Mary's at Kezar Stadium in San Francisco. Games usually ended in riots by the partisan fans. Football was really big at Santa Clara : Nello Falaschi was the first All American, followed by Al Wolff, John Scheill, and Kenny Casanega. Casanega made the most memorable run in 1941 against the Cal team. The game was played in the Cal Stadium, and their wonderful punter, Bob Reinhard, kicked a tremendous punt from Cal's 20 to the Santa Clara 20. Casanega caught the punt on the run, and ran a broken field pattern, avoiding every Cal tackler, for a touchdown. But there was an offside penalty called so Reinhard again kicked the ball to the same place, Kenny caught the ball at the same spot and followed the same route, running for a touchdown and eventually winning the game. In 1947, my classmate Bill "Stub" Crowley punted the football 73 yards in a game against USF. Outstanding football coaches in this era included Clipper Smith, Buck Shaw (later to become the first coach of the San Francisco 49ers), Len Casanova, and Pat Malley. Basketball was also very successful, and George Barsi's "Magicians of the Maplewood" traveled to Madison Square Garden in New York winning against the very best of eastern teams, in the late 1930s.

In 1927 Fr. Bernard Hubbard, the Glacier Priest, made his first trip to explore the wilds of Alaska. This was followed by many discoveries and nearly yearly trips to the far north. To finance these trips, he went on lecture tours all across the United States. At one time, he was the highest paid lecturer in the world. The money Hubbard received for his lectures was used to finance his expeditions and to support the remote Jesuit missions in Alaska. He would appear on stage with his dogs and furs. His exploits were detailed in the Saturday Evening Post magazine, on NBC radio, and in Pathe movie newsreels. When the war broke out, he was immediately called in to advise both the Army and Navy. The Japanese attacked the Aleutian Islands of Kiska and Attu, places he had explored but were relatively unknown by our military. While I had a nodding friendship with the Glacier Priest, I wish that I could have cultivated his friendship because I have since been to many of the same places. Hubbard was a tremendously rugged man who usually took Santa Clara students with him, including football player Red Chisom and San José State graduate Ed Levin (also a football player and professional boxer). Hubbard liked his associates to be capable of carrying heavy back packs and enduring hardship. Always with him were his favorite dogs.

The wonderful movies made by Hubbard of his travel can been seen in the archives in the SCU Orradre Library. Hubbard was also an excellent writer and wrote three books about his adventures. A special exhibit at the de Saisset during the first five months of 2001 featured Hubbard. Hubbard also took more that ten thousand still photos that are now being restored with a grant from the Smithsonian Institution.

By the end of the 1930s the people of the United States believed in isolation from Europe's problems, and Santa Clara was no exception. In 1939 Hitler invaded Poland, and while peace was shattered, a poll of Santa Clara students showed that 95% favored isolation. This attitude changed rapidly as Hitler's blitzkrieg invaded the Low Countries and the Germans invaded Paris. The Nazis had 300 crack divisions ready to fight; Japan had invaded China earlier and manned 120 divisions. Italy was invading Greece and then Ethiopia with 80 divisions. The United States had only 28, poorly equipped divisions. The draft was passed by Congress and our soldiers were being trained with wooden rifles. The Wright Aircraft engine plant received contracts from our allies and was able to produce 1000 aircraft engines in 1940, beginning the huge defense plant effort. U. S. production was a major factor in the final victory of the Allies.

In 1940 I began my freshman year at Santa Clara, although I had been on the campus many years earlier. Standing in the registration line in the old Seifert Gymnasium, I was called up to the Reserve Officer's Training desk. I was advised that it was a requirement for all able bodied students to sign up for the basic two-year ROTC course. On the completion of the two years, a student could either drop out or continue to the advanced course for an additional two years. If one satisfactorily completed the four-year program, he was commissioned a Second Lieutenant in the Field Artillery. This was a decision that became very important because it allowed me to stay in college for three years before I was called up for active duty, whereas young men my age were often drafted unless they made some military commitment. Although the Army ROTC program was the most active on campus, there were also programs with the Navy and Marines in which one could enroll.

By this time, Fr. Walsh had been named president, and tuition was $125.00 per semester, an enormous sum in those late depression times. The next year produced the shock of our lifetime. On December 7, 1941, Japanese naval aircraft bombed Pearl Harbor. Most Americans could not even comprehend that such a thing could happen, and the total devastation was hidden from most of us here. We suddenly and firmly believed that if they could bomb Pearl Harbor, they could also attack the mainland, and we were ill prepared. It was a surprise to read in the newspapers that a blackout was in effect and rationing would soon be started. We were soon under martial law with soldiers standing on downtown corners of San José. General Richardson, commander of the Fifth Army, established his headquarters on North First Street in San José. Many of my high school friends rushed to enlist. Sailor Gene Katt was lying dead aboard the bombed and sunken battleship Arizona in Pearl Harbor and my close friend Bob Burdick joined the submarine corps. Bob Jones and Bob Blackman went to Canada to enlist in the Royal Canadian Air Force to become fighter pilots so they could get into the fight sooner.*

The number of students at Santa Clara was rapidly declining. The seniors were leaving, many commissioned as artillery officers. The law school closed down for lack of enrollment, and only two law professors remained. Seven of the younger Jesuits entered the military as chaplains, and the first women came to the campus. The Engineering Science Management War Training Program was instituted as an evening class, and my mother was one of the first female students on campus.

My curriculum changed as business courses were now replaced with engineering courses; physics and surveying, gunnery and tactics were going to be important to a field artillery officer. My junior class members who had signed up for advanced ROTC were called into active duty as a group, "The Fighting 40." We were sent to basic training and later to officer candidate school. When we were called up, only seven junior students remained from the class of 1940; these seven were either unfit for military duty or were foreign born. Santa Clara received a contract to train enlisted GI's as engineering students, and a reserve officer, one-legged Col. J. Shelborne Robinson, was placed in command of the Army Specialized Training Program. These enlisted men came from line units to be trained as combat engineers at Santa Clara. When this program was shut down, Santa Clara was without students and had the war lasted another year, the school would have gone bankrupt. "The Fighting 40" were returned to Santa Clara for a short time before being sent to officer candidate school. Upon graduation as artillery second lieutenants, we were sent to units as replacement officers. American might finally prevailed, and by mid-1945, the war was over. By that time, the American military had grown to 15 million. Most of us wanted to get out of the service and on with our lives.

After victory in Europe, there was still the war against Japan to win. Troops were being readied for transfer from the European Theater for the invasion of Japan. It was estimated that there would be more than 12 million casualties, Allies and Japanese, with the majority Japanese civilians. When the first and second atomic bombs were dropped, my feeling was one of tremendous relief, that the bombing had saved lives by preventing the invasion. I find little sympathy for the premise that the bomb should not have been dropped, for I feel that my life and 12 million others were saved by its use.

TV Anchor Tom Brokaw's recent book, *The Greatest Generation*, wrote about us as follows:

When the United States entered World War 11, the U. S. government
turned to ordinary Americans and asked of them extraordinary service,
sacrifice, and heroics. Many Americans met those high expectations, and
then returned home to lead ordinary lives.

When the war ended, more than twelve million men and women
put their uniforms aside and returned to civilian life. They went back
to work at their old jobs or started small businesses; they became big-
city cops and firemen; they finished their degrees or enrolled in
college for the first time; they became schoolteachers, insurance
salesmen, craftsmen, and local politicians. They weren't widely known
outside their families or their communities. For many, the war years
were enough adventure to last a lifetime. They became once again
ordinary people, the kind of men and women who always have been
the foundation of the American way of life.

The army cartoonist Bill Mauldin did his very realistic strip of war
wearied GI's Willie and Joe, and he wrote shortly before the end of
the war about all of the soldiers, sailors and marines:

> They are very different now. Don't let anybody tell you they aren't. You
> can't pay in money for what they have done. They need people telling
> about them so they will be taken back into their civilian lives and given a
> chance to be themselves again.

> There will be some good ones and some bad ones. But the vast majority of
> combat men are going to be no problem at all. They are so damned sick
> and tired of having their noses rubbed in the stinking war that their only
> ambition will be to forget it. They don't need pity because you don't pity
> brave men— men who are brave because they fight while they are scared
> to death.

Mauldin wrote those words more than half a century ago, even
before the men headed home from the front lines, and it is as true
today as it was then. They didn't want pity and they did want to
forget. Of course, they could not forget, especially those who'd seen
combat. When they couldn't erase the war from memory they simply
confined it there, refusing to talk about it unless questioned and then
only reluctantly.

After the war, we staggered back to Santa Clara, and I use the
word staggered reluctantly. Those with high combat points arrived
first. We tried to catch up on what happened to our former high

school and college classmates and found that many didn't survive, and those of us who did were to carry lifetime scars. Of my high school classmates, Gene Katt was lying in the ruins of the Battleship Arizona at Pearl Harbor, Bob Jones and Bob Blackmore were missing in their fighter aircraft, the fate of my close friend Bob Burdick was unknown and it wasn't until a half century later that the internet revealed what happened to his sub SS 279, the Snook. Its last patrol was just five months before war's end when it disappeared. College classmate Bob Board had his knee crushed during the invasion of the Philippines, Eugene Towne contracted yellow fever, Second Lt. Charles Pausner was killed in the Battle of the Bulge. What happened to the many others was unknown for as Brokaw wrote "they didn't talk about it and wanted to get on with their lives."

Santa Clara was both the same old place and yet very different. Fr. Gianera was now the president. Fr. Stretch returned to become vice president. Fr. Schmidt was a familiar face and presence who never left the campus, likewise did Fr. O'Connell and Fr. Shipsey. George Sullivan was still the dean of the Engineering School and Dirksen was dean of the Business School. Many of our former Jesuit professors were back. Colonel Fr. Bernard Copeland, S J., was again teaching philosophy as were most of the ex-military chaplains, including Fr. Crowley. Enrollment passed the thousand mark for the first time. The school was bursting at the seams, for the G.I. bill paid for our educations. As Mauldin wrote, "They are very different now." Our prewar classes lacked urgency, but the requirement that undergraduates take four years of philosophy was still important. One of those courses, ethics, was taught by Fr. Fagothey and became important throughout my lifetime. My ethics text is still on my bookshelf and referred to often. We wanted to get that diploma and on with our lives. The age of entrants to the law school went from 21 years old in 1940 to 27 1/2 years when we returned. Many of my classmates had married, had children, and now returned to finish their educations. They assisted in the building of "Veteran's Village", a complex of surplus military metal Butler Huts, that were divided in half to accommodate two young families. At college reunions, many speak of these post-war days as the best of their lives. Jobs were very scarce, for the U.S. was converting from military production to civilian production. New cars were impossible to buy but I managed to buy a beat up 1932 Model A Ford for $150.00. Earl Warren, the Governor of California, gave our graduation address, and as I received my diploma I was still unemployed. As I was walking down the steps of the old "Ship" Auditorium, clutching my sheepskin, Charles Dirksen, the dean of the business school, advised me to apply to Pan American World Airways. I was employed three days later at the monthly salary of $165.00, about one half a lawyer's hourly rate today!

I close with a quote from the 1947 Redwood, our college annual:

> We started in 40, 41,42,43; *The history of the class of 1947 is a history of remarkable men because it tells of these men, first seeking to learn in peace, yet having an eye to war; then gaining that peace, many of them in war, then returning to peace, fulfilling what they first sought to fulfill.*

I wish to acknowledge the sacrifice of my friends during World War II.

A few of the men killed during the war included classmates:

Gene Katt, enlisted soon after graduation from Los Gatos High School was killed when the Japanese attacked Pearl Harbor on December 7, 1941. His body was never recovered and lies today in the Battleship *Arizona*.

Bob Burdick enlisted in the Navy in 1942. He married Jean Wilkes in 1941. He volunteered for the submarine service and was assigned to the

CLASSMATES: Leonard McKay and Hal Turett in the field at Ft. Bragg, 1943. And Lt. McKay with an L4 "Grasshopper" observation plane at Shepard Field, Texas, 1944 (McKay Collection)

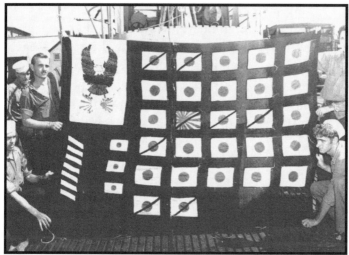

USS SNOOK:
Bob Burdick
(top) was lost at
sea with the
Snook. Left, crew
with battleflag.

Snook, SS 279, a sub that had a tremendous battle record of sinking Japanese ships. Five months before the end of the war it sailed into the midst of a Japanese fleet and the sub and all hands aboard disappeared. His wife never knew what happened to him and waited for five years until the War Department declared him dead.

Bob Jones was one of he passing halfbacks on our high school championship football team. He enlisted in the Royal Canadian Air Force and piloted a fighter plane during the Battle of Britain. He later transferred to the American Army Air Corps and was killed flying.

Bob Blackman enlisted in the RCAF and fought over England and Europe. He too transferred to the U S Army Air Corps and was shot down over the Philippines.

Charles Pausner, was a member of my college "Fighting Forty." He graduated as a second lieutenant in the Field Artillery, and was killed as a replacement officer during the "Battle of the Bulge."

Bob Board and I climbed Yosemite's Mt. Lyell during a summer vacation in 1942. The climb was difficult, but was the last mountain either of us were ever to climb. Bob had his knee crushed during the Philippine Invasion, and I was injured in Europe.

CHAPTER 13

The Ricard Memorial Observatory

A Bridge Across Time

Philip R. Kesten

The Ricard Memorial Observatory at Santa Clara University has a rich and curious history. The building has stood as a Santa Clara landmark for over half a century. The telescope housed in its main dome is famous in its own right and found its way to the Santa Clara campus by a circuitous route. And the man after whom the observatory is named, Fr. Jerome Sixtus Ricard, remains a colorful figure in early days of the South Bay region.

The Man

Fr. Jerome Sixtus Ricard came to California from France in the 1870s. By 1890 the Jesuit priest was teaching philosophy and mathematics at Santa Clara, then Santa Clara College. Ricard had already developed a strong interest in astronomy, and by 1890 had installed an 8-inch telescope in a lean-to building with a roll-off roof. It was to be the first of three observatories on the school's campus.

Fr. Ricard's observations quickly became focused on the sun and sunspots in particular. He built a second observatory in the small vineyard on the south side of the Santa Clara campus to house a telescope and also a heliostat, a device that reflects the sun's rays continuously in a fixed direction using a rotating mirror system. This building, a single cylindrical room topped by a dome with a sliding shutter, still stands today.

By the early 1900s Fr. Ricard had gained a sizable reputation in the popular press for his theories linking sunspots and weather. Dubbed "The Padre of the Rains" for his claim to be able to predict rainfall a month in advance — highly desirable in a region so heavily dependent on agriculture — Ricard was looked on by many as a local celebrity. His popularity grew even after his theories were proven unfounded by scientific study.

In the early 1920s the Knights of Columbus led a fund-raising campaign to honor Fr. Ricard with the construction of a large, new observatory to be built near the heliostat building. Groundbreaking took place in 1925, and three years later a handsome building similar in scale and amenities to the professional observatories of the time was completed. The Ricard Memorial Observatory features a large central dome flanked on each side by a wing topped by a smaller dome. Rising to meet each dome is a poured concrete pier with footings in the subbasement to support whatever telescope might be installed.

And what telescopes indeed! Fr. Ricard had a grand dream for the main telescope, a 26-inch refractor to rival the 36-inch instrument at Lick Observatory on nearby Mt. Hamilton. Early on, however, some in the astronomical community argued that a mirror-based telescope — a reflector — was a more modern and practical device than the traditional refractor with its ground glass lenses at either end of a long tube. Both systems offer advantages and disadvantages, but at that time, the most significant issue was the weight of the optical elements. Because a lens can only be supported at its edges, a piece of glass of even modest size sags under its own weight. This distorts the shape of the glass and, therefore, the images formed using it. Mirrors, however, can be supported from behind, minimizing sag and distortion.

In the end, Fr. Ricard was swayed, and the decision was made to build a telescope with 60-inch diameter mirror. Such a telescope would have been on par with the best in the world, identical to the 60-inch one at the Mt. Wilson Observatory in southern California and not far behind the largest telescope in the world, the 100-inch reflector also on Mt. Wilson. The 100-inch telescope had been built in 1918, only a few years before Ricard was creating the plans for Santa Clara's observatory.

So it was that Fr. Ricard made arrangements to have a 60-inch mirror fabricated. He selected a private individual in Vancouver to do the work, a decision he later regretted. After years of delay, a large, heavy crate arrived from Vancouver at the docks in San Francisco. Inside, however, was only a five-foot in diameter slab of concrete. Some believe that the mirror maker tried but wasn't up to the task; others say his plan from the first was outright sham. In either case, after the crate was delivered he disappeared without a trace. The construction of the Observatory had been completed... a glorious building with no telescope inside. Fr. Ricard died not long afterwards, without seeing his dream realized.

FR. RICARD, S.J., with an earlier telescope in the 1920s. (McKay Collection)

The Telescope

The main dome of the Ricard Memorial Observatory sat empty for nearly 13 years. A telescope befitting the size and stature of the dome and building was finally installed in 1941. The story of its journey to Santa Clara was a circuitous and curious one. Built in 1882 in Cambridge, Massachusetts, the telescope was used first in Rochester, New York, moved to a mountain top in southern California, and then sat in storage for over twelve years before Santa Clara purchased it in 1941.

The saga of Santa Clara's telescope starts in upstate New York about 1880, with Lewis Swift the central figure. Swift owned a hardware store and was a dedicated amateur astronomer. He had discovered a number of comets, for which he was made a Fellow of the Royal Astronomical Society and became highly sought-after as a

public speaker. The people of Rochester took great pride in their
local "Professor" — Swift had been awarded an honorary Ph.D. from
the University of Rochester — and a movement arose to create an
observatory from which Swift could continue his observations.

There would be no small telescope for the city of Rochester! An
order was placed with Alvan Clark and Sons of Cambridge,
Massachusetts, the leading telescope makers of the time, for a 16-inch
refracting telescope. When it was completed in 1882, the 16-inch
Clark was the fourth largest in the world. With it, Swift more than
doubled his own catalog of discovered comets.

The weather in Rochester, however, is not well suited for
astronomical observation. Over the decade or so after the 16-inch
Clark was installed, Swift became increasingly unhappy with the poor
viewing conditions. He knew of the big, new observatories being
developed in California and had been greatly impressed by his visit to
the Lick Observatory.   (Lick's primary telescope at that time was the
younger but larger "sibling" of his own, a 36-inch Alvan Clark
refractor.)   Thus, when his primary sponsor's business collapsed, Swift
packed up his telescope and moved west.

For Swift, "west" was to be a summit of Echo Mountain, now
known at Mt. Lowe. Swift had met Thaddeus Lowe on an earlier trip
to California, and Lowe had persuaded him to join him in his efforts
to create a resort city on Echo Mountain. Lowe had earned a
national reputation as a balloonist — who were viewed then in much
that same way that astronauts are today — and as Abraham Lincoln's
appointed head of the civilian Balloonist Corp during the Civil War.
An inventor and eccentric, Lowe invested his entire fortune creating
a small city on Echo Mountain, complete with residences and
gardens, hotels, and even a casino. Lowe, an amateur astronomer
himself, envisioned a top-flight observatory as an inducement to bring
people up the mountain on the railway he had built.

Patterned to some extent on the first observatory constructed on
nearby Mt. Wilson, the Lowe Observatory was completed in 1894.
Swift continued his observations there until about 1900, and after his
retirement, other astronomers carried out scientific work with the 16-
inch Clark until 1928, when a disastrous windstorm blew the
observatory down. The telescope was saved, but nothing else
remained. The Pacific Electric Company, which had purchased the

resort and the railway from Lowe some years before, put the telescope into storage.

The Ricard Memorial Observatory

And thus it was that the story of Fr. Ricard and the story of Lewis Swift became entangled. In 1941, representatives of the Santa Clara University, then the University of Santa Clara, learned that the Southern Pacific Railway Company had a venerable but powerful telescope in its holdings. Southern Pacific had acquired it through mergers and dealings between the various California rail companies. The university purchased the 16-inch for $2,000, only a fraction of Alvan Clark's original price back in 1882.

The telescope and the observatory saw only limited use in the 1940s and 1950s. In the early 1960s a group of motivated students motorized the dome and its shutters. They also added motors to turn the telescope to follow the motion of stars across the night sky, replacing Alvan Clark's weight-driven system. With the facility modernized to permit easier use, interest in the observatory grew, and through the early 1970s, Santa Clara students sponsored regular viewing nights, often attended by hundreds of people both from the university and general public.

The observatory went dark in 1975. For budgetary reasons, and because university officials believed that growing light pollution of the Santa Clara Valley precluded observations of any useful quality, student access to the domes was denied and all astronomical activity in the building ceased. Because of the perseverance of a new group of students, however, permission to re-open the observatory for astronomy was granted in 1991. In the fall of that year, the university celebrated the renewal of this extraordinary campus resource with "See Stars!," a day of festivities highlighted by an address by Dr. Steven Hawley, astronaut and Associate Director of NASA Ames.

Throughout the 1990s and up to the present, student and faculty continued the work required to modernize and renovate the telescope, its control system, and the observatory. A series of grants allowed the addition of new lenses and a professional-grade digital camera, or CCD array. Although the seeing — as astronomers say — isn't nearly as good as on nearby Mt. Hamilton or at the professional observatories on, for example, Mauna Kea in Hawaii, the new optics and camera permits real scientific research to be carried out.

What about the light pollution that shut down the observatory in 1975? As it happens, the arrangement of the long tube and lenses of Alvan Clark's 16-inch telescope tends to send light that does not originate in the exact direction of the telescope off to the side. That means that bright objects, in particular those in our own solar system, can be studied quite well. In a curious twist of fate, had Fr. Ricard's 60-inch refractor materialized, the different arrangement of tube and optical elements would have rendered it nearly useless next to the bright lights of a city the size of 21st-century San José.

Science!

Perhaps the most spectacular astronomical event in recent memory is the collision of fragments of comet Shoemaker-Levy 9 with Jupiter in 1994. Every powerful ground-based and satellite-based telescope in the world was trained on Jupiter to observe the event. Although the event was interesting to amateurs, there was little likelihood that any of the smaller telescopes could contribute in a meaningful way to the research effort.

The coincidental orientation of the impacts, however, left one opening for observers such as those at Santa Clara University. Every one of the large chunks of comet that had been tracked for a year before the collisions smashed into the planet on the far side from earth. For that reason, ground-based telescopes could only see the effects of a collision after Jupiter turned enough on its axis to allow the impact region to come into view. There was no reason to believe, however, that smaller pieces of the comet, too dim to have been seen from earth, might not be strung out in space behind the larger ones.

Scientists at the Jet Propulsion Laboratory (JPL) in Pasadena predicted that the path of the comet would intersect the earth-facing side of Jupiter about seven days after the last large impact. For this reason, a member of the Santa Clara faculty and a team of students began taking images of Jupiter starting seven days after the last observed impact. While most of the astronomy world was eagerly analyzing the spectacular images and data collected during the predicated collisions, the Santa Clara team recorded nearly 1500 images of Jupiter during a four-day stretch — one image every 12 seconds for all the time Jupiter was visible.

Careful analysis of the Jupiter images revealed a curiosity. On three successive frames, a small bright spot is visible near the edge or limb of the planet, in the exact region predicted by the JPL scientists. In the scientific paper detailing the analysis, the team provided various explanations for this "transient feature," perhaps a cloud in Jupiter's atmosphere or an inadvertent speck caused by the digital camera. But another possibility could not be discounted: that using the hundred-year-old Alvan Clark telescope, a team at Santa Clara University was the only group to observe a comet collision directly from earth. No small feat for a small observatory!

Full circle

In 1882, only a few years after the founding of the school that is now Santa Clara University, Lewis Swift patiently scanned the night sky over Rochester, New York for evidence of undiscovered comets. Over one hundred years later, 3000 miles away but using the same telescope, a team from Santa Clara University watched as a comet met its demise in a fiery impact with Jupiter. With its historic telescope and eccentric history, the Ricard Memorial Observatory is truly a bridge across time.

References Consulted

Bates, Ralph and Blake McKelvey, "Lewis Swift, The Rochester Astronomer," *Rochester History* Vol. IX No. 1, January 1947.

Briggs, John W., "The Santa Clara Telescope Fiasco," unpublished, 1989.

Evans, Charles M., "Air War Over Virginia," *Civil War Times Illustrated*, Vol. 35 No. 5, October 1996.

Hurthere, John, "Ricard Memorial Observatory — 16-inch Clark Refractor," presented at the National Meeting of the Antique Telescope Society, Madison, Wisconsin, 1994.

Rippens, Paul, "Professor T.S.C. Lowe and his Mountain Observatory," *Echo Mountain Echoes* Vol. 3 No.4, Winter 1998.

Watson, Warren, "The People's Astronomer," *Upstate Magazine (Rochester Sunday Democrat and Chronicle)*, January 15, 1984.

Viloria, Theresa, "Out of Mothballs After 18 Years," *San José Mercury News*, July 17, 1991.

CHAPTER 14

City of Santa Clara Sesquicentennial
Ground Zero for Silicon Valley
The Last Fifty Years: A Personal Perspective
Lorie Garcia and Patricia Mahan

The City of Santa Clara, in 2001, may indeed be Silicon Valley Central, and "Ground Zero" may mean the city was at the start of the high-tech, high-flying, high-cost world we live in today. But fifty years ago, Santa Clara was a cozy town with an old-fashioned downtown, surrounded by orchards and agriculture. "Ground Zero" may, in fact, allude to the destruction of that town, wrought by the rapid changes since World War II.

A 1930s aerial photograph reveals Santa Clara as a small town with streets laid out in a grid pattern, fruit packing plants at the town's edge, the railroad tracks defining its north and east boundaries, and miles of orchards and farms to the north and west. The downtown could have come from Henry James: modest, locally owned shops lined both sides of Franklin Street; City Hall dominated one corner, the Bank of America another; the sidewalks bustled with folks going about their daily business. The hard-packed dirt streets served gasoline-powered motorcars and horse-drawn carts alike. With the coming of World War II, however, the industrial and economic needs of the times precipitated changes in Santa Clara — changes that would prove fundamental and drastic.

Just prior to World War II, Moffett Field was established in Santa Clara Valley, to the north of the City of Santa Clara. The naval air base required large numbers of military and support personnel for its operation; at the same time, the war effort demanded developments in aeronautics and new technologies. The people needed housing; the blossoming aeronautics industries needed workers. Like magnets, the towns surrounding Moffett Field, including Santa Clara, drew thousands of people; after the war, the people stayed, the industries expanded beyond military applications, and the growth became unstoppable. From a population of 6,650 in 1940, Santa Clara grew to 9,839 people by the end of the war, then to 11,702 in 1950. The 1952 population count jumped again to 15,800, a twenty-seven percent increase in only two years. During these years, the County of Santa Clara grew at double the rate of the State of California.

The growth of population created a need for land growth as well, and not just in Santa Clara. The early 1950s witnessed a disorderly, avaricious land-grabbing frenzy in most of the cities and towns in Santa Clara County — and nowhere was it worse than in the "Annexation Wars" between Santa Clara and the City of San José, the so-called "silver-backed gorilla" to the east. In 1954, Santa Clara annexed 174 acres in the outlying area north of today's Central Expressway, and zoned this prime agricultural land for industrial development. The Owens-Corning Company built its manufacturing plant in this area, becoming one of Santa Clara's first heavy industrial uses. The land north of the city continued to be the focus of its industrial growth. The orchards to the west of the town were surrendering to large housing tracts built in the suburban ranch style — rambling, single-story homes, with two-car garages, on large lots. Some orchardists saw the future clearly — such as the gentleman who swapped his pear orchard for acres in the Sacramento Valley in a land deal with Intel Corporation. Others hung on in the face of mounting pressures from development, until their orchards were surrounded by houses and could no longer be sustained. Meanwhile, on the city's eastern and southern borders, the annexation wars raged, in a fight with San José to incorporate land, in many cases, block by block. This resulting "cherry stem" approach to annexation — where land not directly contiguous to the cities' borders was acquired in pockets which protruded into the neighboring city — left San José and Santa Clara with ragged adjoining borders, and another page in the continuing saga of conflict between the cities.

Throughout this time, Santa Clara's downtown remained intact,

impervious to the modern influences which were fueling the city's
breakneck expansion to the north and west. School-age children still
walked safely to Toledo's grocery store to buy candy and ice-cream on
hot, boring Saturday afternoons. University Electric displayed the
latest household appliances on well-oiled wood floors; Wilson's Bakery
sold breads and pastries freshly baked that morning; Genova's
Delicatessen packaged sliced prosciutto and mortadella in an
atmosphere redolent with homemade ravioli. Twenty-five cents
bought a viewer entrance to the double feature showing at the Santa
Clara Theater. Neighbors greeted one another on the sidewalks and
merchants extended credit on a handshake. The imposing Federal
Post Office Building on Jackson Street landmarked the center of
downtown.

In the late fifties and early sixties, the housing subdivisions were
as likely to abut an orchard or a creek as anything else, and dug-up
dirt fields separated blocks of homes and nearby streets, as the vacant
lots of obliterated orchards awaited concrete foundations and tilt-up
framing. Children played in these empty tracts, the mounds of dirt
transformed in to "Bicycle Hill" for arduous climbs up and thrilling
rides down. Polliwogs and frogs abounded in the creeks, and it was
child's play indeed to sneak over the back fence and into the water to
catch them.

The changes that would transform Santa Clara, some argue not
for the better, began in earnest with the formation of its
Redevelopment Agency in 1957 and the adoption of its first General
Plan in 1959. Federal redevelopment money was readily and
generously available; and "urban renewal" was the modern by-word in
city planning. The 1959 General Plan called for the ultimate
demolition of more than 30 square blocks in the heart of Santa Clara,
including all of its downtown. In their place, the plan called for
development of a modern shopping mall ringed with garden
apartments suitable for elegant urban living, surrounded by duplexes
and stucco family residences. Ten city blocks were actually cleared —
City Hall destroyed, the old downtown demolished, many historic
family homes razed. The ambitious shopping center plan was gutted
when the major department stores opted to locate on a large open
parcel on the eastern edge of Stevens Creek Boulevard — today's
Valley Fair Shopping Town. City Hall was moved near the El Camino

Real and a separate Police Administration Building was built. Ultimately, the city built Franklin Mall on three square blocks of the scorched area. Grass-roots opposition stalled the remainder of the 1959 plan, and the leveled blocks adjacent to the mall lay vacant and weed-infested for more than twenty years. Only the grand old Post Office building remains of the downtown. As one displaced resident put it, "When I go into Rainbow Travel offices, I'm standing in my own living room." The story of Santa Clara's "Civil War" still rankles; a vintage headline from the San José Mercury News states it well: "Santa Clara Wants Back Its Heart."

At the time downtown was being irrevocably lost, the main thoroughfare of the El Camino Real was being developed as the city's new retail area. Around 1965, a new establishment opened to the delight of teenagers wanting a place to hang out, after buying a hamburger, french fries and a Coke for fifty cents. The garish Golden Arches of this first MacDonald's in the area heralded the future of Santa Clara's commercial development. It foreshadowed El Camino's future as a strip of fast food restaurants, low-end motels, used auto dealers and service stations, dotted with multi-tenant shopping plazas, dominated by large "anchors," like the early Grant's Department Store and Lucky Foods. North of the city, industry continued to develop; although nearer to Alviso, the area was largely wetlands and open fields. Tobacco weed, cattails and Queen Anne's lace bordered the banks of the Guadalupe River and the creeks feeding it. Routinely and almost predictably, the waters of these streams flooded the marshes alongside. The land ended at the southernmost tip of San Francisco Bay, in salt marshes bountiful with native flora and fauna. Shrimping was still done in small boats out of Alviso's port and burrowing owls ranged far and wide over the fields.

The destiny of the city's northernmost area pivoted on the building of Memorex. Built on seventeen acres in 1971, the development brought to Santa Clara a new concept — a high-tech "campus" of many interrelated buildings serving the needs of a single company for headquarter offices, research and development, and product manufacturing. The idea of "clean" industry was attractive to the city: it allowed the development of manufacturing uses which had less impact on land, air, water, and waste than most of the heavy, post-war industries. The city actively pursued these new high-tech businesses, and, in turn, the companies embraced Santa Clara. It offered ample available, buildable land, good water supplies, and low electrical rates from its municipally-owned utilities. The area boomed, bringing jobs and a sound, rich tax base to the city. The decade between 1977 and 1987 saw the building of Intel, Fairchild, National Semiconductor, Hewlett Packard and others. By the 1990s, the city encompassed 19.3 square miles, had more than 100,000 residents housed in 44,000 dwelling units, and, significantly, had a daytime population of 140,000 workers. The impacts of this growth transfigured the topography and natural environment forever. Bunker-like levies channel the river and creeks; office buildings cover the filled-in wetlands; the last of the vast fields have disappeared. Species of native birds and animals relocate (willingly or otherwise) to areas remote from the city. Even the city dump is closed and a municipal golf course built atop its capped land.

Ironically, like most other cities in Silicon Valley, Santa Clara has become a victim of its own success. Nightmarish traffic problems plague every major road, as thousands of employees travel into, out of, and through the city between home and work. The shortage of housing, a problem in itself, causes pricing beyond value, and puts the American dream out of reach for many people working in the area. Forced to buy affordable homes in cities as far as a hundred miles away, these daily commuters add to the traffic congestion. Our natural environment, once the valley's primary attraction, has been irretrievably altered, as open space becomes scarce, air and water quality diminishes, and intense development congests our valley. The city now searches for innovative ways to increase affordable housing and to balance the economic interests of growth with the needs of its residents for decent, affordable homes, clean air and water, and an environment that provides natural beauty and protection of wildlife. In the new millennium, the City of Santa Clara stands again at Ground Zero, with opportunities to preserve the city's history, as embodied in its historic homes and buildings, to support affordable housing with redevelopment funds and special programs, to acquire open space for public use. Physical growth of the city is now impossible; in-fill development and redevelopment must afford the chance to grow in new ways — by spending in ways that add value to the lives of our residents, by building in ways that contribute to resolving regional problems, by managing our precious environment in ways that preserve this valley for future generations. The challenges of the city's future are rooted in the successes — and failures — of its past. The next fifty years should prove at least as interesting as the last.

SECTION V
Epilogue
Santa Clara Past and Future

Today, 150 years after the founding of the City of Santa Clara and Santa Clara University, and just 225 years since the establishment of Mission Santa Clara, Santa Clara stands at the center of the economic world. It is a polyglot society with a new social order, ideas, and technologies. It is a fast paced world epitomized in Moore's Law for Technological Change wherein it only requires 25 years to do what took 200 in the past. For generations who grew up with life dictated by seasonal cycles the past quarter of a century has been numbing. How does a community or a university plan for change in such a volatile setting, a pace that is so fast, and so, complete that to imagine life in Santa Clara in 2012 is difficult and for the bicentennial, impossible.

Santa Clara is a precious place. Children born this year will be making the decisions that will shape tomorrow. Let's hope that the lessons we teach and the legacy we leave will help them. Their answers may lie in their ability to reflect and learn from the past, cherish traditions, and always grasp for ideals.

CHAPTER 15

The Mission Bell's Toll

Michael S. Malone

In the frenetic world of Silicon Valley, where the daily obsession is to shave a microsecond from every transmission, revision, and decision, a vital lesson about time lies unnoticed. As we spend billions struggling to glimpse just one product generation ahead, a prophecy about our future lies with two Ohlone Indian skulls buried to the eyeballs, cranium down, in a box of rice.

At the very heart of Silicon Valley sits Santa Clara University, an oasis of adobe buildings and gardens surrounded by a sea of industrial parks and suburban housing developments.

And at the university's heart, literally and emotionally, is Mission Santa Clara, founded by the Franciscan order in 1777.

Around the mission lie rose gardens, wisteria walks, and one old adobe wall. Each tells a story. But the story told by the rose garden is the most terrible. There, beneath the thorns, and yellow and salmon and red petals, trapped within the deep and gnarled roots, are the skeletons of an untold number of Ohlone Indians, young and old, victims of smallpox and chicken pox, mumps and measles...but most of all, victims of the passage from one era to the next. They are the first valleyites to be sacrificed to the unforgiving passage of time.

The Ohlones ruled the valley for several thousand years. Yet now all that remains of them is a few dusty fragments tucked away in Tupperware bins in the abandoned football team locker room. There, in the remotest building on campus, archaeologist Russell Skowronek manages a staff of two assistants and five student volunteers as they

---

Reprinted by permission of Forbes ASAP Magazine © 1998 Forbes Inc.

race to save the artifacts from the oblivion of asphalt parking lots and poured concrete foundations. What they have found and cataloged is the detritus of America's manufacturing history, a rag-and-bone shop of early California culture: a poker chip, slate pencil, crockery toy marble, shriveled peach pits, the lower half of a glass mustard container, and other shattered and yellowed objects pulled from university grounds and the remains of a privy from a forgotten Santa Clara tannery. And, shockingly, the pair of Ohlone skulls in the desiccant. Sitting in the university's faculty club, Skowronek anxiously stirs his coffee. An energetic man with a long mustache, he speaks quickly, like a man used to not being heard.

"We're sitting right now on ground zero of the modern computer age," he says. "You already knew that. But what you didn't know is that it started 220 years ago."

Skowronek smiles. "Let me explain. Before 1777 the Ohlone Indians lived in a cyclical world. It hadn't changed in 10,000 years, not since the last Ice Age. There was really no sense of time being linear, only circular. The seasons came and went. You hunted or you planted. It was not a time-based world. In fact, despite our arrogance about how much better our lives are today, we estimate that it took only one adult Ohlone just 20 hours per week to feed and shelter his or her family."

It was not a long life, Skowronek continues, nor an especially complex one. The Ohlone lived in clans that rarely interacted — except for the occasional fight or marriage — with neighboring clans just a half mile away. With little east-west trade, clans that lived just a mile from San Francisco Bay might never eat a fish or a clam but instead subsisted largely on deer and on acorns pounded into meal. The early European explorers of the region were frustrated when the guide from one clan would lead them only as far as the next stream and then refuse to go on in fear of losing his life.

"It all ended in January 1777, with the founding of the mission," says Skowronek. "Suddenly, the Ohlone found themselves in time. Western European time. Life at the mission was run by the bell. You got up, ate, prayed, worked, and signed off the day at midnight with the bell. And from the moment the mission bell rang for the first time, the clocks of Santa Clara Valley began — and they kept going faster every year."

It wasn't just the priests who were trapped in this time but the Ohlone as well. Having lived millennia without time, they had no resistance to the temporal march ringing each day from the mission tower.

Mission Santa Clara soon became the locus for all activity in the valley. Suddenly, clans that hadn't moved more than five miles in 500 years were crossing ancient boundaries and making regular visits to the mission to trade. Many chose to stay and live near the mission grounds. Stunted for generations, trade soon flourished, as did communications between clans. For the first time the Ohlone became a distinct tribe but in the process gave up the 50 subdialects and unique styles of family artisanship that had long distinguished them. Their arts and languages hybridized into single, common forms. In listening to the time bell, the Ohlone had embarked on a path from which there was no going back.

The Ohlone's vulnerability to the bell was emblematic of a lack of resistance to many things Western, most horribly contagion. In the first three decades of the mission's existence, hundreds of Ohlone died from epidemics of childhood diseases to which they had no immunity. Those baptized were buried in what is now the rose garden. But many others died from less obvious causes that nevertheless were tied to the Western European pattern of time: diet, overwork, industrial accidents, medicine, and the stress of living in a timed world.

"This new world not only changed the pace of the valley but even its look," says Skowronek. "The daily demands of commerce, faith, and schooling meant you had to build more and more buildings and homes. That meant roof tiles and adobe bricks, and that in turn meant kilns. And kilns meant charcoal, and that meant oak trees. And that deforested the valley floor, which meant no more acorns for the Ohlone. From now on they had no choice but to eat a Western diet and live a Western life."

By 1827 and the end of the valley's first modern era, Santa Clara Mission was home to 1,462 people. Spanish was now the lingua franca.

Tens of thousands of cattle roamed the valley floor, and the first vineyards were planted near the mission. Alta California, because of its unique location on the Pacific Rim, also rapidly became a center for trade in a global economy: The priests wore silk vestments from

China, and mission residents regularly bought items imported from Acapulco and Mexico City, the Philippines, Spain, and even England.

The second revolution in valley life, which occurred in the decade after 1845, was as profound as the first, and it teaches the same lessons. One is that technological change not only produces wholly new types of products but it also forces the reorganization of the society around it. Furthermore, this reorganization is not just structural but temporal. Its participants physically and culturally restructure the world and society, and inhabit an irrevocably new timescape with its own unique rhythms and cycles.

The third lesson is the most disturbing: When a society encounters such a point of inflection, it divides into two groups. One group, usually the majority, which cannot or will not cross over to the new world, is lost. The other, the minority that does cross over, to be joined by the next generation and new arrivals, establishes a new identity so complete as to erase all traces of the people they were before.

"You see it at the mission during the first half of the 19th century," says Skowronek. "You start out with 50 clans, and almost overnight they become Ohlone Indians. Then come the Catalonian Spanish priests and the mestizo soldiers. Before long, they are Californians. Then, in the 1840s, the Anglos arrive. They are squatters — at least until the Bear Flag Revolt and the gold rush. Then they become 'pioneers.' "It would be easy to say these are merely changes in nomenclature, mixed with some public relations. But in fact, these name changes represent a fundamental transformation. These before-and-after groups, even when they include the same people, inhabit very different worlds."

No group felt this change more than the Ohlone. The few who had survived the first revolution in time had, within a few years, stopped being Indians and became, in an odd metamorphosis, Mexicans. "Then," says Skowronek, "after U.S. statehood, they became, basically, nothing.

They were disenfranchised, dehumanized. And in response they simply disappeared. They hid as best they could in the ethnic population, losing their Ohlone identity. Their descendants wouldn't emerge again until it was safe, in our time."

Meanwhile, the Spanish/Californians, too, became Mexicans and were largely marginalized as the valley filled with new immigrants — Irish, Italian, Yugoslavian (Americans) — who easily adapted to the new pace of life.

One of these was a German, Jacob Eberhard, who bought a tannery, itself the descendant of a tanning works that was as old as the mission, from his father-in-law. Lasting nearly 170 years until finally closing its doors after the Second World War, the tannery was the most enduring business in valley history. Eberhard brought the latest inventions and consumer products to the factory and his own home. By 1880 his home featured a privy and new Edison lights, and the tannery had become a giant complex of a dozen buildings beneath a towering, belching smokestack. The tannery was a foul-smelling, unpleasant place to work — and wasn't very popular at the new college campus across the street when the wind shifted.

Nevertheless, it was on the cutting edge of American technology in the years after the Civil War. Leather was the plastic, the silicon, of the 19th century, and nobody made it better than Eberhard.

At its peak, the factory shipped 900,000 pounds of cow, calf, and sheep hides throughout the world, most notably to the shoe factories of Lowell, Massachusetts. But Eberhard wasn't just a mass producer of rendered flesh; he produced some of the best saddle leather on the planet, the finest of which became part of a bejeweled, silvered, and gilded $10,000 saddle ordered by the 101 Wild West Show. It was, according to contemporary accounts, "the most beautiful and high-priced saddle in the United States."

The world of the Eberhard Tannery in the 1880s was one of alarm clocks and pocket watches, factory whistles and train schedules. This was the new timescape, and those who could adapt to its regime survived.

Those with a gift for it thrived. Once again, the new time transformed the landscape. An added level of complexity had been bolted to the manufacturing process.

Now there was a hierarchy of order processing, from customer to retailer to distributor to manufacturer to supplier (like Eberhard) and back again. This system demanded the rapid transfer of information and material, and soon the valley was crisscrossed with telegraph wires and railroad tracks. And where they and the cattle ranches met, towns appeared. The mission faded in importance to the commercial centers of the valley. Increasingly, the mission became an object of nostalgia for the past, not a part of the active present.

The valley floor itself was now one vast cattle ranch, with the last of the great oak trees felled or killed by grazing.

Living in hovels, the surviving ancient Ohlones died out. Meanwhile, in 1881 Martin Murphy Jr., founder of what is now Sunnyvale and owner of most of the ranch land in the valley — indeed, the largest private landowner in the world — celebrated his golden wedding anniversary by inviting the entire state to a party. An arrogant man celebrated not just his own wealth and power but also the victory of the industrial world. Trains were chartered from around the state; hundreds of cattle were slaughtered. Eberhard was there, as were all of the successful businessmen of Santa Clara Valley. This was their moment, the high watermark of their era.

Yet even as they were celebrating, that era was coming to an end.

Within a decade the cattle ranches would almost be gone, replaced by miles of fruit trees. Technology had once again sped up the clock.

Thanks to artesian wells and water pumps, mass production, marketing, and reliable railroads and highways, Santa Clara Valley was now the Valley of Heart's Delight, with the most prosperous orchards in the nation. The valley moved on corporate time, the punch clock, and the Taylor Method: In the vast new Del Monte and Libby canneries, workers were shown time-motion films on how to cut apricots and boil cherries and pit prunes.

The flats of goods were wrapped in colorful promotional labels, sold according to Chicago Board of Options Exchange prices, and shipped by rail to markets in Minneapolis and Manhattan.

The children of the deceased Martin Murphy and Jacob Eberhard now lived in turreted gingerbread homes in downtown San José and sent their well-dressed sons to Santa Clara University and their daughters to the College of Notre Dame. The local towns swelled with the new cannery workers from Portugal and Eastern Europe, who deposited their wages at the new Bank of Italy (soon to be Bank of America).

Mansions now lined the Alameda from the old mission to San José, the very path once taken by the Franciscans.

And in the spring, the streets would whiteout from a blizzard of blowing fruit blossoms. Busy drivers, rushing to work in the new corporate time, complained about the nuisance to city magistrates.

Once again, as time accelerated and the valley floor was transformed, and as the production process grew more subtle and complex, the people again changed. The aging pioneers, now distinguished but anachronistic, were trotted out at museum openings and interviewed by the local paper about how it was in the old days. And thanks to a new generation of writers like Jack London and local publications like Sunset magazine, a cult of nostalgia sprang up, creating an enduring myth of graciousness out of the hard life of the mission era. By the 1920s, houses in a growing number of new valley developments featured walls painted in adobe hue, tile roofs, and even little ersatz bell towers — along with a garage to house that most representative object of the new timescape.

Yet even as the Valley of Heart's Delight was celebrating its newfound luxury, two young men, Bill Hewlett and David Packard, were turning on the switch of their new audio oscillator, in whose high-frequency waves could be heard the squeal of the valley's next era. Then, in 1955, two years after a feeble Eberhard Tannery finally shut its doors, William Shockley, armed with a team of brilliant young men and a Nobel Prize for creating the transistor, returned to his old hometown to reset the clock and, in doing so, annihilate the valley of his childhood. It is a curious fact, long known to biologists, that every animal — from the torpid giant tortoise to the frantic housefly — is given as its birthright about 1 billion heartbeats. Even that cynosure of the ephemeral, the mayfly, gets its 109 as a larva before its brief fling at flight.

Why a billion — 2 at most — and not more? The answer seems to lie in some kind of clock within the cells. It is as if the Almighty, with uncharacteristic democracy, ordained that every species would have its same threescore and ten, the same span of experiences, no matter how quickly or slowly it was forced to live them. Clotho may change the content of each life's thread, but Lachesis always draws out the same length for Atropos to cut. And all of our vast and costly struggles — medicine, nutrition, safety, genetic engineering — to extend this deadly timer will, it seems, at most improve our fateful number of heartbeats by a factor of two.

But in the digital, solid-state world that is the new metronome of valley life, it is a different story. The modern integrated circuit chip will soon be able to perform approximately 1 billion operations per second. One gigahertz. A billion electronic heartbeats: the equivalent of a lifetime in a single second. And, of course, at the end of those billion beats, there won't be a tiny electronic death but another billion-beat second, and another. And, since silicon is incredibly stable and invulnerable to almost everything but cosmic rays, there will be a billion more of these digital lifetimes for each chip — more than all the generations of life on earth — before it goes dark.

This is the new clock, our clock, the timepiece of the valley's digital era. This is the mission bell that tolls quicker than the synapses can arc across our brains, that counts out an eternity of silicon days in the time it takes to blink your eye. And thanks to Moore's Law — that defining rule of our lives and augury of our future superfluity — this new silicon clock will grow faster and faster, doubling in speed every few years, until it too produces whole cosmologies of change that are beyond human comprehension. And what then? What happens when the next clock resets the time once again? Who gets through the next time, and what do they become?

Look at any newspaper, magazine, or television show; surf the Net; shop at the local department store; listen to the words you use in daily speech: Silicon Valley is now the center of the world, the greatest creator of new wealth and employment in human history, the dynamo of innovation transforming the modern world, the creator of a new paradigm that is redefining the way we speak, live our daily lives, even how we see the world. And in this digital universe, Silicon Valley is the new Greenwich: We build the clocks and set the pace; the world revolves around our time. We are sui generis, we are unique in all the world and all of history, we are without precedent, and without end. The '90s have been our golden age — this has been our great party, and we have invited the whole world to attend. We speak knowingly of long booms and perpetual prosperity as if God himself has blessed our good works with immortality.

Yet the lesson of the past is that none of this is new, only the magnitude. In fact, in the 220 years of modern Santa Clara Valley history, there have been three other such eras. Each of them was kicked off by a technological revolution, each of them operated to a different and faster clock, each of them was global in scope, each of them transformed the nature of the valley itself and the self-image of its residents, and each effectively erased all real memory of what came before. And at the moment of each era's greatest arrogance and self-assurance, each was within a decade or two of coming to an end. The clock shifted again and they were as effectively erased as Minos or Carthage. Their children lived in a different world, spoke different words, and bore different names. If the cycles of the past hold, the end of Silicon Valley and of the digital revolution as we know it lies sometime in the years just beyond 2010.

And then? The clocks reset themselves once more, this time perhaps to the speed of nucleotides forming and re-forming a trillion times each second in biological computers, or quantum dots, or perhaps one vast global computer, humming away in 100 billion interconnected computers and chips, bearing all the world's knowledge in a new kind of silicon consciousness.

But whatever the clock, the pace will be unimaginably fast. And under such a blazing discipline, who among us will be able to cross over to the other side? A few will, perhaps our children and our children's children who have spent their entire lives as navigators of cyberspace.

But it is also not hard to imagine that no one, at least no one human, will enter this new world, or the next one that arrives in the final decades of the 21st century.

Who, or more accurately what, will this new era, this new timescape, belong to? Intuitively, we already know: the machines themselves. Chips can live a lifetime in a second, then live a billion lifetimes more. For them the pace of this new clock is almost pastoral. Eventually, anthropomorphic software agents will be our surrogates into this world...until they need us no more. They will in time take over cyberspace as their own universe — real ghosts in the machine. Unlike us, they will be able to change their identities and their roles in microseconds and, thanks to Moore's Law, will grow ever smarter and faster and more capable of dealing with this hyperaccelerated timescape.

Then the tool will become the toolmaker, and perhaps the toolmaker the tool. And the numerous objects of our lives will become the broken relics in some future cyberarchive.

We have entered into a kind of Faustian bargain with time: Just join the world of the clock, and we'll give you progress, we'll give you hope. And medicine. A longer life span. Libraries of knowledge. The ability to reach around the world. And fly to the moon. Just listen for the bell and attend to its call...

We have listened, and we have been rewarded in extraordinary ways.

But it has come at an enormous cost — perhaps none greater than the one that lies ahead. Time is about to speed up again. Soon the pace will leave us behind.

And then, as for the Ohlone, the mission bell may signal the end of our day.

CHAPTER 16

Santa Clara University
2025
Paul Locatelli, S.J.

Not even Hegel could predict the future.
— *paraphrasing Cardinal Hans Urs Von Balthasar*
If then a University is a direct preparation for this world,
let it be what it professes. — *Cardinal John Newman*

As Cardinal Newman urged more than a century ago, we must educate for the world that will be, not one that has already passed into history.[1] When asked to predict what a Santa Clara education will look like in 25 or 50 years, I am reminded that not even Hegel could predict the future. And, one only has to look at the past ten years to realize such a prediction is fraught with uncertainty. With the world community rapidly changing in so many ways, science and technology advancing into new areas, and political economy evolving in new global patterns, educating for contemporary society demands a constant revitalization of the curriculum and pedagogy. Of course, some key underlying principles remain.

Past as Prologue

In the course of its history, Santa Clara has experienced a number of defining moments. These are times when a decision enhanced its fortunes and expanded its vision. The founding of Mission Santa Clara in 1777 on the banks of the Guadalupe River, although charged by some as having a "fatal impact" on the indigenous culture and the lives of native Americans, is one of those moments, as is March 19, 1851. That date marks the founding of Santa Clara College by two intrepid Italian missionaries, Fathers John Nobili and Michael Accolti, who began their missionary work in the Northwest. They came to begin the first institution of higher learning in this raw Gold Rush land of California.

By adding the schools of engineering and law in 1912, Santa Clara College was transformed into a university. In 1926, the school of business opened, and the high school branch of the college moved down the Alameda to become Bellarmine College Preparatory. Another defining date was 1959: the schools of business and engineering began to offer graduate programs that would serve the needs of the growing number of working professionals as the Valley of the Heart's Delight was quickly becoming Silicon Valley. Of course, the fall of 1961 began one of the most transformative periods in the university's history: the formal admission of women into its undergraduate program. (For a few years, women studying nursing at O'Connor Hospital had been taking courses at Santa Clara.) The law school and the graduate programs had already anticipated that move by going co-ed a few years earlier.[2]

The admission of women markedly improved academic quality, in large part by adding a female perspective to the social and intellectual dialogue; it also afforded women the opportunity of a Jesuit education. That sea change parallels the current one that began roughly 10 years ago. Santa Clara began a concerted effort to increase its diversity and enroll more students of color as well as increase the ethnic diversity among the faculty and staff. In the time since then, students of color have increased from less than twenty percent of the student body to close to forty percent of both the undergraduate and graduate programs in 2001.

All of these decisions demarcated Santa Clara's past while enriching its future. Both the past and present help to understand the role that history will play in shaping the Santa Clara of the 21st century. The decisions of today do not stand in isolation from the past or from the future; they will either enhance our Jesuit, Catholic tradition or detract from it; their purpose is at least twofold — to enhance and enrich the excellence of Jesuit education and to ensure this education prepares responsible, moral citizens for contemporary and future society.

A Living Tradition with a Humanistic Orientation.

Nobili and Accolti brought a 300 hundred-year old educational legacy to this valley. Then, as now, academic and moral excellence was indispensable to a Santa Clara education. Ignatius of Loyola, the founder of the Jesuits, would not accept anything less. He was convinced that God was glorified in the search for knowledge, truth and wisdom. He also believed that God and truth could be found not only in monastic solitude, but also in the thick of daily life — in cities and marketplaces, in halls of power and at the intersection of ideas, and among the poor.

Santa Clara can be proud of its history. But too frequently when people talk about tradition, they idealize the past and try to hold onto it, to replicate it in the present. In fact, tradition must be vital and dynamic, containing elements of innovation — with a forward looking spirit like that exemplified by Ignatius and our founders. When women were admitted to Santa Clara, some alumni saw this as destructive of its tradition. Others saw it as an enhancement and development of tradition, as Santa Clara sought to reflect in fullness the society it hopes to serve.

Tradition is as much about the future as it is history. Decisions are made, they pass into history, but they affect the future. Tradition, then, is a living reality that incorporates creativity into the every peak and valley of the university, particularly in quality of learning. Understanding tradition means educating for the contemporary world, not for some past time or place.

The rapidly changing world places new obligations upon our curriculum and pedagogy. Our location at the heart of Silicon Valley, for example, is an ever-present reminder that we must integrate the latest technologies into a humanistic education. Conversely, in this rapidly changing world, we must temper technology and the professions with ethical and humanistic principles.

In this context, we must constantly ask ourselves: how should Santa Clara change to meet the needs of a 21st-century society? What will tradition at Santa Clara look like two generations from now? How have changes of the past 50 years influenced the Santa Clara education of tomorrow?

Then, as now, a Santa Clara education is humanistic in

orientation, but its meaning has expanded. More narrowly defined in the past, a humanistic education emphasized the arts and sciences, and saw eloquence and rhetoric as qualities of an educated person. In 1951, the emphasis was even more narrowly focused on knowledge of the arts and humanities. Today, science and technology have greater emphasis, and there is a conscious commitment to the development of the skills needed to think and act critically, morally, creatively about our world. This perspective led to changing the curricular requirement from a course in both scholastic philosophy and theology each term to a liberal arts, humanistic core. The aim is to provide students with the ability to ask the question, "How can I fashion a more humane society?" The pedagogy for learning how to ask and act on such a vision is in one of our guiding principles: learning to integrate rigorous inquiry, creative imagination, reflective engagement with society, and a commitment to fashioning a more humane and just world.

New Pedagogies of Engagement and Literacy

The way students learn will continue to change in a number of ways. Student learning will include greater collaboration between students and faculty, through which students will become engaged in their own learning and in research. This will lead to a greater emphasis on active learning which integrates rigorous analysis and reflective experience.

Learning at its best will engage the reality of the world. Community-based learning means an academic pursuit that integrates community experience with structured academic reflection. Students learn to learn with and from people, particularly those with different class and cultural backgrounds, to gain a deeper and broader understanding of the subject matter and an enhanced sense of civic responsibility.

In both collaborative and community-based learning, an interactive learning process benefits students, faculty and the community. The students of the future must move from the simple acquisition of knowledge to developing the skills to use that knowledge, by being engaged with reality, for the benefit of the world. It is the difference, for example, between knowing about physics and being a physicist, knowing about art and being an artist, knowing about law and being a lawyer, and the list goes on. In any field of study then, the student will benefit by learning with and from their professors, peers, and members of the community.

What remains constant is the need to think critically and creatively, but the understanding of literacy has been expanded as new ways of learning have emerged. At Santa Clara's centennial in 1951, learning was limited to verbal literacy in all disciplines, including the sciences, mathematics, and engineering. That emphasis shifted first to include visual literacy with the introduction of television and now digital literacy to reflect the changes in technology. Students today must learn to balance and connect verbal, visual, and digital literacy.

Verbal literacy was more individually focused, with the ability to read and analyze texts as the path to learning. Somewhat oversimplifying the case, education was seen as what students would learn from books and lectures and discussion in the classroom. Today, this is insufficient as the emphasis has shifted to learning that includes reading, watching, using the Internet, and debating as a learning community; in some cases, that learning community incorporates the broader community.

Digital literacy means more than knowing how to acquire information from the internet; it must have a social dimension. Using information technology is a means to an end where learning will continue to become even more group-oriented and socially organized, as John Seely Brown and Paul Duguid point out in their illuminating book, *The Social Life of Information*.[3] The intellectual life will continue to emphasize a variety of skills, and in this context, Santa Clara's emphasis on "compassion" becomes even more relevant for the future. The life of the mind does not simply focus on the acquisition of knowledge but what one does with that knowledge as we face and solve the great questions challenging our world.

A Faith Commitment Leading to Social Justice.

In general, a Jesuit education has always stressed the education of the whole person, intellectually and emotionally, spiritually and physically. At Santa Clara's centennial in 1951, educating the whole person focused on the individual, the development of the person as a responsible, ethical "citizen" for the greater glory of God.

Today, Jesuit education has expanded its horizons. The shift is from a personal quest to stressing the relationship of the individual to the world, including a concern and preferential option for the most marginalized of society. The new quest focused more on making the *community* whole, not merely the person. Fr. Peter-Hans Kolvenbach, the superior of the Society of Jesus, challenges us to the new ideal of a well-educated solidarity with the real world.[4] This notion of solidarity also echoes Pope John Paul II's Eastern European experience before he became pope. The accent balances and integrates the community and individual such that one's personal good is inextricably bound with the common good. The question, "How should I live?", has become "How should all of us live together in this time and place?" The moral dimension asks further, "How will we address the great problems of life, such as poverty, the growing gap between rich and poor, and human rights in our nation and throughout the world?"

This larger perspective of educating the whole person of solidarity in the real world means educating for justice — a justice emerging from our commitment to society and to faith. This view preserves the original principle of St. Ignatius of Loyola to integrate learning with living to leaven society for good and for the greater glory of God but takes our commitment of 'faith doing social justice' to center stage in the new world. Our faith commitment demands promoting social justice, which means both undergraduates and graduates will learn to address new and changing questions, for example, of global and local human rights, ecology, discrimination, dignity of the poor, and ignorance.

Santa Clara's moral and religious imperative remains clear. Ethical reasoning and ethical actions will continue to be important but, like learning itself, will require greater connection to the great questions about contemporary questions and problems. For Santa Clara, faith serves as the wellspring of our ethical and social justice principles; genuine faith require us to engage in rational interreligious dialogue. Ideally, dialogue will connect rather than separate people of different faith traditions.

Santa Clara believes that for one to develop the "right" relationship with God, the biblical definition of justice, one must have "right" relationships with people. One cannot establish a right relationship with God and be indifferent to the injustices of this world. In fact, having the right relationship with other people in all walks of life will measure our relationship with God. Justice and ethics, then, have both a social and a faith dimension. This is where the university's commitment to educating for conscience will play a greater and greater part because as our world becomes more and more complex, so will the ethical and moral dilemmas we face.

A New and Changing World

Two trends that will continue to influence education are technology and globalization. On the front edge of the 21st century, technology is in its early stage of development. In a few decades we have seen the rapid development of integrated circuits, the microprocessor and personal computer, and the internet. Each of these developments changed the nature of learning, providing, for example, greater access to knowledge, pedagogical tools for learning, and a new form of literacy. New waves of innovation in technology — mobile internet, biotechnology, and nanotechnology, for example — at this moment are emerging; each development will influence the curriculum and pedagogy. Within a decade, there will be other waves of innovation. As these changes emerge, Santa Clara will be a place that incorporates the use of these technologies but also will critique them by raising humane and ethical implications. The aim is to find ways for technology to benefit the common good.

As with technological innovation, the shifting concepts of globalization expand our horizon to reflect on and discuss new questions regarding our planet and our world. In 1951, whatever ecological concerns there were tended to focus on saving redwoods and preserving our natural resources. Today, we express concern for the whole environment, from conservation to acid rain, ozone layers, and global warming. Similarly, we see economic development in a world with less defined borders as contrasted with the clearly defined nation-states and political blocs of the early Cold War period. This change resulted from more than the collapse of the Berlin Wall in 1989. If the campus concerns in 1951 were relatively parochial, today, located as we are in the heart of Silicon Valley, we view the world through a special window opening on the entire world and a transnational economy. Technological and economic exchange are turning our planet into a global society.

How can and will we balance a world that is moving toward a global market economy while preserving the best values of local cultures? As the earth becomes more and more connected through an economic eco-system, how can we establish a complimentary social eco-system? And how will we deal with an interdependent market economy that does not address the pressing issue of world poverty?

Politically, multinational corporations will continue to aggregate more power than some smaller nation states, especially the emerging or developing nations. As a result of these changes, frustration and anger against the United States have been reflected at a number of international conferences where multinational organizations, and the United States in particular, are accused of destroying local cultures.

When we look at all these challenges, it is clear that the world of the future will be more dynamic and, perhaps, chaotic than ever before. The changes will come so rapidly that it is foolhardy to try to predict them, except to say that these changes require the university to become more connected than ever before. The university must more and more interact not only with its local community, but also with the world. It will adopt a more external focus and be seen less and less as an isolated ivory tower. It will more and more interact with society, both in an effort to teach to a broad audience and, at the same time, to learn from society.

A More Diverse People Living Together.

The notion of diversity will present the challenge of balancing the impulse toward one global culture with the desire for maintaining a diversity of cultures. Santa Clara will remain committed to maintaining a diverse university community, particularly in its student body. At its founding, Santa Clara was diverse. The college bulletin was published in both Spanish and English through the 1860s. But by the time Santa Clara turned 100 in 1951, its population was almost all-white. There were only a few Hispanics and Asians. By the 1980s, as the ethnic composition of California was changing, the decision was made that the population of the university community ought to reflect greater ethnic diversity. Today, it does so and even reflects a much broader outlook when we consider that both graduate and undergraduate programs include students from roughly 80 countries and students of color represent 40 percent of the student body.

Increasingly, we recognize that this Valley's creativity and richness has its roots in many cultures. We must appreciate that this diversity is a fabric in which many different strands of ethnicity, religion, and history overlap. We have Vietnamese, Italian, and Hispanic Catholics; Eastern European Jews; Scotch-Irish Baptists and African American Methodists; Japanese Buddhists and Indonesian Muslims, to name but a few of these layered identities. A history of immigration did not produce a homogenized nation but a multicultural one.

Related to cultural plurality is class plurality. The financial disparity between those with great wealth and those with only minimal levels of income is increasing. That class mix in our student body becomes a problematic for learning. Namely, how can people of different socio-economic classes learn from each other? Learn to live together as one community? And learn to how to narrow the "class gap?"

Cultural and class plurality shapes our community and challenge our pedagogy and research. We learn from each other with students, faculty and staff, who bring their own culture, values, and perspectives to learning. In the dialogue between learning and culture, we must constantly ask: "How do we educate for culture, learn from culture, yet critique cultural trends and humanize culture?" "How can education change structures, so that self-determination and economic well-being are available to the poor of this world?"

Learning in this context is learning to understand the cultural and class realities of our world and also to appreciate the good in all the cultures that make up our common culture. Learning also includes addressing existing class differences so that the poor begin to live as full members of the community, rather than on the edge.

The University: Other Characteristics of Our Future

Some characteristics we now assume will change and others will remain relatively stable. I believe the university's size is ideal and so will remain relatively constant over the next ten years; the current enrollment is appropriate for what we want to be and do and for the size of the faculty and campus. The student body itself, however, will become a bit more national and even international, and diverse.

There will be fewer Jesuits at the university but that should not affect our Jesuit Catholic character. Advancing the Jesuit, Catholic mission of education will depend on a deeper partnership between lay and Jesuit colleagues. In the future, lay colleagues, who are just as committed to the Ignatian philosophy of education as are the Jesuits, will assume greater responsibility for a Jesuit, Catholic education at Santa Clara.

There is a discussion in higher education today about the future of traditional colleges. Some see a movement away from campus settings to virtual campuses. This is sometimes described as the conflict between "bricks" and "clicks." This is not the Santa Clara of the future, because this is not an either-or, but rather a both-and situation. Both technology and a locus (campus) are means for the community to learn.

This learning community must integrate technology into the humanistic education it offers. Education in general, and a Santa Clara education of the whole person in particular, cannot all happen over the internet. If the pedagogy of engagement and of interpersonal and interdisciplinary dialogue are important to learning, so are both technology and community. Thus, while the web can connect people in many ways, it lacks the appropriate personal and social dimension. For the Santa Clara of the future, there will be both bricks and clicks; there will be more and more networking but not at the expense of personal contact among students and faculty and staff.

The university will also continue to stress educating students for leadership so that upon graduation Santa Clara alumni and alumnae will be men and women who are personally reflective of who they are, what they want to become, and what they want to do in their careers and lives. With self-understanding, they will become forces for and of integrity in their communities.

Educating for this new world means much more than uncritically accepting things as they are. We must understand the intricacies of global economics, politics, digital electronics, and biotechnology, while never forgetting the plight of the poor, the fragile, and the disenfranchised of our society. Our Jesuit legacy now calls us to educate women and men to be leaders who exhibit the three intertwined dimensions of a Santa Clara education: competence, conscience, and compassion. Only at the nexus of these three traits will we find the solutions to the problems that will face us.

Finally, our graduates will possess a vision and quest for life. This will permit them to look beyond the narrow vision of the here and now and look to the bigger picture, the broader vision. Two stories illustrate this point. When President Kennedy announced the space program, he did not simply say that the United States would build rockets (the immediate vision), he said the United States would put a man on the moon in ten years (the broader vision). The other story also reflects the importance of having a vision for your life, for what you are doing and where you are going. Two bricklayers were asked what they were doing. One said: "I am laying bricks." The other: "I am building a cathedral." It's all in the individual's vision. And, I hope, in an institution's vision.

Endnotes

1. John Henry Newman, *The Idea of a University*, ed., George N. Shuster (1959).

2. For a full description of Santa Clara University's history see Gerald McKevitt, S.J., *The University of Santa Clara: A History 1851-1977* (1979).

3. John Seely Brown and Paul Duguid, *The Social Life of Information* (2000).

4. Peter-Hans Kolvenbach, S.J., "The Service of Faith and the Promotion of Justice in American Jesuit Higher Education," A lecture at Santa Clara University, October 6, 2000.

About the Authors

Constance Cortez received her BA and MA in Art History from the University of Texas at Austin where she specialized in PreColumbian Maya Art. She completed her Ph.D. in Art History at UCLA in colonial indigenous visual culture of Mexico.

Cortez currently publishes in three fields: Pre-Columbian Art, Colonial Art of Mexico, and Contemporary Chicano/a Art. Her most recent studies in Contemporary Chicano/a Art include an edited volume entitled *Imágenes e Historias/Images and Histories: Chicana Altar-Inspired Art* (Constance Cortez, ed.. Medford, MA : Tufts University Gallery. 1999.) and "The New Aztlán: Nepantla (and Other Sites of Transmogrification)" in *The Road to Aztlán* (Virginia Fields, ed. Los Angeles: Los Angeles County Museum of Art. 2001.).

Cortez is currently an assistant professor of Art History at Santa Clara University, located in Silicon Valley.

Paul J. Fitzgerald, S.J., has been an Assistant Professor of Religious Studies at Santa Clara University since 1997. He earned a doctorate in Sociology of Religion from the Sorbonne in Paris, where he studied the role of the Church as a school of citizenship. He also holds a pontifical doctorate in ecclesiology from the Institut Catholique in Paris. His research and teaching interests include Historical Ecclesiology, Theology of the Laity, and Peace and Justice Studies. His recent publications include: "Faithful Sociology: Peter Berger's Religious Project." *Religious Studies Review* 27/1, 2001; and with Dr. Kieran Sullivan, "Preparing for Marriage: What Pastoral Marital Counselors Should Know about Religious Belief, Psychological Health, and Marital Outcome." *INTAMS Review* 7/1, 2001.

Lorie Garcia is a seventh generation Californian whose ancestors came to the San Francisco Bay Area in1776 as members of the Juan Bautista De Anza party, and whose family has resided here since then. A historian, she specializes in the history of Santa Clara and has written and lectured on this subject. Currently Lorie serves as chairman of the Santa Clara County Historical Heritage Commission, as vice-chair of the City of Santa Clara Planning Commission and as the Planning Commissioner board member of the California Chapter of the American Planning Association.

George F. Giacomini, Jr. received his bachelor's degree at Santa Clara University and did his graduate work at the University of California, Berkeley. Currently Associate Professor of History and Assistant to the President, he began teaching at Santa Clara in 1962. He also served as Dean of Students and Vice President for Student Services in the 1970s. He recently co-authored with Gerald McKevitt, S.J., *Serving the Intellect, Touching the Heart: a Portrait of Santa Clara University, 1851-2001*.

Carl H. Hayn, S.J., received his B.A. (1939) and M.A. (1940) from Gonzaga University; his S.T.L. (1948) from Alma College; his Ph.D. (1955) from St. Louis University. He has served as a National Science research fellow at St. Louis University and conducted post-doctoral work at Oak Ridge Institute of Nuclear Studies and at Washington State University. Fr. Hayn is past president of Northern California section of the American Association of Physics Teachers and currently serves as the director of the Harvard Project Physics and in-service program for high school teachers.

Robert H. Jackson (Ph.D. History University of California Berkeley) is the author/coauthor/editor of nine books and more than forty journal articles, including *Indian Population Decline: The Missions of Northwestern New Spain, 1687-1840* (1994); *Indians, Franciscans, and Spanish Colonization: The Impact of the Mission System on California Indians* (1995); *The New Latin American Mission History* (1995); and *Race, Caste, and Status: Indians in Colonial Spanish America* (1999). He is currently working on a comparative study of missions in northern Mexico and Paraguay.

Philip R. Kesten is an Associate Professor of Physics and Chairman of the Physics Department at Santa Clara University in Santa Clara, California. He holds a B.S. in physics from the Massachusetts Institute of Technology and received his Ph.D. in High Energy Particle Physics from the University of Michigan in Ann Arbor, Michigan.

Paul Locatelli, S.J. became the twenty-seventh President of Santa Clara University in 1988. He received his undergraduate education at Santa Clara, his doctorate in accounting from the University of Southern California and is a certified public accountant. In 1962 he entered the Society of Jesuit and was ordained a priest in 1974. Prior to becoming President, he taught in the accounting department and served as Academic Vice President at Santa Clara, and was Rector at Loyola Marymount University. He serves on numerous local and national boards including the Presidents Council of the Association of Governing Boards, American Leadership Forum, Joint Venture: Silicon Valley Network, Executive Committee of the Association of Independent California Colleges and Universities (chair 1992-94) and the Association of Jesuit Colleges and Universities (chair 1994-2000).

Born and raised in Santa Clara, **Patricia Mahan** is a graduate cum laude of San Jose State University, with degrees in Speech-Communication, English and education. She obtained her Juris Doctor from Santa Clara University School of Law in 1980 and maintains a private practice, specializing in tax and estate planning. She served on the West Valley-Mission Community College Board of Trustees (1985-1992) and was elected to the Santa Clara City Council in 1994. Patricia is married to John V. Boyles, a detective sergeant for the City of San Jose Police Department, and has one son, Colin Mahan Boyles, age 11. For the past 12 years, the family has worked to restore Pat's grandmother's home, a 105-year old Victorian in the Old Quad section of Santa Clara.

Michael S. Malone has been called "the Boswell of Silicon Valley" by the *San Jose Mercury News*. He was raised in Silicon Valley and holds a bachelor's degree in combined sciences and an MBA from Santa Clara University. In his eclectic career he has been an instructor on moral values at the Santa Clara Law School, a rock record reviewer, a B-movie critic, even a saloon reviewer. He hosted *Malone*, a half-hour interview program that ran for nine seasons and was seen on PBS stations nationwide. Beyond the television programs, Malone is best known as an author. His first book, *The Big Score: The Billion Dollar Story of Silicon Valley* (Doubleday), was named one of the top 10 business books of 1985 by *Business Week*.

The book grew out of Malone's years at the *San Jose Mercury News* as the nation's first daily high tech reporter, where he co-authored the first investigative stories on toxic waste contamination, workplace drug abuse and espionage in Silicon Valley. *The Big Score* went on to become the basis for the KTEH documentary series *Silicon Valley*, which aired on PBS in 1987. Another documentary hosted and written by Malone, *Future Tense*, earned a 1996 cable television Telly award.

In the past decade Malone's articles and editorials have appeared in such publications as the *New York Times* (where he was a columnist for two years), the Wall Street Journal, the Economist, Forbes ASAP and Fortune. He was featured as a lead essayist (with Tom Wolfe and Mark Helprin) in the celebrated *Forbes ASAP* Big Issue (1996).

About his book, *Going Public* (HarperCollins), published in 1991, Inc. magazine wrote that it "contains all the suspense and intrigue of a Robert Ludlum thriller." In 1992, Malone co-authored (with William H. Davidow) *The Virtual Corporation* (HarperCollins), which became the subject of a cover story in *Business Week* and was one of the most influential business books of the decade. *The Microprocessor: A Biography* (Telos/Springer-Verlag) was published in September 1995 and was the winner of a Critic's Choice award. *Virtual Selling* (Free Press), co-authored with Tom Siebel, was published in February 1996. *Intellectual Capital*, co-authored with Leif Edvinsson, was published in March 1997. His latest nonfiction book, *Infinite Loop: How the World's Most Insanely Great Computer Company Went Insane*, about Apple Computer, was published by Doubleday in February 1999. It was named one of the top tech and business books in 1999 by the Library Journal.

In August 1998, Malone was named editor of *Forbes ASAP*. He is now Editor at Large. He also has a weekly column on ABCNews.com called "Silicon Insider." He also is the host/interviewer in a sixteen part PBS documentary *Betting It All: The Entrepreneurs.*

Leonard McKay, Businessman, Historian and Author.
Leonard McKay was born in San Jose, attended local schools, and graduated from Santa Clara University. As a youngster he worked in the fields, particularly picking prunes, cutting "cots" and later did cannery work. As a businessman for more than 44 years, he ran Smith McKay Printing from 1953 to 1983 and is the present owner of Memorabilia of San Jose, since 1984. Leonard is the past president of the California Pioneers, Historic Landmarks Commission and San Jose Rotary Club. He is the author of five books, many articles and was featured for three years as "Mr. San Jose" on the now defunct Sunday Night with Tom McEnery radio show.

Randall Milliken graduated from the University of California at Berkeley in 1973. He subsequently received the M.A. from Sonoma State University and the Ph.D. from the University of California at Berkeley. A staff ethnohistorian and archaeologist with Far Western Anthropological Research Group in Davis, he also serves on the committees of graduate students at various California universities. He is the author of *A Time of Little Choice*, the definitive study of tribal interaction with the San Francisco Bay area missions prior to 1810.

Ann-Marie Sayers is Tribal Chair Person of Indian Canyon, founder of Costanoan Indian Research, Inc. She successfully reclaimed ancestral lands using the Indian Allotment Act of 1887. Visit Chair Person Sayers and Indian Canyon at: www.indiancanyon.org.

Robert M. Senkewicz is Professor of History at Santa Clara University, where he teaches courses on early American History and California History. He is the author of *Vigilantes in Gold Rush San Francisco* (1985). He and Rose Marie Beebe edited, translated, and annotated a work originally written in 1851 by Antonio María Osio: *The History of Alta California* (1996). They also edited a documentary history of *The Californias, Lands of Promise and Despair: Chronicles of Early California, 1535-1846* (2001).

Russell K. Skowronek is Associate Professor of Anthropology in the Department of Anthropology and Sociology, and Campus Archaeologist, at Santa Clara University. He holds MA degrees in Anthropology and History from Florida State University, and a Ph.D. in Anthropology from Michigan State University. Professor Skowronek has conducted research on the Spanish colonial world in Spain, Florida, South Carolina, the Caribbean, Latin America, and the Philippines. He is a Research Collaborator with the Smithsonian Center for Materials Research and Education studying the supply, production and exchange of earthenwares on the Spanish Borderlands.

Skowronek is the author of numerous articles on the Spanish Borderlands. They include:"Global Economics in the Creation and Maintenance of the Spanish Colonial Empire," in *Research in Economic Anthropology*; "The Spanish Philippines: Archaeological Perspectives on Colonial Economics and Society," in the *International Journal of Historical Archaeology*; "Empire and Ceramics:The Changing Role of Illicit Trade in Spanish America," and "Ceramics and Commerce: The 1554 flota Revisited," both in *Historical Archaeology*; in *Ethnohistory* "Sifting the Evidence: Perceptions of Life at the Ohlone Missions of Alta California;" and "Archaeology at Santa Clara de Asís: The Slow Rediscovery of a Moveable Mission," in the *Pacific Coast Archaeological Society Quarterly*. He has also penned a booklet for the California Mission Studies Association titled, *Identifying the First El Pueblo de San José de Guadalupe: Some Archaeological, Historical, and Geographical Considerations*.